MIXING METHODS IN SOCIAL RESEARCH

Sara Miller McCune founded SAGE Publishing in 1965 to support the dissemination of usable knowledge and educate a global community. SAGE publishes more than 1000 journals and over 800 new books each year, spanning a wide range of subject areas. Our growing selection of library products includes archives, data, case studies and video. SAGE remains majority owned by our founder and after her lifetime will become owned by a charitable trust that secures the company's continued independence.

Los Angeles | London | New Delhi | Singapore | Washington DC | Melbourne

MIXING METHODS IN SOCIAL RESEARCH

Qualitative, Quantitative and Combined Methods

Ralph Hall

Los Angeles | London | New Delhi
Singapore | Washington DC | Melbourne

Los Angeles | London | New Delhi
Singapore | Washington DC | Melbourne

SAGE Publications Ltd
1 Oliver's Yard
55 City Road
London EC1Y 1SP

SAGE Publications Inc.
2455 Teller Road
Thousand Oaks, California 91320

SAGE Publications India Pvt Ltd
B 1/I 1 Mohan Cooperative Industrial Area
Mathura Road
New Delhi 110 044

SAGE Publications Asia-Pacific Pte Ltd
3 Church Street
#10-04 Samsung Hub
Singapore 049483

Editor: Alysha Owen
Editorial assistant: Lauren Jacobs
Production editor: Victoria Nicholas
Copyeditor: Sharon Cawood
Proofreader: Jill Birch
Indexer: David Rudeforth
Marketing manager: Susheel Gokarakonda
Cover design: Shaun Mercier
Typeset by: C&M Digitals (P) Ltd, Chennai, India
Printed in the UK

© Ralph Hall 2020

First published 2020

Library of Congress Control Number: 2019945239

British Library Cataloguing in Publication data

A catalogue record for this book is available from the British Library

ISBN 978-1-4462-8201-4
ISBN 978-1-4462-8202-1 (pbk)

CONTENTS

ABOUT THE AUTHOR

Ralph Hall MA PhD AM is an Emeritus Professor in the School of Social Sciences at the University of New South Wales, Sydney, Australia. He has taught research methods to both undergraduate and graduate students in the social science and policy programme in the School since 1990. His research interests include the role of peer mentoring in facilitating incoming students' adjustment to academic study, the work–study experience of students in addition to research designs in social research with particular reference to mixed methods. He has co-edited one book with Lynn Scott, namely *Global Issues: Perspectives on General Studies* (Macmillan, 1987) and authored two, namely *Impacts: Contemporary Issues and Global Problems* with Roger Bell (Macmillan, 1996) and *Applied Social Research: Planning, Designing and Conducting Real World Research* (Palgrave Macmillan, 2008). In 2019, he was awarded an AM (Member of the Order of Australia) for services to education as an academic and to the community.

PREFACE

The use of mixed methods in social research is now well established. Texts on mixed methods began appearing in the late 1990s and particularly in the first decade of the 21st century.

This was a period in which mixed-methods research needed justification and many of these books launched into a defence of mixed methods as an alternative to straight quantitative or qualitative research. That time has now passed and mixed methods are now accepted as legitimate research designs. The need for a defence is no longer necessary.

The aim of this book is to integrate mixed methods into the mainstream of research methods texts. Mixed methods will be presented along with single methods and the circumstances in which each method could be considered appropriate outlined. It is now time that mixed methods is not seen as an additional course to standard research methods but is included throughout all research methods courses. It is intended that this book will contribute to the integration of mixed methods in all research methods courses.

The approach adopted here assumes that the reader has some basic knowledge of research methods and data analysis so that introductory accounts of these are not included. The focus here is on how these methods are integrated into mixed-methods research.

Part 1 deals with the nature of social research and why mixed methods has emerged as an approach to doing research. This part also deals with the arguments that have been advanced for using mixed methods and the debates over methodology that gave rise to mixed methods.

Part 2 deals with the research planning process and sets out the major research methods used in the social sciences and how these can be combined in mixed-methods designs.

Part 3 sets out the methods available for collecting social science data and how these can be combined in mixed-methods research.

Part 4 deals with organizing and analysing the data that has been collected, and Part 5 deals with ensuring quality in research, reporting findings and strategies for convincing stakeholders of the value of mixed-methods research.

This book is based on the experience gained from some 25 years of teaching research methods to advanced undergraduate students in a social science programme and to graduate students in a policy studies degree at the University of New South Wales. Many of the graduate students were already employed in research roles and appreciated the applied focus of the courses I taught. Their feedback, as well as that from my undergraduate students, has been helpful in framing my views about teaching research methods, for which I am grateful.

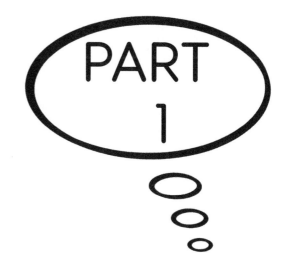

PRINCIPLES OF MIXED-METHODS RESEARCH

Part 1 of this book examines the nature and purpose of social research and outlines the emergence of mixed methods as a major development expanding the scope and power of social research methods.

Chapter 1 outlines the types and goals of social research methods, distinguishes between methodologies and methods, introduces the notion of paradigms and traces the emergence of mixed methods. The aim of this chapter is to acquaint readers with the developments in social research that led to the emergence of mixed methods.

Chapter 2 develops the notion of paradigms further and their application to mixed-methods research. The relevance of paradigms to research is outlined with particular reference to mixed methods.

1

THE NATURE OF SOCIAL RESEARCH AND THE EMERGENCE OF MIXED METHODS

INTRODUCTION

In this chapter, the nature and origins of social research are described and the various forms it takes discussed. It is important for intending users of social research to understand the context in which the methods of social research have been developed and applied so that they are aware of their uses and limitations.

Social research methods are used in a number of quite distinct social sciences. They are not exclusive to any one particular social science such as sociology. Each of the social sciences uses research methods in ways deemed to be most suitable to their fields of study.

Research methods have traditionally been differentiated in terms of whether they involve the collection of quantitative or qualitative data. Quantitative data is data where concepts are measured on a numerical scale. Examples of such concepts would be a rating of a teacher's effectiveness, say, on a 7-point scale, or asking people to indicate their agreement with an attitude statement by assigning a numerical value to represent their opinion. Qualitative data is data for which no numerical measure has been assigned. Such data can be textual as in a description of the effectiveness of a teacher by a former student, visual as in a picture or film segment, or observational as in a description of children interacting in a playground.

In some social sciences, such as psychology, until recently quantitative methods have predominated, while, in others, for instance anthropology, qualitative methods have been more widely used. But all social sciences use both.

Newer, emerging fields within the social sciences such as criminology, evaluation and policy analysis have embraced a wide range of research methods. Indeed, evaluation has pioneered the use of mixed-methods research, as will be outlined later in this chapter. An example of an evaluation study using mixed methods is provided in Box 1.1. What this study shows is how a range of research methods can be used in a single study to provide information – in this case, about the success of a programme whereby changes to the environmental conditions are made, designed to increase physical activity in communities as a way to improve public health.

Mixed methods refers to the combination of quantitative and qualitative methods in the one study. The term is of recent origin but, as pointed out by Fetters (2016) and Maxwell (2016), there is a long history of studies combining qualitative and quantitative methods. What is new about mixed methods is that it systematizes the ways in which these methods can be fruitfully combined.

The background to the emergence of mixed methods as a research strategy has been the longstanding debate between proponents of quantitative methods and those of qualitative methods as being most appropriate for the social sciences. This debate will be described in more detail later in this chapter. But, to understand the debate, a discussion of research methodology and the influence of philosophical positions about what constitutes knowledge, is needed.

Before discussing these debates, some general background about the nature and goals of social research is outlined. This is followed by a discussion of debates around research methodology and the emergence of mixed methods.

==== **BOX 1.1** ====

AN EXAMPLE OF AN EVALUATION STUDY USING MIXED METHODS

Brownson et al. (2012) reported an evaluation of a programme termed Active Living by Design (ALbD) to increase physical activity in 25 communities across the USA. The programme was designed to modify the environment so as to promote increased healthy lifestyle changes through physical activities such as walking, cycling, and so on. To evaluate the outcome of this programme, the authors used eight research methods comprising quantitative and qualitative methods. These were: a survey of partnerships in the 25 communities to identify capacity to identify social and public health problems; a concept-mapping exercise involving selected community representatives to determine priorities for creating change to increase physical activities; a progress reporting system designed to document activities and accomplishments; key informant interviews with individuals who have expertise or experience in implementing changes; focus group interviews with individuals representing various sub-groups in the communities to find out what changes had been implemented and how successful they had been; photos and videos of completed projects; environmental (community) audits to determine whether environmental conditions for increased physical activity had changed as a result of the programme; and direct observations of community members using facilities provided by the programme.

The evaluation using all these methods found that the programme had succeeded in increasing physical activity in those projects that had been completed at the time the evaluation was conducted. Some large-scale changes were still in progress and thus couldn't be evaluated.

The authors added that using mixed methods enabled the effects of changes to be more clearly identified by overcoming the limitations of any one method.

CATEGORIES OF SOCIAL RESEARCH

It is important to identify the type of social research being planned as each type has a different focus and aim.

Three major categories of social research have traditionally been identified. These are: **basic research**, **strategic research** and **applied research**. While the differences among these can sometimes be blurred, the general thrust of each is usually evident in any particular research project. The characteristics of these three types will now be outlined.

Basic research is research conducted with the aim of extending knowledge in the field in which the research is conducted. It is said to be curiosity driven. That is, a researcher seeks to answer questions posed by gaps in knowledge arising from existing research. It is not designed to provide solutions to practical problems nor is it designed to further the goals of governments or other organizations. This does not mean, however, that basic research does not have any practical application. Indeed, many basic research findings across a wide range of scientific areas have provided breakthroughs in providing solutions to practical problems. It is, of course, likely that furthering knowledge in any scientific area will lead to useful applications, but this is an incidental consequence of basic research rather than its goal.

Much basic research involves theory testing. That is, social scientists devise theories to explain social processes, deduce predictions from these theories and conduct research to test these predictions. Should the predictions be confirmed by the research findings, the theory is supported; whereas if the predictions are not confirmed, the theory is either rejected or modified.

When basic research is conducted to test theories, the focus of the research is specific and tends to be narrow. The methods used tend to be single methods such as the randomized control trial, to be discussed in Chapter 5. Mixed methods have not typically played a major role in such research.

Basic research is conducted primarily in universities or research centres and is funded predominantly by government grants.

Strategic research is research conducted in specific areas considered to be important by governments. It shares many features in common with basic research but tends to be more narrowly focused – for example, research focused on ageing where the aim is to understand the problems faced by elderly citizens so that governments can devise programmes to address these problems.

Strategic research is conducted predominantly in research centres established either by governments or non-government organizations such as philanthropic, service provider or other non-profit organizations to conduct research in a specific area considered to be important to policy. An example of such a research centre is the Johns Hopkins Center on Aging and Health at the Johns Hopkins University in Baltimore, Maryland. This centre was established in 1998 to conduct research aimed at improving the health of older adults. An example of a non-university research centre is the Social Impact Research Center located in Chicago, Illinois. This centre is part of the Heartland Alliance programme, a non-profit organization in the USA dedicated to ending poverty.

While strategic research is focused on a particular policy area, it tends to be broader in scope than basic research. Mixed methods are more likely to play a role in the conduct of strategic research than in basic research, although, as we will see, mixed methods are increasingly being used in all forms of research.

Applied research is research conducted to address specific issues or problems considered to be of practical significance. The focus of applied research is on problem solving rather than on expanding the knowledge base in a discipline or area of research. Bickman and Rog (1998: x) have defined applied research as research which 'uses scientific methodology to develop information to help solve an immediate, yet usually persistent, societal problem'.

Applied research is usually commissioned by governments, industry or non-profit organizations with interests in specific social issues or problems to gain more information on the nature of the issue or problem. These organizations fund the research and decide the questions to be answered. The funding body then awards the contract to the applied researcher who then reports the findings to that body.

Programme evaluation can be regarded as a form of applied research since it is aimed at determining whether a programme, such as a mental health rehabilitation programme, is effective. The evaluation outlined in Box 1.1 is an example of such a piece of applied research.

Action research is a form of applied research that aims to bring about social change. Participatory action research (Kemmis and McTaggart, 2003) likewise aims to confront and overcome irrationality, injustice, alienation and suffering by involving local communities in research to improve their social conditions.

Mixed methods have played a major role in applied research, particularly in programme evaluation, as we have seen. This is because finding solutions to social problems involves collecting information from as many sources and in as many forms as necessary to understand the problem and find possible solutions.

While there are other classifications of varieties of research (e.g. Bulmer, 1978, 1986), the one presented here is widely accepted.

The main features of these types of social research are summarized in Table 1.1.

Table 1.1 Main varieties of research and their typical distinguishing characteristics

Typical features	Type of research		
	Basic	Strategic	Applied
Purpose	Expanding knowledge	Expanding knowledge in a limited field of study	Practical application of findings
Motivation	Curiosity driven	Policy relevance	Problem solving
Location	Mainly universities	Mainly research centres	A wide range of settings including private consultancies
Funding	Mainly government grants	Government and many non-government organizations	Government and private sector grants
Utilization	Improving understanding and testing theories	Assisting organizations to improve policy	Finding solutions to social problems

GOALS OF SOCIAL RESEARCH

Social research is conducted for a range of purposes, which impact on the nature of the research methods used. Most analyses of research distinguish three main goals: exploration, description and explanation (e.g. Babbie, 2016; Neuman, 2011). All three goals employ both single-method and mixed-methods research designs. These goals are described as follows.

Exploration

Exploratory research is aimed at gaining information about a topic that very little is known about. The topic may be a new one or one that has become important due to changing social or economic conditions, such as the use of social media by employers to profile employees or job applicants. This topic has gained in importance as some employers are accessing social media such as Facebook to gain information about their employees without the knowledge of their employees, resulting in concerns about potential breaches of privacy (see Box 1.2).

━━━━━━━ BOX 1.2 ━━━━━━━

AN EXPLORATORY STUDY OF PROFILING EMPLOYEES ONLINE

A study by McDonald, Thompson and O'Connor (2016) analysed data from a survey of the UK and Australia to study the prevalence of profiling and the extent to which employees are informed

(Continued)

of this practice. In some cases, the study found that employers have asked for the passwords of their employees' social media accounts.

The study also examines employee responses to such practices, including the extent to which they take action to protect their privacy by limiting access to their social media accounts.

Exploratory studies often form the basis for more specific follow-up studies. They set the groundwork for further research on the topic. They seek to establish the main areas and issues that are in need of more detailed investigation.

Description

Descriptive research aims to identify the major characteristics of a field of research. It focuses on the 'what', 'how' and 'who' questions rather than the 'why' questions.

Descriptive studies are the most common type of research in the social sciences. This is because they identify the key characteristics of the social situations under investigation. Knowing these characteristics is necessary before any explanatory research can be undertaken. That is, we need to answer the 'what', 'how' and 'who' questions before we can ask the 'why' questions.

Explanation

Explanatory research focuses on the 'why' questions. It aims to determine the causes of social phenomena. It uses research methods designed to establish causal mechanisms, often through testing predictions from theories that propose causal relationships.

Explanation is often seen as the ultimate goal of social research because it goes beyond description into establishing cause–effect relationships in the social sciences or through confirming predictions from social theories.

Explanatory research can be either basic or applied. Some evaluation research, for example, seeks to establish why programmes work or why they do not (explanatory), rather than simply establish whether or not they work (descriptive).

Explanation as a goal of social research is an optimistic one, since social processes are extremely complex and don't lend themselves to simple explanations. Hence, most explanatory research involves testing theories about social processes.

Alternative formulations of research goals

The goals set out above are very general and other, more specific ways of categorizing goals of social research have been proposed. For example, Ragin and Amoroso (2011) identify seven goals of social research, as set out in Box 1.3.

━━━━━━ BOX 1.3 ━━━━━━

GOALS OF SOCIAL RESEARCH ADAPTED FROM RAGIN AND AMOROSO (2011)

1. Identifying general patterns and relationships: this goal involves identifying social phenomena that are common to a range of situations. Achieving knowledge that can be generalized beyond specific situations is seen as a goal of all science so that it brings social science into line with other sciences.
2. Testing and refining theory: testing existing social theories and using the results of these tests to refine or even abandon theories is seen to be an important goal of social research. By refining theories, an understanding of social phenomena can be advanced.
3. Making predictions: using social theory and knowledge to predict future trends is also a goal of social research. At the present state of knowledge in the social sciences, prediction of rates such as use of illicit drugs in a city or region is more realistic than is the prediction of specific events.
4. Interpreting culturally or historically significant phenomena: cultural and historical events are important landmarks in the development of human society so that understanding their significance is a goal of social research.
5. Exploring diversity: social and cultural diversity is a characteristic of human societies and so an understanding of the nature of such diversity is an important goal of social research.
6. Giving voice: enabling marginalized groups in society to be heard can reveal aspects of society that cannot otherwise be uncovered. Hence, giving voice to such groups and individuals can also be seen as a goal of social research.
7. Advancing new theories: social research often produces evidence that is not explicable under existing theories so that developing new theories to accommodate such evidence is another worthwhile goal of research.

Still other goals can be identified. One goal that is a common feature of much social research is achieving *understanding*. Researchers study a particular social or cultural event in order to gain an in-depth understanding of that event. This goal is implicit in goals 4, 5 and 6 in Box 1.3, but many researchers feel the need to make this goal explicit.

SOCIAL RESEARCH METHODOLOGIES AND PARADIGMS
Methodologies and methods

A research project will involve choosing one or more research methods in order to collect data. What determines which research methods are used in any particular study is the research methodology adopted by a researcher. A **methodology** is a set of principles that identifies what practices count as research. A method is the practice by which research is conducted. The aim of a methodology is to set out the criteria by which research is conducted, whereas the aim of a research method is to generate data to answer **research questions**. The methodology, then, is the theory that tells us what constitutes a research method and the method is the means by which we conduct research.

Quantitative and qualitative research can be seen as two competing methodologies that seek to decide what counts as knowledge in the social sciences. These are set out in Table 1.2, along with a mixed-methods methodology.

As can be seen from Table 1.2, mixed methods combines the features of quantitative and qualitative research and in this sense is not subject to the limitations of either.

While all forms of research can be either descriptive or exploratory (see above), much quantitative research is said by its proponents to be aimed at explanation. Whether it can achieve this goal is a matter for debate. Indeed, qualitative researchers challenge this goal and instead substitute a form of 'in-depth' understanding of social phenomena. This 'understanding' is a form of description that seeks to provide insights into social realities through an analysis of textual data obtained by in-depth interviews or group discussions. They argue that attempting to quantify social concepts is misplaced and only serves to oversimplify them. Social reality, they claim, is complex and cannot be reduced to measurable concepts.

Mixed methods is an attempt to overcome this divide by incorporating both approaches into the social research methodology. To do this, advocates of mixed methods accept that some concepts can be meaningfully quantified while others cannot. By combining both in a research project, they claim that the goals of explanation and understanding can be achieved. In this sense, it can be argued that mixed methods may provide a resolution of the 'paradigm wars', as discussed in the next section.

Table 1.2 Defining characteristics of quantitative, qualitative and mixed methodologies

	Methodology		
Defining characteristics	**Quantitative**	**Qualitative**	**Mixed**
What counts as data?	Social concepts are defined as variables which can be measured	Social concepts are textual or observational and as such are not measurable	Some social concepts are measurable while others are not
How is research conducted?	Social measurements are made in an objective, neutral manner	Social concepts are obtained through methods designed to provide textual data	Social concepts are obtained either by measurement or by methods designed to yield textual data
How are social concepts analysed?	Social measurements are related through statistical analysis	Social concepts are analysed by detailed textual analysis	Social concepts are analysed by both statistical and textual analysis
What is the aim of research?	Explanation, description or theory testing	Understanding, theory testing, description	Explanation, description, theory testing and understanding

PARADIGMS AND THE 'PARADIGM WARS'

What became known as the 'paradigm wars' throughout the 1980s was the debate between proponents of quantitative methodology and those of qualitative methodology as to which was the appropriate way to conduct social research.

Quantitative research had dominated some social sciences through the early part of the twentieth century, particularly education, psychology and some areas of sociology until qualitative researchers began challenging the assumptions underlying quantitative research. There are many good summaries of this debate, such as those of Gage (1989), Sale, Lohfeld and Brazil (2002), or in the collection of articles in Reichhardt and Rallis (1994), so only a brief description will be given here.

Quantitative research was built on a number of assumptions, including:

- Research should be objective and value-free.
- Social concepts are defined as variables which are measureable.
- Social scientific knowledge progresses through the establishment of relationships among these variables by the application of inferential statistics.
- The aims of social research are explanation and prediction.

These assumptions became identified with the paradigm called **positivism**. A **paradigm** is a set of concepts that specify how science should be conducted and what counts as knowledge (see Box 1.4). The concept of a paradigm and its relevance to the social sciences will be discussed in more detail in Chapter 2.

━━━━━━ BOX 1.4 ━━━━━━

PARADIGMS IN RESEARCH

What is a paradigm?

Paradigms play an important role in the mixed-methods literature for reasons outlined in the text. The term has been adapted from Kuhn (1970), whose book The *Structure of Scientific Revolutions*, first published in 1962, stimulated a whole new field of discussion about the nature of scientific progress. Kuhn defined a paradigm as 'universally recognized scientific achievements that, for a time, provide model problems and solutions for a community of practitioners'. Science progresses, according to Kuhn, by paradigm shifts, where a new paradigm emerges when the existing paradigm outlives its usefulness and is discredited. Although Kuhn did not consider the term applicable to the social sciences, it has been widely used in this context. As Morgan (2007) points out, it has been given at least four different meanings in the social scientific literature: a world view; an epistemological stance; shared beliefs among a community of researchers; and model examples of research. Although Morgan

(Continued)

(2007) argues that the third of these is closest to what Kuhn defined as a paradigm, he does acknowledge that the second meaning, namely a paradigm as an epistemological stance, has been the most commonly used meaning in discussions of social science methodology.

The positivist approach to research only admits as knowledge evidence that has been collected through the application of 'scientific method', interpreted as making objective, value-free observations. So the quantitative researcher is more likely to use methods that provide this kind of data, such as experiments, surveys, or observational studies that involve collecting quantitative data.

Qualitative research, on the other hand, has long been associated with anthropology and some areas of sociology and psychology. Qualitative researchers maintained that social interaction is a complex meaningful phenomenon and as such cannot be reduced to objective quantitative measures. They argue that social phenomena are different from natural phenomena in that social interactions involve meaning in a way that natural phenomena does not. So methods that are applicable to the study of natural phenomena are of little or no use in the study of social phenomena.

Those supporting qualitative research have argued against positivism and instead supported the paradigms of **interpretivism** or **constructivism**. Many quantitative researchers have also rejected positivism and have moved to a paradigm referred to as **post-positivism** in an attempt to relax some of the contested claims of positivism, such as objectivity of observations and value freedom of research. These paradigms are outlined in Table 1.3. Both interpretivism and constructivism focus on the meaning and understanding of social phenomena and this must take into account the context in which the phenomena occur. For this reason, qualitative researchers are most likely to use methods such as field studies, case studies or in-depth interviewing, where complex qualitative data is obtained.

Table 1.3 Four paradigms for social research

Paradigm	Key features	Typical methods	Data type
Interpretivism	Social reality conveys meaning and the goal of social science is to interpret meaning	Field study Case study	Qualitative
Constructivism	Reality is socially constructed; social constructions are the subject matter of social science	In-depth interview	Qualitative
Positivism	Observations are to be objective and value-free and in accordance with scientific method	Experiment, Survey	Quantitative
Post-positivism	Values and bias are present in all observations but efforts should be made to limit their impact	Mixed methods	Quantitative and qualitative

The debate between positivism and its critics intensified during the 1970s and 1980s. It was the establishment of mixed methods during the 1990s that, to some extent, sidelined the dispute. As a consequence, additional paradigms were adopted by researchers in order to overcome the limitations of those set out in Table 1.3. These paradigms include pragmatism and realism and will be discussed in Chapter 2.

THE EMERGENCE OF MIXED METHODS

Although researchers had been using mixed methods long before the 1990s, it was not until then that it became recognized as a third paradigm for social research. Much of the development of mixed methods research has emanated from the field of programme evaluation. Evaluating social programmes is a complex task requiring the development of measures of programme performance as well as stakeholder consultation involved in delivery of the programme to gain a fuller understanding of its aims and mode of operation. Evaluators found that they needed both quantitative and qualitative data to answer all the questions posed by the evaluation, making programme evaluation a fertile ground for the development of mixed methods.

Jennifer Greene has been one of the pioneers of mixed methods in the field of evaluation and in an early paper (Greene, Caracelli and Graham, 1989) developed a framework for mixed-methods designs that has been influential in later work on these designs.

'Mixed methods' has come to be defined as the use of both qualitative and quantitative methods in the same project. Those advocating mixed methods argued that the advantages gained from combining both forms of research were so great that the paradigm wars became irrelevant. The rationales offered for this view will be discussed in Chapter 3, but it is worth pointing out now that they have defused the debate over quantitative and qualitative methods.

The advantages claimed for using mixed methods are set out in Box 1.5. They do not specifically address the issues raised in the paradigm wars but rather present practical reasons for their use. This does not of course mean that the philosophical positions that gave rise to the paradigm wars can just be swept aside, but that practical considerations need to be addressed.

Mixed methods gained support from a wide range of social research areas in the 1990s. By the first decade of the 21st century, specialist mixed-methods texts had appeared, notably Teddlie and Tashakkori (2009), Cresswell and Plano Clark (2007) and Greene (2007), and in 2007 *The Journal of Mixed Methods* was launched. From a relatively obscure beginning, mixed methods has now become accepted as an integral part of the research methods establishment.

━━━━━━━━━ BOX 1.5 ━━━━━━━━━

ADVANTAGES OF USING MIXED-METHODS RESEARCH

1. Mixed methods enables researchers to answer a wider range of research questions than in single methods. It is not confined to answering just one type of research question but can answer both quantitative and qualitative questions as well as those that involve both forms of data in the one question.
2. Using mixed methods can provide stronger inferences. Teddlie and Tashakkori (2009: 34) argue that mixed methods can utilize the strengths of different methods and offset any weaknesses these methods may have by themselves.
3. Using mixed methods can identify any divergent findings that occur due to the use of both quantitative and qualitative methods. Such findings may arise due to the methods addressing different aspects of a problem which would not have been identified in a single method. Addressing such inconsistencies in mixed-methods research is dealt with in Chapter 16.
4. Researchers can integrate findings from qualitative and quantitative methods in the one study, thereby providing more comprehensive information about the issue being researched.

AN OVERVIEW OF THE RESEARCH PROCESS

An overview is useful for gaining a broad perspective on the research process to see how the various components get put together. In particular, it helps identify when using mixed methods rather than a single method in a research project is appropriate.

A research project can be divided into the following stages:

*   Choosing the research topic
*   Reviewing the literature on the topic
*   Formulating the research questions to be answered
*   Deciding whether the research questions can be answered by analysing existing (secondary) data or by collecting new (primary) data
*   Deciding on the conceptual and theoretical framework to be adopted
*   Choosing the research design
*   Gaining funding for the project
*   Gaining ethical approval for the study
*   Selecting participants for the study
*   Conducting the research project
*   Undertaking the data analysis
*   Reporting and communicating the findings from the research.

An illustration of these stages is provided in Box 1.6, which describes the design and conduct of a research project as part of an advanced undergraduate course in research methods at the

University of New South Wales supervised by the author. This example illustrates that steps 5 and 6 in particular are intertwined and a decision on step 5 was actually not made until after step 6 in this case.

BOX 1.6

AN EXAMPLE OF A RESEARCH PROJECT TO ILLUSTRATE THE STEPS INVOLVED IN THE CHOICE, DESIGN AND CONDUCT OF RESEARCH

1. Choosing the research topic: the general topic of road safety was set by the supervisor. The first meeting discussed areas of interest and the topic of road safety in school zones was chosen. School zones are areas in the immediate vicinity of a school. Sponsorship was then obtained from the state Roads and Traffics Authority (RTA).
2. Reviewing the literature: peer-reviewed journals and reports by Road Safety centres and agencies were accessed to provide a basis for constructing research questions.
3. Formulating the research questions: the aim of researching road safety in school zones was to find out to what extent drivers, parents and children observed safety rules in these zones. The list of research questions will not be reproduced here due to space requirements but they concerned the behaviour of drivers, parents and children during the operation of the zones (morning and afternoon when schools start and finish) and the views of these groups along with teachers about the effectiveness of the operation of the zones.
4. Deciding whether the research questions can be answered by existing data or not. Since there were no studies on the operation of these zones, primary research was indicated.
5. Choosing the conceptual and theoretical frameworks: this proved to be a difficult step due to the variety of viewpoints about such frameworks present in the group. Largely because a mixed-methods methodology was adopted in step 6, it was agreed that to combine both quantitative and qualitative data a post-positivist paradigm seemed to be most appropriate. No particular theoretical perspective emerged from the literature review.
6. Choosing the research design: a mixed-methods methodology was chosen since it was agreed that quantitative data was needed to document the extent to which traffic regulations were observed and qualitative data was needed on the views of parents and teachers on the effectiveness of the rules. The research methods to be used included an observational study of drivers, parents and children in the school zone. Mainly quantitative data was obtained, dealing with the extent to which safety rules were observed. Interviews were conducted with teachers and parents to gain their views about the operation of the zones and these interviews yielded the qualitative data.
7. Gaining funding for the research: the research was funded through teaching grants to the course. The Roads and Traffic Authority was prepared to provide funding but this was not needed.

(Continued)

8. Gaining ethical approval: an ethics application was submitted to the university ethics committee and approval obtained.
9. Selecting participants for the study: four school zones were chosen within the Sydney metropolitan area, two on main roads and two in side streets to ascertain any differences in observation of rules. Parents were interviewed as they arrived to collect their children and teachers were interviewed depending on availability.
10. Conducting the research project: students were allocated to zones to collect data using an observational protocol to collect the observational data and an interview schedule to collect the interview data.
11. Undertaking data analysis: quantitative data was analysed using SPSS on university computers and interview data was coded using NVivo.
12. Reporting and communicating findings: students each wrote their own reports as part of their course requirements and the supervisor put together the best of the reports to compile a report for the RTA. Selected students presented the finding to a seminar at the RTA offices after the course was completed.

These stages will be outlined in detail throughout this book.

CONCLUSION

This chapter has explored the nature of social research and outlined the emergence of mixed methods as a way to overcome the paradigm wars and combine the benefits of qualitative and quantitative methods in the one study.

At this stage, the notions of paradigms and paradigm wars have been introduced in a preliminary way to explain why mixed methods emerged as a reaction against the seemingly entrenched oppositions between positivists on the quantitative side and interpretivists and constructivists on the qualitative side. More details are provided in Chapter 3 where paradigms for mixed-methods research are discussed.

CHAPTER SUMMARY

The social sciences use a range of research methods to advance knowledge in their respective areas. These methods may be either qualitative or quantitative or a mixture of both. In the latter case, the approach is called mixed methods.

Social research can take on a variety of forms. The three main forms of research are: basic research, which is conducted to expand knowledge in an area; strategic research, which is conducted to investigate areas of special interest to government policy; and applied research, which is conducted to solve practical problems.

There are also three main goals of social research: exploration, description and explanation. Exploratory research opens up new fields about which little is known; descriptive research aims to provide a picture of the main features of a field of study; and explanatory research aims to answer 'why' questions or to test theories about the social phenomena under investigation.

Quantitative research tended to dominate the social sciences until the latter part of the 20th century until qualitative researchers challenged its legitimacy as the main research methodology. This led to a period referred to as the 'paradigm wars' where each side attacked the assumptions and methods of the other. The emergence of mixed methods effectively ended this conflict and heralded a new era of social research where both quantitative and qualitative methods could be integrated to provide a unified approach to research.

FURTHER READING

Creswell, J. W. and Plano Clark, V. L. (2011) *Designing and Conducting Mixed Methods Research*, **2nd edition. Thousand Oaks, CA: Sage Publications.**
This is the second edition of a pioneering text on mixed methods. Chapters 1 and 2 cover in more detail the background to mixed methods than has been included in this chapter.

Neuman, W. L. (2011) *Social Research Methods: Qualitative and Quantitative Approaches*, **7th edition. Boston, MA: Pearson Education.**
This is a widely used introductory text that provides some useful material in Chapters 1–4 on the contents of this chapter.

Reichhardt, C. S. and Rallis, S. F. (eds) (1994) The qualitative–quantitative debate: New perspectives. *New Directions for Program Evaluation*, **No. 61. San Francisco, CA: Jossey-Bass.**
This is a useful collection of early articles on the quantitative–qualitative debate as it related to the field of evaluation. It predates the emergence of mixed methods but many of the articles advocate combining these methods.

Schoemaker, P. J., Tankard, J. W. Jr. and Lasora, D. L. (2004) *How to Build Social Science Theories*. **Thousand Oaks, CA: Sage Publications.**
This book provides a very systematic approach to theory building and testing in the social sciences, a topic that was only touched on briefly here in the discussion of explanatory research.

2

DEFINING PARADIGMS IN MIXED-METHODS RESEARCH

INTRODUCTION

In Chapter 1, the concept of a research paradigm was introduced and the debate between qualitative researchers adopting interpretivist or constructivist paradigms and quantitative researchers adopting a positivist or post-positivist paradigm was outlined. This debate came to be called the 'paradigm wars'. Proponents of each paradigm argued that the paradigm they supported was the only viable one for the social sciences. The positivist and post-positivist paradigms, on the one hand, and the interpretivist and constructivist paradigms, on the other, were said to be incompatible (Howe, 1988).

This 'incompatibility thesis' was used to justify conducting either quantitative research (positivism or post-positivism) or qualitative research (interpretivism or constructivism) since it was argued that there was a necessary connection between the research approach and its supporting paradigm.

The emergence of mixed methods challenged both the incompatibility thesis and the claim that there is a necessary connection between research methods and paradigms.

A consideration of paradigms is of particular importance in mixed-methods research because it combines quantitative and qualitative methods and so needs to address the issues involved in doing this.

In this chapter, we will examine the notion of a paradigm and its application to social research methods and outline the ways in which paradigms have been applied to mixed-methods research.

PARADIGMS

The notion of a research paradigm was originally proposed by Thomas Kuhn in his book *The Structure of Scientific Revolutions* (Kuhn, 1970). In this book, he characterized science as going through a series of paradigm shifts during which assumptions on which scientists had relied to engage in scientific work were challenged, resulting in a new conception of what constituted scientific research. A paradigm then was the set of assumptions, often not articulated, on which scientists relied to conduct their research.

The components of a paradigm are set out in Table 2.1. What defines a particular paradigm is the stance it takes on one or more of these components.

The concept of a paradigm has, however, been interpreted in a number of ways. Morgan (2007) has identified four meanings of the term. These are:

- paradigms as world views
- paradigms as epistemological stances
- paradigms as shared beliefs among members of a specialty area
- paradigms as model examples of research.

Table 2.1 Components of a paradigm

Component	Description	Application in mixed-methods research
Ontology	Ontology is concerned with establishing what exists, with the nature of existence. It addresses the question of whether objects exist independently of minds (realism) or whether they are mental entities and hence mind-dependent (idealism)	Are the entities studied in quantitative and qualitative research the same or different?
Epistemology	Epistemology is concerned with the nature of knowledge and how it is produced. It addresses the question of whether all knowledge is derived from the senses (empiricism) or whether some knowledge is derived from logic (rationalism), or whether knowledge is socially constructed (constructivism)	Is the knowledge produced by quantitative research of the same kind as that produced by qualitative research?
Axiology	Axiology is concerned with the nature of values and value judgements	Are there differences in the value components in quantitative and qualitative research?
Methodology	Methodology is concerned with the systematic analysis of methods used in research	How can quantitative and qualitative methods be meaningfully combined in the one study?

The world-view meaning is by far the broadest, most all-encompassing way of thinking about the world, including values, what constitutes reality (ontology) and how this reality can be known (epistemology).

The other meanings are more restricted than the first. Paradigms as epistemological stances treat a paradigm as a set of assumptions about what constitutes knowledge. Two stances that were adopted in the social sciences and gave rise to the paradigm wars are positivism and constructivism (see Chapter 1, Table 1.3) and these have fundamentally different positions on epistemology.

The third meaning, namely paradigms as shared beliefs, does not rely solely on epistemological beliefs but also encompasses research practice and has been applied to whole disciplines such as sociology.

The fourth meaning – model examples of research – is the most specific and least common amongst social scientists, most likely because there is little or no agreement on what constitutes model research.

Morgan (2007: 50) considered the second meaning as being most widely held in the social sciences, since it highlights the assumptions that most differentiate those espousing qualitative or quantitative methods. The first view is also widely adopted as many researchers extend their assumptions beyond just epistemological ones.

The term 'world view' seems to be rather broad and all encompassing, but since the other three views tend to be too restrictive this will be the view of paradigms adopted here.

Table 2.2 summarizes these views.

Table 2.2 Views about paradigms

Views about paradigms	Characteristics	Advantages	Disadvantages
As world views	Ways of thinking about the world	Enables inclusion of a wide range of beliefs	Can be too broad
As epistemological stances	Views about the nature of knowledge	Focuses on the key assumptions about knowledge	May neglect some important issues
As shared beliefs	Beliefs about how research should be conducted	Avoids philosophical issues	Difficulty in characterizing beliefs
As model examples of research	Examples regarded as high-quality research	Provides clear statement of what constitutes good research	Too narrow; limited application

Source: adapted from Morgan, 2007: Table 1

RELATIONSHIPS BETWEEN RESEARCH METHODS AND PARADIGMS

The paradigm wars, as has been pointed out, were fought over claims as to what was to be the appropriate paradigm for the social sciences as well as the most appropriate form of data to be collected. In this debate, the form of data was identified with the paradigm: quantitative data with positivism and qualitative data with (mostly) constructivism.

Subsequent critics of this debate point out that there is nothing inherent in the form of data to identify it with any particular paradigm (see Teddlie and Tashakkori, 2010).

While quantitative data provides very limited scope for interpretation under a constructivist or interpretivist paradigm, it does not require a positivist paradigm for its interpretation. Alternative paradigms to be described in this chapter, such as post-positivism, pragmatism or realism, can readily accommodate quantitative data as well as qualitative data.

Indeed, qualitative data in all its forms can be interpreted under a wide range of paradigms. It is how the data is conceptualized, rather than its form, that constitutes the paradigm.

This separation of data form from paradigmatic identification is crucial to mixed-methods research which relies on being able to combine qualitative and quantitative data in the one study. In the next section, paradigms that have been applied to mixed-methods research will be outlined.

PARADIGMS IN MIXED-METHODS RESEARCH

Two approaches have been taken to the application of paradigms to mixed-methods research. These are:

- the multiple paradigm approach
- the single paradigm approach.

The multiple paradigm approach

The multiple paradigm approach adopts different paradigms for quantitative and qualitative data. This approach has been favoured by Greene (2007) and Greene and Hall (2010). They call it the *dialectic stance*. A problem with this stance is that it needs to address more clearly how it can deal with incompatible paradigms. Greene and Hall (2010) provide an example where the researcher adopts a constructivist stance for the qualitative data and a critical realist (see below) approach for the quantitative data, but don't provide any guidance as to how the conflicting assumptions in these approaches are to be reconciled.

The single paradigm approach

The single paradigm approach adopts the same paradigm for quantitative and qualitative data. Single paradigms that have been suggested for mixed methods research are pragmatism, post-positivism and realism. Mertens (2003) has proposed an alternative paradigm which she calls the *transformative–emancipatory paradigm*. In her own words, 'The transformative–emancipatory paradigm places central importance on the lives and experiences of those who suffer oppression and discrimination' (Mertens, 2003: 159). This insistence on addressing issues of discrimination and oppression has led to the claim that rather than being a paradigm this approach is better seen as a purpose of research (Tashakkori and Teddlie, 2003: 680). This is the view that will be adopted here so that the single paradigms for mixed methods research are pragmatism, post-positivism and realism to be described next.

Pragmatism

Pragmatism has gained considerable support amongst mixed-methods researchers and has most likely become the most widely supported paradigm. It derives from the writings of American philosophers of the 19th and early 20th centuries, notably Charles Peirce, John Dewey and William James. In philosophy, it asserts that the meaning of a concept lies in its practical consequences. It justifies mixed methods by focusing on the practical results of using the approach rather than on any epistemological issues.

Pragmatism has been proposed as an approach to mixed-methods research by Biesta (2010), Johnson and Onwuegbuzie (2004), Maxcy (2003), Morgan (2007) and others.

As a philosophical approach, it has been criticised by Russell (1945) on the grounds that we cannot know the consequences of action to assess their usefulness until after the actions have been performed. Thus, the meaning of a concept cannot be defined in advance of its use and only then if this use has practical consequences.

A version of this critique in mixed-methods research has been advanced by Mertens (2003: 159) when she argued that 'The value of pragmatics that drives the desire to adopt a mixed methods stance in research is seen as inadequate and unexamined because it does not answer the question "Practical for whom and to what end?"'.

Despite these criticisms, pragmatism has gained a lot of adherents because it is perceived to straightforwardly solve the conceptual problems of combining qualitative and quantitative methods by pointing to the practical usefulness of the outcomes.

Post-positivism

Many predominantly quantitative researchers accepted many of the criticisms levelled against positivism and proposed amendments to positivism to accommodate these criticisms, hence the emergence of post-positivism.

Post-positivism rejected the controversial elements of positivism, namely:

* that research must be value-free in order to qualify as scientific
* that observations must be objective in order to be accepted as research data
* that the goal of research is the accumulation of facts, leading to the construction of empirical laws.

Post-positivists accept that values are inextricably intertwined with the research process but seek to identify these values and ascertain their effect on research outcomes. They also acknowledge an element of subjectivity in observations. Adopting a range of methods to examine an issue can assist in ascertaining the impact of subjectivity so that post-positivists are amenable to the use of mixed methods.

The role of theory in research is also emphasized by post-positivists. Theory testing is an integral part of post-positivist research. Post-positivists do not see scientific progress as the construction of empirical laws.

Post-positivists share a realist ontology with positivists. They assert the existence of an independent and external reality which scientific research seeks to uncover. This has led to the development of more specific assumptions about that external reality, resulting in the development of a realism paradigm largely overtaking post-positivism.

Realism

Realism has gained support from mixed-methods researchers, following its widespread use in the field of evaluation (see Mark, Henry and Julnes, 2000).

Realism is basically an ontological position (see Table 2.1) that does not make any particular commitment to other components of a paradigm without additional assumptions. Consequently, there are several versions of realism in the social sciences and it is not always clear which one is being applied to mixed methods. These include **critical realism** (Maxwell and Mittapalli, 2010; McEvoy and Richards, 2006) and emergent realism (Mark, Henry and Julnes, 2000).

There are even differences among critical realists. For example, McEvoy and Richards (2006) adopt Bhaskar's (1978) version, which divides reality into levels, while others, such as Maxwell and Mittapalli (2010), don't.

Furthermore, although Maxwell and Mittapalli (2010: 151) adopt a realist ontology, they adopt a constructivist epistemology, for instance 'critical realism retains ontological realism while accepting a form of epistemological relativism or constructivism'. This is not a position most realists would endorse, since it implies that even if there is a reality out there we cannot know anything about it since our knowledge is socially constructed.

Thus, adopting a realist paradigm for mixed-methods research is incomplete without specifying the other components set out in Table 2.1.

Critical realists accept that values cannot be removed from research. This has been a major problem with positivism, which asserts that research is value-free. That is, researchers espousing a positivist paradigm claim that research must not be influenced by values, a claim that has been discredited many times. As indicated above, *post-positivism* is a modification of positivism that recognizes the influence of values in research but otherwise retains the other components of positivism.

How critical realism differs from post-positivism is that it deliberately incorporates those values that contribute to social progress and critiques ideologies that stand in the way of this.

RELEVANCE OF PARADIGMS TO RESEARCH

It is of course possible to conduct research without any reference or regard for a paradigm and many researchers do just this. In such instances, it is likely that there is an implicit paradigm that is being used, sometimes without the researcher being aware of the paradigm they have adopted.

This practice may not necessarily result in any problems with the research but it does run the risk of inconsistencies in reporting and interpreting findings. This can particularly occur in mixed-methods research where findings from qualitative and quantitative research are being compared. Here it is possible to interpret these findings using different paradigms for each. This is not necessarily a problem since the *dialectic stance* outlined above permits this, but researchers need to be aware that they are using the dialectic stance so that they are able to apply it appropriately.

Mixed-methods researchers using a single paradigm, such as that discussed above, need to be clear about which paradigm they are using and to apply it consistently throughout the analysis and interpretation of the findings. Only if this is done will the research achieve coherence.

It should be clear from this discussion that there is no 'best paradigm' for mixed methods research. Alternative paradigms may be appropriate for different research problems so that no one paradigm is applicable to all mixed-methods research.

CONCLUSION

Paradigms divide researchers over what they judge to constitute valid research. There is no way of deciding whether one paradigm is in any sense 'better' than another. Choice of a paradigm is a matter of personal conviction, determined by one's views about what constitutes reality and how it can be researched.

The 'paradigm wars' discussed in this part have not been resolved, nor will they be. The important point for researchers is that a knowledge of the paradigms and their implications for research, is essential for engaging in the conduct of social research.

CHAPTER SUMMARY

Research paradigms are the guiding principles under which research is conducted. They provide researchers with a justification for deciding what it is they are researching, how to go about their research and how to interpret their findings.

Researchers do not always acknowledge the paradigm they have adopted but one is always implicit in the way research is conducted and findings are interpreted.

The emergence of mixed-methods research has highlighted the significance of paradigms by combining methods that traditionally have involved competing paradigms. The challenge for mixed-methods researchers is to justify the combination of qualitative and quantitative methods in the one study in the face of these competing paradigms. This chapter has described how mixed-methods researchers attempt to do this, either by adopting different paradigms for the quantitative and qualitative components of their research, the dialectic stance of Jennifer Greene, or by adopting a single paradigm that accommodates both quantitative and qualitative components such as pragmatism, post-positivism or realism, outlined above.

Pragmatism focuses on the practical usefulness of combining qualitative and quantitative methods, stressing the benefits derived from this process. Post-positivism and realism share a common realist ontology but differ in the way reality is conceived.

There is clearly no agreement over a 'best paradigm' for mixed-methods research but rather a realization that alternative paradigms may be appropriate for different problems.

FURTHER READING

Creswell, J. W. and Plano Clark, V. L. (2011) *Designing and Conducting Mixed Methods Research,* **2nd edition. Thousand Oaks, CA: Sage Publications.**
Chapters 1 and 2 deal with the paradigm debate and paradigms for mixed-methods research.

Hall, R. (2013) Mixed methods: In search of a paradigm. In T. Le and Q. Le (eds), *Conducting Research in a Changing and Challenging World.* **New York: Nova Publishers.**
This chapter discusses the paradigm issues in mixed-methods research.

Morgan, D. L. (2007) Paradigms lost and pragmatism regained: Methodological implications of combining qualitative and quantitative methods. *Journal of Mixed Methods Research,* **1, 48–76.**
This article summarizes the various meanings of paradigm and their application to mixed-methods research.

Tashakkori, A. and Teddlie, C. (eds) (2010) *Sage Handbook of Mixed Methods in Social and Behavioral Research,* **2nd edition. Thousand Oaks, CA: Sage Publications.**
Part 1 of this book contains a series of articles dealing with the paradigms discussed in this chapter.

PLANNING SOCIAL RESEARCH

Part 2 deals with planning social research using mixed methods. Planning issues involve the selection of a research problem, conducting a literature review to ascertain the state of knowledge in the chosen area, choosing an appropriate conceptual and theoretical framework, deciding on the research questions to be addressed and choosing the research design to be used.

Throughout this part, and indeed in the rest of the book, distinctions are drawn among the concepts of research design, research methods and data collection procedures. These distinctions are not always drawn in the research methods literature, often leading to some confusion over their use. A research design is the overarching concept that includes the methods used, sampling procedures, data collection and analysis. The research method is defined here as a broad concept identifying the general approach to conducting research, including sampling and data collection procedures. At the most specific level, sampling and data collection procedures deal with the actual conduct of the research.

Chapter 3 deals with establishing the research problem, including conducting the literature review and identifying the aims and research questions. It will also include a discussion of how research quality can be addressed.

Chapter 4 outlines the theoretical and conceptual frameworks appropriate to social research. Alternative approaches to theory construction will be outlined as well as concept development in both qualitative and quantitative research.

Chapter 5 outlines the major research methodologies involved in social research, namely qualitative, quantitative and mixed, and describes each of the research methods available to social researchers. This will be followed by an account of how research methods are linked to research questions.

Chapter 6 outlines a rationale for the use of mixed methods, describes how quantitative and qualitative research methods are combined to form mixed-methods designs, and details a proposed classification of these designs.

3

DEFINING THE RESEARCH PROBLEM AND REVIEWING THE LITERATURE

INTRODUCTION

Defining the research problem involves choosing a research topic, reviewing the existing literature, deciding on the aims of the research and obtaining funding.

Research questions must then be formulated and it is these that determine the research design to answer them. Research questions play a central role in deciding whether mixed methods are needed.

In this chapter, the process of setting up a research project will be outlined. The major steps involved are:

1. Choosing the research topic
2. Reviewing the existing literature
3. Deciding on the conceptual and theoretical framework to be adopted
4. Formulating the research questions to be answered
5. Deciding whether to analyse existing data or collect new data
6. Deciding on the research methods
7. Gaining funding for the research
8. Gaining ethics approval for the project.

Steps 1, 2, 4, 5, 7 and 8 will be dealt with in this chapter, and steps 3 and 6 in the following chapters.

Embedded in all stages of the research process is the issue of research quality. No researcher can afford to neglect consideration of how to achieve credibility of research outcomes and this only comes with attending to quality matters early in the research process.

It is now recognized that this process of ensuring quality differs for quantitative and qualitative research. The chapter will conclude with an outline of the research quality issues for both qualitative and quantitative research and for mixed-methods research.

CHOOSING THE RESEARCH TOPIC

Research projects can be either self-initiated by the researcher or in response to a research brief issued by a funding body.

Basic research is most often conducted in universities by academics or postgraduate research students. Applied and strategic research can also be conducted in universities but also in private research consultancies or research institutes.

Ideas for self-initiated research derive from a number of sources, including:

- priorities set by a research team or centre
- previous research experience by a researcher
- collaboration with research colleagues through personal communication or conference attendance
- further research suggestions in published studies.

Much applied and strategic research is commissioned by governments, government agencies, large charitable organizations or peak industry bodies. In such cases, the topics are determined by the organization commissioning the research. This is set out in a *research brief* or *request for proposal* (RFP) as it is usually termed in the USA.

The research brief or RFP should contain at least the following information:

- details about the organization commissioning the research
- background to the research required, including reasons it is needed by the organization
- aims and objectives of the research
- a timetable for completing the research
- funds allocated for the project
- deliverables by the researcher, such as presentations, preliminary and final reports
- date and contact details for the submission of proposals.

The research brief might also include suggestions or even requirements for the conduct of the research. In this case, often little discretion is given to the researcher so that, unless mixed-methods designs are included in the brief, there may be little or no scope for their use.

Research briefs may be found on websites of government agencies or large non-profit organizations. There are also websites devoted to research briefs. For example, the RFP Data Base (www.rfpdb.com) lists requests for proposals current in both the USA and Europe. In Australia, the website Austenders (www.tenders.gov.au) lists the government research briefs available for tender.

In all forms of research, familiarity with the literature on the topic is essential for understanding the issues that need to be addressed in future research. This familiarity is gained from a review of the literature as well as through the previous experience of the researcher.

REVIEWING THE LITERATURE

Conducting a literature review enables researchers to identify areas where further research on a chosen topic is needed. Literature reviews can differ in their focus. Cooper (1998) identified three main areas on which a literature review can focus:

- Integrative research review: focuses on past research findings with a view to identifying directions for future research
- Methodological review: focuses on methods used to research a problem or an issue with a view to critiquing existing methods and suggesting improved methods
- Theoretical review: examines and critiques the theories that have been used to explain findings in an area with a view to identifying better theoretical approaches.

Key issues in any literature review include:

- Accessing the literature: researchers need to decide how extensively they intend to cover the literature on the topic they are researching. Papers directly on the topic published in peer-reviewed journals should be the top priority as these are considered to be the highest quality articles because they have passed through a rigorous review process by experts in the field. Books on the topic are also of high priority, although most of the material in books has most likely already been published in peer-reviewed journals. Papers in non-peer-reviewed journals may be included but these are of lower priority since they have not passed through a rigorous review process.
- Organizing the review: researchers need to decide how the review will be organized. Themes could be based on the theories used in the literature, on methods used, on concepts explored or on a chronological sequence of research published. The organization to be used will depend on the topic and the nature of the literature.

If an integrative research review is conducted, it:

- identifies the research reported on the topic under consideration
- brings together the main findings from that research
- points out areas of agreement and disagreement in the research findings
- identifies strengths and weaknesses in the research reports
- locates knowledge gaps in the research
- indicates where future research is needed.

An integrative review may also include the theoretical approaches that have been taken in the literature, identify any problems in applying theories and point to promising alternative or modified theoretical developments.

There is no simple format for a literature review as each topic has its own particular set of issues, sub-topics and theories. There are, however, a variety of sources that contain suggestions about setting out literature reviews. Some of these are presented in Table 3.1.

The first two of these sources in the table are relatively brief but provide useful suggestions about writing the review and can readily be located on the internet. The third is a book on the topic now in its seventh edition. It is a very comprehensive account of the process of writing a review.

Table 3.1 Some guidelines for writing a literature review

Source	Content
Guidelines for writing a literature review: www.duluth.umn.edu/~hrallis/guides/researching/litreview.html	A step-by-step guide to writing a literature review with reference to other sources
How to write a literature review: library.bcu.ac.uk/learner/writingguides/1.04.htm	Suggestions about what to include in a literature review and how to structure it
Writing literature reviews: Galvan, J. L. (2017) *Writing Literature Reviews: A Guide for Students of the Social and Behavioral Sciences*, 7th edition (Routledge)	A comprehensive guide for writing literature reviews

Locating literature sources

Deciding what literature to include in a literature review can present difficulties for a researcher. On the one hand, the researcher would not wish to miss important contributions, while, on the other hand, she would not wish to waste time on unimportant or poor quality literature. However, distinguishing important from unimportant contributions is not simple.

A useful starting point is to use the established credibility ratings of literature sources. A credibility hierarchy of sources is set out in Table 3.2. Peer review is the major contributor to the credibility of sources. Peer review involves a paper submitted for publication being sent to experts in the field for review. The paper is only published if the experts agree that it is worthy of publication. They may require amendments to the paper or further research to be conducted before the paper is published or they may recommend it not be published at all.

There are a number of alternative rankings of sources so that the ranking in Table 3.2 should be read as indicative only. Disciplines tend to produce credibility hierarchies specific to their discipline.

Even the highest credibility sources can publish papers that have later turned out to be discredited by subsequent publications, sometimes where fraud has been identified (see Box 3.1). It is not easy to identify fraudulent research, particularly when it is published in prestigious journals. Where research reports findings that contradict previous research or findings that other researchers have not been able to replicate, caution needs to be exercised.

Table 3.2   Research sources and their credibility

Source	Credibility	Comments
Papers published in top-ranking peer-reviewed journals	Highest	Journal rankings can be found in most university libraries
Research books published by reputable publishers	High	Identifying reputable publishers can be a problem
Papers published in middle-ranking peer-reviewed journals	High	Journal rankings can be misleading as some journals that receive middle rankings are often regarded as high quality
Published conference proceedings where papers are peer reviewed for inclusion	High	The conference website will provide details of the review process
Papers published in low-ranking peer-reviewed journals	Medium	Having a low ranking does not necessarily mean the papers published are not of high quality
Reports by government agencies and research centres	Medium	These may or may not be peer reviewed. The quality of such reports can be variable
Papers published in non-peer-reviewed journals or conference proceedings	Low	Lack of peer review means that the research is not subject to scrutiny by experts in the field so there can be no guarantee of quality
Internet sources not produced by reputable publishers	Lowest	Much of what is called research that appears in internet sources is not subject to any professional scrutiny

━━━ BOX 3.1 ━━━

EXAMPLES OF RESEARCH FRAUD

Example 1: Effect of personal contact on voters' attitude towards gay marriage

In December 2014, LaCour and Green published findings that personal contact by gay advocates had a lasting influence on the attitudes towards gay marriage of those interviewed. Attempts to replicate these findings were not successful and further investigations revealed that the data had been fabricated. The paper has since been retracted.

(Continued)

Example 2: Racial stereotyping

Dutch social psychologist Diederik Stapel was found to have fabricated data in a number of studies, ranging over areas of social psychology including racial stereotyping. Stapel had also sent his fabricated data sets to colleagues for further analysis and publication and supervised a number of graduate students, some of whom also used his data. As of December 2015, *Retraction Watch* had reported 58 retractions of articles published by Stapel.

Writing the review

Detailed guidelines for writing literature reviews can be found in the sources included in Table 3.1. Some issues to be focused on by mixed-methods researchers are included here:

- References to justifications for using mixed methods may need to be included as not all researchers are familiar with these arguments.
- Research on the topic using mixed methods should be highlighted where it is relevant to the research aims.
- The review needs to be clearly focused on providing a rationale for the proposed research and why the use of mixed methods is appropriate.

RESEARCH QUESTIONS

Research questions are those formulated by the researcher that the research project aims to answer. They are the main focus of the research.

Research questions should be distinguished from *aims* and *hypotheses*. Aims are the broad statement of purpose of the research, whereas hypotheses are specific predictions about research findings. Examples of these distinctions are shown in Table 3.3.

Table 3.3 Example of differences among aims, research questions and hypotheses in a study of paid work undertaken by full-time students

Aim	To ascertain problems faced by full-time university students who are engaged in part-time work
Research questions	1. What percentage of full-time students work in paid employment during term time? 2. Are full-time students working more hours per week in paid employment now compared to a decade ago? 3. What is the relationship between hours worked per week and grades achieved by full-time students? 4. What coping strategies do full-time students who work more than 20 hours per week adopt to balance their work and study? 5. Do full-time male and female students experience different problems in combining work with study?

| **Hypotheses** | 1. | There is a negative correlation between hours worked per week by full-time university students and their time spent in study. |
| | 2. | Female full-time students report more problems in combining work and study than do male full-time students. |

Source: Hall (2010)

Types of research questions

Classifications of research questions range from a simple two-type classification of descriptive ('what' questions) versus explanatory ('why' questions) to multi-type classifications based on research purpose (see White, 2009, Ch. 2) or on data type (qualitative or quantitative).

A classification that does capture the main differences in research questions is as follows: descriptive, correlative, comparative, casual, evaluative.

Descriptive questions

Descriptive questions are concerned with establishing what the case is. They ask 'what', 'when', 'where' and 'how much' questions. They can be qualitative or quantitative. The fourth research question in Table 3.3 is a qualitative descriptive question. The first research question in Table 3.3 is a quantitative descriptive question.

Descriptive questions are by far the most common research questions asked in the social sciences.

Correlative or relational questions

Correlative or relational questions are concerned with relationships among concepts. The third research question in Table 3.3 is a quantitative correlative question. Establishing relationships among concepts is a common goal of social research so that such questions play a prominent role in research.

Correlative questions are descriptive rather than explanatory. They establish only whether a relationship exists, not whether the relationship is causal.

Comparative questions

Comparative questions are those that ask whether differences exist among two or more groups on a **dependent variable** or variables (quantitative) or on some descriptions of experience (qualitative). The second research question in Table 3.3 is a quantitative comparative question, while the fifth research question is a qualitative question.

Causal or impact questions

Causal or impact questions seek to establish cause–effect relationships. Such questions are often quite difficult to answer since establishing a causal relationship requires ruling out all other possible causes and this is not easily achieved in social research due to the complexity of the relationships being studied. This difficulty has led some social researchers to argue that causal questions are just not appropriate in social research.

Evaluative questions

Evaluative questions are concerned with assessing the value of a programme or practice. Evaluation has increasingly become an integral part of social research with many books and journals devoted to it (e.g. Newcomer, Hatry and Wholey, 2015). Evaluative questions ask whether an intervention has been effective, has achieved the goals set for it or can be improved. Answers to such questions necessarily contain value judgements.

Qualitative and quantitative research questions

Research questions can also be classified according to data type, namely quantitative or qualitative questions. Quantitative research questions are those that are asked about a dependent variable. Qualitative questions are those asked about outcomes that are not quantified. As Onwuegbuzie and Leech (2006: 482) state, qualitative questions 'tend to seek, to discover, to explore a process or describe experiences'. In this sense, they tend to be descriptive but may be comparative, as, for example, question 5 in Table 3.3.

Research questions in mixed-methods research

Mixed-methods research entails both qualitative and quantitative research questions. It has been suggested by Onwuegbuzie and Leech (2006) and by Creswell and Plano Clark (2011) that there are also mixed-methods research questions. According to Onwuegbuzie and Leech (2006: 483), mixed-methods research questions are those that 'combine or mix both the quantitative and qualitative research questions'. Answers to such questions will involve either a quantitative or qualitative analysis and in that sense can be allocated to a quantitative or qualitative question without the need to invoke a separate category of research question. Onwuegbuzie and Leech (2006: 485) give as an example of a mixed-methods research question: 'What is the difference in levels of statistics performance between freshmen whose negative experiences while enrolled in the statistics course were extreme and freshmen whose negative experiences while enrolled in the statistics course were not extreme?' The answer to this question will be a quantitative comparison of performance on the statistics course between the two groups and as such will be a quantitative comparison question. The groups themselves will have of course been established by a qualitative research method so that a mixed-methods design will be necessary to answer the question, but the question itself is clearly a quantitative one.

Creswell and Plano Clark (2017, Ch. 5) provide a number of mixed-methods research questions as examples. But these examples tend to be interpretations of findings rather than research questions or value statements that can't be answered by reference to data. An example of the former is 'In what ways do the qualitative data help to explain the quantitative results?' and an example of the latter is 'Is the instrument that has been designed based on the qualitative data a better instrument than existing instruments?'

Whether a separate class of research questions is necessary to incorporate mixed-methods designs is yet to be decided. What needs to be emphasized here is that research questions need to be carefully chosen so that they enable integration of the answers into the mixed-methods framework adopted. These frameworks will be discussed in the next chapter.

DECIDING WHETHER TO ANALYSE EXISTING DATA OR COLLECT NEW DATA

In some instances, the research questions may be answered by analysing existing data rather than collecting new primary data. This involves a distinction between primary and secondary data.

Primary data is original data that has not previously been collected. **Secondary data** is data that already exists. It includes previous research studies, statistical data collected by government agencies and administrative records of organizations.

If the research questions can be answered from existing information, there is no need to collect new, primary data. A wealth of data exists in previous research reports and surveys conducted by government agencies, such as the General Social Survey (GSS) conducted in the USA every second year (see Box 3.2).

Accessing secondary data can be plagued by problems, including:

- gaining access to the information: documents containing the required information may not be available or access to them is denied
- document quality: documents produced by organizations often reflect the biases and assumptions of those responsible for their production so that information of importance to the researcher may not be included.

Researchers need to assess the worth of secondary data and, if found lacking, then new primary research will need to be conducted. The remainder of this chapter will be concerned with primary research.

━━━━━ BOX 3.2 ━━━━━

THE GENERAL SOCIAL SURVEY AS AN EXAMPLE OF SECONDARY DATA

The General Social Survey (GSS) has been conducted in the USA since 1972 by the National Opinion Research Center (NORC) at the University of Chicago. Residents aged 18+ are randomly chosen to participate and the questions cover a wide range of attitudes, practices and concerns as well as demographic information about the participants. The data from the survey is available to researchers to analyse and report trends in US attitudes and practices. Special topics such as crime, civil liberties, morality and social mobility are also included. According to NORC, the programme has two major goals:

- to conduct basic scientific research on the structure of American society
- to distribute up-to-date, important, high quality data to social scientists, students, policy makers and others.

GAINING FUNDING FOR THE RESEARCH

For some research projects, funding is available and so is not an issue. This is usually the case for postgraduate research projects and by individual researchers working in an institutional environment, such as a university, where the project is small scale and does not require substantial funds. In such cases, a detailed research proposal may not be necessary, although postgraduate students will need to prepare a proposal for their research to be approved.

Where funding needs to be accessed, a researcher will need to submit a research proposal to gain the necessary funding. The key elements of a proposal are set out in Box 3.3. Some additional information may be required for commissioned research tenders as specified in the research brief.

━━━━━ BOX 3.3 ━━━━━

KEY ELEMENTS OF A RESEARCH PROPOSAL

A research proposal should include at least the following:

1. Aims and importance of the research: this section should set out the main aims of the research and give some guidance on why it is important.
2. Background: this section should include sufficient information on the background to the research project to justify its conduct. It should include a review of the key literature in the field.

3. Research questions: the research questions to be investigated should be stated here, related to the aims of the research as set out in section 1.
4. Research design and methods: a detailed account of the methods to be employed in the project and how they will answer the research questions. Where mixed methods are to be used, a rationale for their use needs to be included.
5. Schedule: this section sets out the timing for the various components of the research. It is often included as a chart.
6. Ethics approval: the steps taken to gain ethical approval for the project.
7. Budget: in applied research, the funding body usually specifies the amount allocated for the research so the researcher only needs to specify how this is to be spent. In basic research, the researcher needs to compile a budget to show how the funds are to be spent to conduct the research project.
8. References: a list of all references used in the proposal.
9. Appendices: additional material can be added as appendices to the main proposal. These may include background information such as the CVs of the researcher/s.

ADDRESSING QUESTIONS OF RESEARCH QUALITY

For the findings of research to be accepted by the scientific community as well as by the general public, they need to have credibility. To achieve credibility, research must satisfy the established standards of quality. Quality standards differ for qualitative and quantitative research and additional standards have been proposed for mixed-methods research.

Quality concepts in quantitative research

In quantitative research, the concepts of validity and reliability have been developed to assess quality. Validity refers to the soundness or quality of the conclusions drawn from a research study, whereas reliability refers to the extent to which findings can be repeated in similar studies.

Campbell and Stanley (1963, 1966) further developed the concept of validity by distinguishing between internal and external validity.

Internal validity refers to the extent to which a research study enables cause–effect relationships to be established from the findings of the study. For this to be achieved, there needs to be control over the conditions under which data is collected. This control is considered to be maximized in randomized control trials where factors that might impact on the findings are carefully controlled.

External validity refers to the extent to which findings from a research study can be generalized to other populations or settings. This is achieved by drawing random samples from a population for inclusion in the research so that findings can then be generalized to the population from which the sample is drawn.

An additional validity concept has been added to these by Cook and Campbell (1979), termed **statistical conclusion validity**. This concept refers to the extent to which statistical inference procedures used in a study are adequate to detect relationships or differences among variables measured in the study.

Validity in quantitative research can also refer to the measures used in the research, in which case it is referred to as *measurement validity*. Likewise, reliability is also used in the context of measurement. This use of validity and reliability will be discussed in Part 3.

Quality concepts in qualitative research

Assessment of quality in qualitative research is more controversial than in quantitative research due to the wider range of paradigms adopted by researchers (see Chapter 1). This has resulted in three positions on quality criteria among qualitative researchers. These are:

(i)   Adapt the concepts of validity and reliability so that they are appropriate for qualitative research. This approach has been taken by Golafshani (2003).

(ii) Develop a set of concepts to assess the credibility of qualitative research different from those used for quantitative research. This approach has been taken by Lincoln and Guba (1985) amongst others.

(iii) Abandon attempts to develop a single set of criteria for qualitative research since qualitative research does not follow any particular set pattern, and attempting to apply set criteria of quality tends to force research into a common format (see Denzin, 2011).

Of these three approaches, the second has gained most support amongst qualitative researchers. One of the early attempts at this was by Lincoln and Guba (1985) who developed quality criteria for qualitative research to replace those adopted by quantitative researchers. The criteria developed by Guba (1981) and extended by Lincoln and Guba (1985) are set out in Table 3.4.

Table 3.4   Criteria for establishing trustworthiness of qualitative research, developed by Guba (1981) and Lincoln and Guba (1985)

Criteria	Definition	Strategies for achieving trustworthiness
Credibility	The extent to which all relevant viewpoints have been included in the research	• Prolonged engagement with participants • Triangulation • Member checks
Transferability	The extent to which the findings can be applied to other settings	• Providing information about context of the research • Ensuring 'typical' participants

Criteria	Definition	Strategies for achieving trustworthiness
Dependability	The extent to which the research is conducted consistently	• Ensuring researchers are well trained in collecting data
Confirmability	The extent to which the findings adequately reflect the situation, rather than the views of the researcher	• Peer reviews, which provide an independent assessment of the research

Quality concepts in mixed-methods research

Teddlie and Tashakkori (2009) point out that mixed-methods researchers need to employ not only the quality standards for qualitative and quantitative research but also standards for combining qualitative and quantitative methods in the one study.

They distinguish two families of criteria for evaluating quality in mixed-methods research, namely *design quality* and **interpretive rigour**. The latter set of criteria applies specifically to the inference process and will be discussed in Chapter 16. Design quality is more relevant to the early stages of the project and is broken down into four components, as set out in Table 3.5.

Table 3.5 Design quality components for mixed-methods research

Component	Description
Design suitability (appropriateness)	Appropriateness of the methods for answering the research questions
Design fidelity (adequacy)	Adequacy of the procedures for capturing the meanings, effects or relationships
Within-design consistency	Extent to which the components of the design fit together
Analytic adequacy	Adequacy of the data analysis procedures for answering the research questions

Source: adapted from Teddlie and Tashakkori (2009, Table 12.5)

Research quality needs to be addressed at the design stage. Once the research is under way, it may well be too late to correct for poor quality in any of the components.

CONCLUSION

Research questions are the focus of a research project and need to be carefully formulated. Vague or ambiguous research questions will undoubtedly lead to a research design that will be unable to answer them.

CHAPTER SUMMARY

This chapter has outlined the early steps involved in designing a research project. They include choosing the research topic, conducting literature reviews, formulating the research question(s) and gaining funding for the research.

These steps must be followed by all researchers, regardless of the research methods to be used. It is not until the research questions are formulated that mixed-methods designs are considered.

Research quality issues have been outlined for quantitative, qualitative and mixed-methods research. Mixed-methods research encounters the additional problem of not only ensuring quality in the qualitative and quantitative components but also in the ways in which these are combined.

FURTHER READING

Galvan, J. L. (2017) *Writing Literature Reviews. A Guide for Students of the Social and Behavioral Sciences*, **6th edition. New York: Routledge.**
A comprehensive guide to writing literature reviews and a useful supplement to any text on research methods.

Hammersley, M. (2011) *Methodology: Who Needs It?* **London: Sage Publications.**
A discussion of methodology that goes well beyond the scope of this chapter but contains much useful information to situate some of the discussion here.

Schoemaker, P. J., Tankard, J. W. Jr. and Lasora, D. L. (2004) *How to Build Social Science Theories*. **Thousand Oaks, CA: Sage Publications.**
A comprehensive discussion of the role of theory in social science research.

Teddlie, C. and Tashakkori, A. (2009) *Foundations of Mixed Methods Research*. **Thousand Oaks, CA: Sage Publications.**
Chapter 12 discusses research quality issues.

White, P. (2009) *Developing Research Questions: A Guide for Social Scientists*. **Houndmills, Basingstoke: Palgrave Macmillan.**
An excellent discussion of research questions, which sets out in detail how to write them.

4

CONCEPTUAL AND THEORETICAL FRAMEWORKS IN SOCIAL RESEARCH

INTRODUCTION

The **conceptual framework** for a research project is the set of concepts used in the research project, including their definitions and type. It also includes the paradigm within which the researcher is operating, although this is not always made explicit. Paradigms were discussed in Chapters 1 and 2. In many cases, researchers do not acknowledge the paradigm within which they are operating but this does not mean they are not using one.

The **theoretical framework** is the connections that are proposed to exist among the concepts used in the study. It provides a framework for specific theories that share concepts and theoretical mechanisms.

The relationships that exist among paradigms, theoretical and conceptual frameworks and methodologies are depicted in Figure 4.1.

Paradigms permeate all levels of the research process as they provide the principles that guide researchers. Both theoretical frameworks and methodologies (see Chapter 1) adopted in a research project are influenced by the paradigm adopted by the researcher. For example, a researcher who adopts a constructivist paradigm (see Chapter 2) will choose a qualitative methodology and theoretical and conceptual frameworks that incorporate only qualitative concepts.

Note that phenomenology has been included in Figure 4.1 as a qualitative methodology but it must be recognized that this is just one of many interpretations of its role in social research. It is generally understood to involve the study of conscious experience, although how this is done is the subject of much debate.

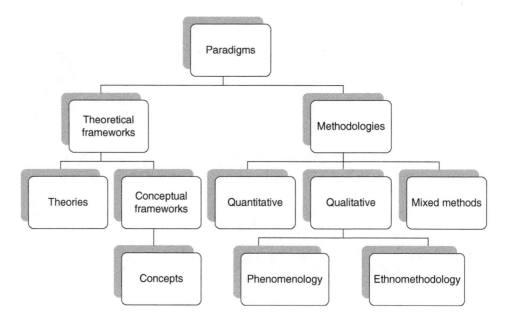

Figure 4.1   Relationships among paradigms, theoretical and conceptual frameworks and methodologies

Ethnomethodology has also been included as a qualitative methodology. It focuses on how people make sense of their everyday life through the application of commonsense reasoning.

Choice of a conceptual and theoretical framework for a research project is influenced by:

- The existing literature on the topic: existing research may have been conducted from within a particular theoretical framework. A researcher may choose to continue using this framework to extend its application or propose an alternative approach.
- The paradigm adopted by the researcher: researchers tend to operate within an existing paradigm although this is not always made explicit. The paradigm adopted will influence both the conceptual and theoretical framework used in the research project.
- The theoretical approach of the researcher: a researcher may choose to bring to bear a theoretical approach to a topic not previously applied to that topic or may adapt a theory that has worked well on a related topic.

In this chapter, both conceptual and theoretical frameworks used in social research, and their relationships to paradigms, will be outlined.

THE THEORETICAL FRAMEWORK

The theoretical framework adopted in a research project is more general than specific theories. It includes the assumptions that exist in the paradigm adopted for the research project as well as the major concepts employed. Particular theories form an integral part of the theoretical framework. Some writers, such as Neuman (2011: 85), do not distinguish between theoretical frameworks and paradigms, whereas Imenda (2014) does. The distinction will be supported in this book. Theoretical frameworks do adopt some paradigmatic assumptions but are focused on social processes, whereas paradigms, as defined in Chapter 1, are not concerned with any particular domain of social activity.

There are many definitions of theoretical frameworks, two of which are included in Box 4.1. The definition by Imenda does not seem to distinguish a theoretical framework from a theory, whereas Neuman's definition does.

BOX 4.1

DEFINITIONS OF A THEORETICAL FRAMEWORK

'[A] theoretical framework is the application of a theory, or a set of concepts drawn from one and the same theory, to offer an explanation of an event, or shed some light on a particular phenomenon or research problem.' (Imenda, 2014: 189)

A theoretical framework is 'a very general theoretical system with assumptions, concepts, and specific social theories.' (Neuman, 2011: 85)

Some major theoretical frameworks used in the social sciences are described in Table 4.1. The frameworks included here are not meant to be exhaustive of all theoretical frameworks employed in the social sciences, but the table does identify some of those most often in use.

There may also be some debate over the inclusion of, say, **post-structuralism** as a theoretical framework rather than as a paradigm. The reason for including it as a theoretical framework is that it includes reference to social entities and how they should be studied.

Table 4.1   Some major theoretical frameworks used in the social sciences

Framework	Description
Structuralism	**Structuralism** refers to the view that social processes can only be understood by their relation to overarching social systems or structures. This view was prominent in anthropology due to the work of Claude Levi-Strauss, in psychoanalytic theory by Jacques Lacan and in social science by Louis Althusser.
Post-structuralism	**Post-structuralism** was a reaction against what was a perceived deterministic approach of structuralism. Social processes cannot be understood by locating them in a larger system, but are better seen in relation to the discourses that construct knowledge about these processes. The development of post-structuralism is usually attributed to the work of Michel Foucault.

(Continued)

Table 4.1 (Continued)

Framework	Description
Feminist theory	**Feminist theory** focuses on gender inequalities in societies where women have experienced discrimination in social, political and economic spheres. As a theoretical framework, feminist social theory was developed in the late 1960s by writers such as Shulamith Firestone, Betty Friedan and others.
Symbolic interactionism	**Symbolic interactionism** is a framework that focuses on how individuals construct meaning through their communications with others. It is attributed to George Herbert Mead, but was developed by Herbert Blumer after Mead's death in 1931. This framework asserts that humans derive meaning from the social interactions they have with others and social institutions, and that they act on the basis of these meanings (see Charon, 2010).

Theories

As Abend (2008) points out, there is very little agreement in the social scientific literature over what is meant by the term 'theory'. He identified seven distinct meanings of the term. For the purposes of using theory in research, the second and third meanings would seem to be most appropriate. Putting these together, theory can be seen as either an explanation of a particular social phenomenon through identifying causal, structural or individualistic relationships, or as providing an original interpretation or a new understanding of a social process or event.

There is a wide range of social theories available for use. These theories differ on a number of characteristics:

1. Level of analysis
2. Focus of theorizing
3. Direction of inference
4. Domain of application.

Level of analysis

Social theorists distinguish three levels of theory:

*   macro-level theory
*   mid-range theory
*   micro-level theory.

Macro-level theory

Macro-level theory is at a high level of abstraction, encompassing whole societies, social institutions or sectors of society, or historical periods. Researchers may generate their research topics from such theories but the concepts are too general to guide researchers in formulating specific research projects. Some of the major macro-level theories in use in the social sciences are described in Table 4.2.

Table 4.2   Macro theories in the social sciences

Macro theory	Description
Structural functionalism	**Structural functionalism** sees society as composed of a system of interrelated components which work together to bring about stability. These components satisfy the needs of the system as a whole and act to shape society. Functionalism as a theoretical methodology was developed by social theorists such as Emile Durkheim, Robert Merton and Talcott Parsons, among many others, in the early part of the twentieth century.
Conflict theory	**Conflict theory** sees social structures as products of conflict between social classes where the conflict arises from economic inequalities between these classes. It is seen to originate in the work of Karl Marx but has been developed by later theorists such as C. Wright Mills.
Social positions theory of social structure	Blau (1977) sees social structure as a multidimensional space of social positions in which individuals are located, and these positions are instrumental in determining social relations. Structural parameters such as age, race, education and socioeconomic status are the axes in the space that underlie the distinctions individuals make in their social relations.

Mid-range theory

Mid-range theory deals with social processes at a societal level. The concepts involved are less general than those of macro theory but still quite removed from the specific situations that researchers study. The notion of mid-range theory was introduced by Merton (1949) to propose a level of theorizing intermediate to the broad general theories, referred to here as macro-theories, and the more specific empirical generalizations from research, which he did not see as theory at all.

An example of mid-range theorizing suggested by Risjord (2019) is the theory of planned behaviour originally proposed by Ajzen (1985). In this theory, planned behaviour, in contrast with spontaneous behaviour, is seen to be a consequence of intentions, which in turn are determined by attitudes, subjective norms and control beliefs. What makes this a mid-range theory is that the concepts employed to explain planned behaviour are a step removed from the observations and are seen as causing the behaviour.

Micro-level theory

Micro-level theory focuses on the more specific aspects of social life and uses concepts that can more directly relate to the research project. An example of a micro-level theory is *self-efficacy* *theory*, derived from Bandura's social cognitive theory (see Bandura, 2001). It refers to people's beliefs about their ability to perform tasks. Measures of self-efficacy have been devised and used as independent variables in research (see Box 4.2).

To be useful in social research, a theory needs to be able to generate testable predictions in the form of hypotheses. These are predictions about the outcomes of a piece of research based on assumptions in the theory about the factors likely to contribute to the outcomes. A study by Reed, Mikels and Lockenhoff (2012) (Box 4.2) provides an example where decision-making self-efficacy theory generated predictions about the range of choices made by individuals when presented with a choice situation.

A researcher can adopt a theoretical framework at any of the above levels to either frame the research topic (usually via macro or mid-range theories) or to test specific predictions from a (micro-level) theory.

In this sense, a theory is explanatory. It helps us understand why events happen by identifying the factors that give rise to them.

▬▬▬ BOX 4.2 ▬▬▬

A STUDY OF SELF-EFFICACY THEORY IN DECISION MAKING

Reed, Mikels and Lockenhoff (2012) tested predictions from self-efficacy theory that individuals with high decision-making self-efficacy (DMSE) would prefer more choices when they expect to be able to make effective decisions than those with low DMSE. They conducted two studies to test this prediction. The first study involved participants rating their confidence in making decisions in a number of domains (e.g. hospitals, holidays, restaurants) and completed a choice preference measure indicating how many options they would prefer when making decisions in each domain. In the second study, decision-making self-efficacy was manipulated by providing either positive or negative feedback about the decisions that needed to be made (choosing the best photo printer). Choice was varied by asking participants their preference for the number of photo printers they wished to choose from, varying from four to twenty. In both studies, high DMSE was associated with higher levels of choice.

There are however, challenges to this division of social theories. For example, Knorr-Cetina (1981) has proposed that developments in what she calls 'methodological situationism' and the 'cognitive turn' have called into question the micro–macro division, and she suggests a reconstruction of macro-social theory based on micro-sociological foundations. This and other challenges to the division of levels of analysis have led to an ongoing debate among social theorists as to the value of this distinction. There are, nevertheless, theorists who still support macro-social theories, so the debate is far from being resolved.

Focus of theorizing

Theories can focus on explanation or on **interpretive understanding** as implied in the definition of theory offered above. Explanatory theories seek to establish either cause–effect relationships or some form of structural or individual explanation, whereas interpretive understanding theories seek to attain a greater depth of understanding of the situation under investigation.

Causality

A causal connection is one in which one event (the cause) brings about the occurrence of another event (the effect). For example, high blood alcohol levels of drivers can be seen as a cause of motor vehicle accidents (although not the only cause). Requirements for **causality** are set out in Box 4.3.

Although many social scientists seek to establish causal connections, others claim that the nature of social reality is such that causality is not possible to determine, if indeed underlying causes are operating at all (see Hughes and Sharrock, 1997, Chapters 5 and 6). It is an issue to which we will return in later chapters.

━━━━ BOX 4.3 ━━━━

REQUIREMENTS FOR CAUSALITY

There are three requirements for causality. For an event to be a cause of another, the following requirements must be met:

1. The two events must occur together (constant conjunction).
2. The cause must occur prior in time to the effect.
3. Other possible causes must be ruled out.

These requirements date back to the British philosopher John Stuart Mill in the 18th century.

Causal explanations are used in both quantitative (e.g. in randomized control trials; see Chapter 5) and qualitative methods (e.g. in qualitative comparison analysis; see Chapter 14).

Structural explanation

A **structural explanation** is one in which an event is located within a larger system, which imposes constraints on its occurrence. These constraints set limits on what actions are possible in a particular situation. As pointed out by Haslanger (2016: 127), social constraints 'set limits, organize thought and communication, create a choice architecture; in short, they structure the possible space for agency'.

Social structures include macro-structures such as a political system as well as micro-systems such as families, schools or workplaces. In general, they are components of a system that operates as a whole in regulating the behaviour of individuals occupying positions within the system.

Haslanger (2016: 122) provides an example of a structural explanation of why women are economically disadvantaged relative to men by attributing this disadvantage to a 'self-perpetuating economic structure that systematically disadvantages them'.

Individualistic explanation

Individualistic explanations are contrasted with structural explanations just as micro-social theories are contrasted with macro-social theories (see above). An individualistic explanation of a social phenomenon locates the explanation within the motives, values or intentions of individuals. Proponents of this approach argue that all social processes can be explained by recourse to individual actions and that there is no need to invoke higher-level structures in the explanation.

The debate between proponents of structural and individual explanations is far from being resolved.

Interpretive understanding

Interpretive understanding as a goal of theorizing is supported by those who claim that explanation is not appropriate for the social sciences. Instead, social research should be aimed at gaining an understanding of the meaning people attribute to their social experience. What is now called interpretive sociology was developed in the early 20th century by the German sociologists Max Weber and George Simmel. It was a reaction against positivism, which was seen by interpretive theorists as neglecting the real subject matter of social science, namely, the ways in which people make sense of their situations by attributing meaning to them.

Interpretive understanding draws on qualitative methods of research and on the paradigms of interpretivism and constructivism. Schwandt (2003) identified three perspectives on researching the understanding of human action, which he identified as interpretivism, hermeneutics and social constructionism. These perspectives, he argued, provide different ways of addressing the aims and methods of qualitative inquiry. He notes that there is little agreement on the purposes of the interpretive perspective, nor over how interpretive understanding is to be conceptualized. This lack of agreement does not, however, deter the pursuit of interpretive understanding through qualitative inquiry.

Direction of inference

Direction of inference refers to the inference process embedded in a theory. This can either be deductive or inductive. A **deductive inference** is one in which a conclusion is drawn logically from two or more premises. A deductive theory, then, is one in which predictions about empirical consequences are drawn from the theory. These consequences can then be tested by conducting research to determine whether or not the predictions hold. If they do, then the theory is confirmed, whereas if they do not hold then the theory is falsified. Confirming a theory does not mean that the theory is proven since other tests of it may disconfirm other predictions.

For a deductive theory to be worth considering as being able to make a contribution to social science, it must be testable. That is, predictions from the theory must be capable of being tested by an appropriately designed research study. As Berkson (1989) points out, many social scientific theories have turned out to be untestable, leading social scientists into 'a swamp of confusion about their relation to observation and experiment' (p. 157). Berkson continues his discussion of testability by suggesting ways in which social theories can be modified to produce new testable versions of them. He concludes by arguing (p. 170): 'Only when theories of social science become testable, and pass the tests, will they bring to social problems the kind of powerful insight that has enabled the natural sciences spectacularly to promote the development of technology and medicine.'

An inductive theory is one in which the theory is constructed from empirical findings. This is done by a researcher collecting observations on a topic of interest and developing theoretical concepts to explain the findings. Inductive theories are often developed from qualitative research, using an approach referred to as 'grounded theory'. This approach, originally devised by Glaser and Strauss (1967), analyses qualitative data by constructing codes to extract concepts which reflect meaning in the data, and combines these codes into theoretical terms. This process will be described more fully in Chapter 14.

Domain of application

The domain of application of a theory refers to the entities or units of analysis included in the theory. These can range from characteristics of individuals such as their attitudes or values, to characteristics of whole societies such as their ethnic, social class or age structure. Psychological and micro-social theories deal with the individual and small group characteristics, whereas macro-social theories deal with social structures.

THE CONCEPTUAL FRAMEWORK

As stated above, the conceptual framework for a research project specifies the types and nature of the concepts used in the project.

Concepts can either be qualitative or quantitative. The major differences between these types are outlined in Table 4.3. Both types are integral to social research. Although some commentators claim superiority of one over the other, there are no definitive grounds for these kinds of claims. Indeed, mixed-methods research recognizes the important role of both types of concepts by incorporating them in the one study.

It is also often claimed that quantitative and qualitative concepts derive from different paradigms, qualitative from interpretivism or constructivism and quantitative from positivism or post-positivism. It was argued in Chapter 2 that these claims are oversimplifications. Not all qualitative researchers adopt an interpretivist or constructivist paradigm and, likewise, not all quantitative researchers subscribe to positivism or even post-positivism. These are extreme positions and proponents of mixed methods have developed alternative frameworks that can accommodate both types of concepts.

Table 4.3 Major differences between qualitative and quantitative concepts

Characteristics	Qualitative concepts	Quantitative concepts
Measurability	Not measurable	Measurable
Defining features	Rich textual definition	Measure on a scale
Relation to context	Linked to their real-world context	Defined independently of context
Subjectivity	Subjective	Objective
Researcher involvement	Involved	Detached
Origin	Collected by in-depth interviews, focus groups, field observations	Collected by experimental methods, surveys or secondary statistical data

Conceptual frameworks also differ for quantitative and qualitative concepts. An example of a conceptual framework for quantitative concepts is shown in Figure 4.2 below, and for qualitative concepts a mind map, as shown in Figure 12.1 (in Chapter 12).

Quantitative and qualitative concepts require different defining features and are incorporated into research in quite different ways, as outlined below.

Quantitative concepts

Types of measurable social concepts

Social concepts that are measurable can be classified into those that characterize individuals, those that characterize outputs and outcomes of programmes and those that characterize societies. These are referred to as the *units of analysis*. These units of analysis differ in their level of aggregation from characteristics of the individual at the lowest level, to groups of individuals, such as families, to regions such as cities or states, to nations at the highest level.

Where data is aggregated at a high level, conclusions can't be drawn about relationships at a lower level. This is referred to as the *ecological fallacy*. For example, the incidence of motor vehicle theft may be higher in areas of a city characterized by high unemployment. It cannot be concluded from this finding that the unemployed are stealing the motor vehicles without data at the level of individuals responsible for the theft. To do so is to commit the ecological fallacy.

There are, of course, many characteristics of individuals, organizations and societies that are not measurable, and for such concepts qualitative data analysis is appropriate.

Measuring characteristics of individuals

Those characteristics of individuals that are considered measurable include:

- Physical characteristics such as height, weight and age: these are measured on standard **measurement scales** involving mass, length and time.
- Physiological characteristics such as physical capabilities, reaction times: measured by achievement outcomes such as time to run 100m, or time to press a button to measure reaction time.
- Socially defined characteristics such as occupation, education, income, marital status, ethnic affiliation: measured by using existing measures such as annual salary in $, years of education completed, occupational classification, and so on.
- Personal characteristics such as attitudes, opinions, motives, personality traits, values: measured using questionnaires or rating scales.
- Intellectual characteristics such as abilities and aptitudes: measured using ability and aptitude tests.
- Behavioural characteristics such as leadership, impulsivity, aggressiveness: measured using rating scales either by self or others.

Measuring organizational performance

Although economic performance is the most common measure of organizational performance, many organizations, particularly those in the public sector, conduct human service programmes, such as rehabilitation schemes for the mentally ill, or job training programmes for the unemployed. Economic performance is not an appropriate measure for such organizations; rather, some measure of the success of such programmes is required. This is an area in which social scientists can play a role in determining through the conduct of evaluations of them. Programme evaluation is a major area of research in which social scientists, along with other professionals, are major contributors (see, for example, Rossi, Lipsey and Freeman, 2004).

To evaluate a human service programme, some measure of the effectiveness of the programme is needed. The results of such programmes are conceptualized as outputs and outcomes.

An *output* of a programme is the product of the programme. That is, it is the immediate result of programme operation, such as the number of individuals completing it.

An *outcome*, on the other hand, is a measure of the success of the programme. That is, it provides information on whether the programme has achieved useful results, or has satisfied the programme goals. An example of this difference between outputs and outcomes is shown in Box 4.4.

While outputs are usually quite readily available and measurable, outcomes can be more complex and difficult. For example, in Box 4.4, measuring whether women have gained a higher quality of life as a result of completing the shelter programme would be difficult to quantify.

Social scientists are increasingly being called upon to evaluate social programmes of the kind shown in Box 4.4, so that an awareness of measurement issues in this area is important.

■ BOX 4.4 ■

OUTPUTS AND OUTCOMES OF A PROGRAMME FOR A SHELTER FOR WOMEN VICTIMS OF DOMESTIC VIOLENCE

A programme to provide shelter for women who are victims of domestic violence would have the following outputs and outcomes:

Outputs

- the number of women and children admitted to the shelter per week
- the number of women admitted to the shelter who have completed counselling sessions
- the number of women with children admitted to the shelter who have accessed childcare.

Outcomes

Women who have completed the programme offered by the shelter:

- are satisfied with the services they have received from the shelter programme
- are better placed to access support services in the community
- have stable, affordable and safe housing
- have developed strategies for enhancing their safety
- have gained a higher quality of life.

Learn more at: www.endvawnow.org/en/articles/1465-output-and-outcome-indicators.html

---

Measuring characteristics of societies

For some research projects, measures of social conditions at a national or regional level are needed. In the 1970s, dissatisfaction with the existing focus on economic indicators led to the development of *the social indicators movement*. This movement advocated the development of indicators to show trends in social conditions to evaluate the effectiveness of government policies on social reforms. Governments now produce a range of social indicators to monitor social conditions.

Examples of social indicators produced by governments include:

- The unemployment rate: this indicator, produced by most countries, provides a measure of employment and unemployment in a country. It is usually broken down into age groups and gender as well as region.
- Life expectancy: this indicator provides an indirect measure of the health status of a country on the assumption that the longer the life expectancy, the better the health care in a country.
- Hospital beds per 1,000 people: another health indicator that measures the level of health care in a country on the assumption that the more hospital beds provided, the better the health care.
- Government expenditure on education as a percentage of GDP: this indicator is an indirect measure of the level of education in a country.

Another example of a social indicator is provided in Box 4.5.

BOX 4.5

THE GLOBAL MULTIDIMENSIONAL POVERTY INDEX (MPI)

The MPI is a poverty index developed by the Oxford Poverty and Human Development Initiative and the United Nations Development Program in 2010. It weights ten indicators in three areas to calculate the index. The three areas are health, education and living standards.

Further details can be found at: www.un.org/en/ga/second/65/docs/foster.pdf

Types of quantitative concepts

Quantitative concepts are called 'variables' since they are measurable. That is, a quantitative concept can take on a number of values on a measurement scale. For example, the concept 'time spent on domestic tasks' might be measured on a scale of hours per day undertaking domestic tasks which can take values from zero to twenty-four.

In quantitative research, variables are considered to be independent, dependent or intervening:

An **independent variable** is one which is either manipulated by the researcher, such as time spent awake in a sleep deprivation study, or a background variable such as the age of participants which is seen to be relevant to the research outcomes.

A **dependent variable** is one which the researcher is seeking to explain or understand. It is seen as a consequence of the independent variables, such as performance on a simulated driving test where the independent variables might be hours of sleep deprivation (manipulated by the researcher) and age and gender of the participant (background variables).

An **intervening variable** is one that mediates in some way the relationship between the independent and dependent variables. Intervening variables can be either **mediator** or **moderator** variables (Donaldson, 2001). A mediator variable is one that is affected by the independent variable and in turn affects the dependent variable. A moderator variable is one that affects the strength of the relationship between the independent and dependent variables. The relationships among these variables are shown in Figure 4.2. Two independent variables are shown. Independent variable 1 might be previous work experience which is unaffected by either moderator or mediator variables. Independent variable 2 could be level of skill training. Gender is an example of a moderator variable. Skills training may work better for females than males, so gender moderates the relationship between skill training (the independent variable) and job performance (the dependent variable). Two mediator variables are shown in Figure 4.2. These could be self-efficacy and self-confidence. Both might be improved by skills training and these in turn impact on job performance.

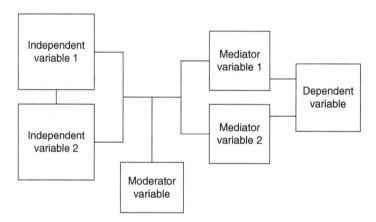

Figure 4.2   Relationships between independent variables, moderator variables, mediator variables and the dependent variable

Note: Independent variable 1 is unaffected by either the moderator or mediator variables.

The aim of quantitative research then is to ascertain the effect independent variables, including moderator and mediator variables, have on the dependent variable. Usually, statistical inference methods are used to estimate these effects, as will be explained in more depth when data analysis is discussed.

Qualitative concepts

In *qualitative research*, concepts are defined holistically. They involve in-depth descriptions rather than the assignment of numbers. Qualitative concepts are complex textual descriptions that are not fixed but change as the researcher develops more comprehensive ideas about the subject of the research. They are designed to convey meaning by elaborating the complexities of the ideas underlying the concepts by placing them in their social context.

An example of a qualitative research concept is 'the experience of homelessness by mothers'. This concept involves feelings of powerlessness, loss, fear and anxiety amongst the homeless mothers that are not readily captured as quantitative variables. Box 4.6 describes a study by Tischler, Rademeyer and Vostanis (2007) of homeless mothers, using qualitative methods.

■■■■■■■■ BOX 4.6 ■■■■■■■■

A STUDY ILLUSTRATING THE DEVELOPMENT OF A QUALITATIVE CONCEPT

Tischler et al. (2007) conducted a qualitative study into the experience of homelessness by mothers. They interviewed mothers attending homeless centres in Birmingham, UK, focusing on their experience of homelessness. The interviewees reported feelings of powerlessness, loss and isolation. Most mothers were estranged from their families due to domestic violence, child abuse and family conflict. They suffered poor mental health and depressive symptoms and tended to avoid problems rather than deal with them. The authors concluded that their qualitative study enabled 'rich, detailed information' to be gathered about the experience of homelessness among the mothers included in the study.

THE ROLE OF THEORY IN MIXED-METHODS RESEARCH

There is very limited discussion on the application of theory in mixed-methods research. Kelle (2015) outlined some potential applications of theory in sequential mixed-methods designs. In a sequential qualitative–quantitative design, he suggested that the qualitative component be used to develop theoretical concepts which can then be examined further in the quantitative component. Alternatively, in a sequential quantitative–qualitative design theoretical concepts developed in the quantitative component can be further explored in the qualitative component in order to further develop these concepts. At this stage, these suggestions have not been applied to any particular theory but remain speculative.

CONCLUSION

This chapter has outlined the basic principles of theoretical and conceptual frameworks. The proliferation of such frameworks in the social sciences means that researchers will only be able to master a small proportion of them. What is important, however, is that the researcher has an understanding of the major perspectives on social theory to enable positioning of any particular theory or theoretical framework within these perspectives. This chapter has sought to outline these perspectives so as to provide researchers with the basic knowledge needed to evaluate and use particular theories in their research.

CHAPTER SUMMARY

A conceptual framework is a set of concepts and their types that define a particular area of research. A theoretical framework is the relationships that are postulated to exist among the concepts employed, including the theory or theories that specify the theoretical mechanisms operating.

Major theoretical frameworks in the social sciences include structuralism, post-structuralism, feminism and symbolic interactionism.

Theoretical frameworks subsume particular theories. A theory can be seen either as an explanation of a particular social phenomenon or as providing an original interpretation of a new understanding of a social process or event. Theories vary on a number of characteristics, including level of analysis, focus of theorizing, direction of inference and domain of application.

Concepts can be either quantitative or qualitative. Quantitative concepts are those that are measurable on a scale and are termed variables. Variables can be independent, dependent or intervening and the relationships among these are shown in Figure 4.2. Qualitative concepts are holistic and involve in-depth descriptions rather than the assignment of numbers.

Researchers need to understand the basic structure of conceptual and theoretical frameworks in order to be in an informed position to choose particular theories in their research.

FURTHER READING

Inglis, D., with Thorpe, C. (2012) *An Invitation to Social Theory*. Cambridge: Polity Press.
Includes a wide range of social theories and paradigms. Uses the term paradigm to include what are called either macro-social theories or theoretical frameworks in this book.

Laustsen, C. B., Larsen, L. T., Nielsn, M. W., Ravn, T. and Sorenson, M. P. (2017) *Social Theory: A Textbook*. Oxford: Routledge.
An account of social theories organized by topic area. Contributions of influential theorists on each area are discussed in pairs, enabling a comparison of approaches.

Neuman, W. L. (2011) *Social Research Methods: Qualitative and Quantitative Approaches*. Boston, MA: Pearson Education.
Chapters 2 and 3 contain a discussion of theory and methodology.

5

CHOOSING THE
RESEARCH DESIGN

INTRODUCTION

The research design is the overall structure of the research project for collecting new data. It includes the research method or methods to be used, the instruments by which data is to be collected, the participants from which data is to be collected and the actual data collection procedures to be adopted. Thus, a research design consists of the following components:

1. The research methodology to be adopted
2. The research method or methods chosen
3. The instruments used to collect data
4. The sampling procedure used to select participants
5. The data collection procedure adopted.

Components 1 and 2 will be dealt with in this chapter and components 3–5 will be dealt with in Part 3.

THE RESEARCH METHODOLOGY

A research methodology was defined in Chapter 1 as 'a set of principles that identifies what practices count as research'. Three methodologies for research were identified:

1. Qualitative research: qualitative methodology conceptualizes research as the collection of rich textual information in order to gain an understanding of the object of the research, whether that be an event, social interaction or the views expressed by an individual.

2. Quantitative research: quantitative methodology conceptualizes research as the collection of measurements of concepts in order to identify the relationships or differences among these measurements.

3. Mixed-methods research: mixed-methods research involves the combination of two or more of the above methods in the same study. For a study to qualify as mixed methods, at least one of the methods must be quantitative and one qualitative. Experimental methods and surveys are predominantly quantitative, whereas case studies and ethnographies are predominantly qualitative. Hence, a typical mixed-methods design would combine a survey with a case study or an ethnography. Mixed-methods designs will be discussed in Chapter 6.

This list does not exhaust the range of possible methodologies, but for the purposes of this chapter these are the main focus.

The decision to use a particular methodology will depend critically on the paradigm adopted by the researcher and the nature of the research questions asked.

The decision to use a mixed-methods design derives from the research questions. Research questions drive the whole research process so great care needs to be taken in their formulation. Mixed methods are indicated when the research questions need both qualitative and quantitative methods to answer them. The situations in which this takes place will be discussed further in Chapter 6.

RESEARCH METHODS

Research methods are the procedures chosen in order to answer the research questions. In some books, research methods are lumped together with data collection methods and in other books research methods are identified as the research design. It is useful to distinguish all three concepts, particularly in the context of mixed-methods research, so that usage of these terms is clear.

The research method, then, is the overarching procedure in which data collection takes place. The main research methods used in the social sciences are:

1. Experimental methods
2. Survey methods
3. Case studies
4. Ethnographic studies
5. In-depth interviews.

The first two are regarded as mainly quantitative methods, whereas the last three tend to be mainly qualitative. It is always possible, however, for both kinds of data to be collected in any of the methods, so that classifying methods as quantitative or qualitative can be misleading. Nevertheless, experiments and surveys are predominantly quantitative methods, while case studies, ethnographies and in-depth interviews are predominantly qualitative.

It is important for researchers to understand the strengths and limitations of these methods and the situations in which they are appropriate to use. This is particularly the case with mixed-methods research. A researcher planning to use mixed methods needs to know which methods are appropriately mixed and the conditions under which mixing them leads to a sound research design.

Experimental methods

Experimental methods have been widely used in the social sciences, largely because of their capacity to isolate factors that might contribute to an outcome and control them. The features of an experiment that enable this are as follows:

1. An outcome of interest (the dependent variable) and the factors thought to be responsible for its occurrence (the independent variables) are identified.
2. These independent variables are either varied systematically or controlled.
3. Observations of the dependent variable are made under controlled conditions so that the effects of the independent variable/s can be determined.
4. Conclusions are then drawn about the effects or lack thereof of the independent variables on the dependent variable.

The experimental method has been used extensively in psychology where psychological processes have been studied in the laboratory in order to gain control over the multitude of variables influencing behaviour. This has led to criticisms of the method as being too far removed from reality, having little relevance to behaviour in the real world.

Experimental methods have, however, been used in 'real world' settings, particularly to study the impact of social programmes. Box 5.1 illustrates a classic example of such an experiment. This study used a **randomized control trial** method to ascertain the effects of class size. In such studies, participants are assigned randomly to the conditions included. This random assignment is designed to eliminate factors that might influence the results, such as home environment, previous skill attainment, and so on.

━━━━━ BOX 5.1 ━━━━━

EXAMPLE OF A 'REAL WORLD' EXPERIMENT – THE TENNESSEE CLASS SIZE STUDY (MOSTELLER, 1995)

In the mid-1980s, a randomized field trial known as Project STAR (Student–Teacher Achievement Ratio) was initiated to assess the effects of class size in elementary schools on student achievement.

(Continued)

In the study, over 6,000 kindergarten students were randomly assigned to one of three class structures as follows:

- regular class sizes of 22–35 students with one teacher
- regular class sizes with a teacher and a teacher's aide
- small class sizes of 13–17 students with one teacher.

Students remained in these classes until the end of year 3. The study found that the small class size resulted in higher levels of student achievement than either of the other two conditions.

Types of experimental methods

There are two major types of experimental design, namely the randomized experiment and the **quasi-experiment**. In the randomized experiment, the units of analysis are randomly allocated to the conditions being observed, as in the example in Box 5.1, whereas in quasi-experiments random assignment is either not possible or plausible.

Randomized experiments

In the randomized experiment, two or more groups are formed by randomly allocating the units of analysis (usually individuals) to each group. In the example in Box 5.1, the units of analysis are classes rather than individuals.

Each group then receives a different treatment devised by varying one or more independent variables systematically. In the example in Box 5.1, the independent variable is class size with or without a teacher's aide. This conflates two independent variables, namely class size (large or small) and teacher's aide (present or absent), but they are not separated in the design outlined in Box 5.1.

Usually there is a control group, which is defined as the existing method. So, in the above example, regular class size with one teacher is the control group. The purpose of the control group is to provide a reference outcome to which the treatment groups can be compared.

The simplest form of the randomized experiment is the two-group design depicted in Table 5.1. In this design, there are just two groups designated as the experimental group and the control group. The control group receives no treatment or the pre-existing treatment, whereas the experimental group receives the treatment to be evaluated. If the treatment is, say, a new drug for the treatment of asthma, then the experimental group receives the drug and the control group receives either a placebo (something that resembles the drug but has no effect) or the existing drug. Comparison of the results from the two groups provides evidence on the effectiveness of the treatment.

Table 5.1 The simple two-group randomized experiment

Group	Condition	Treatment	Measure
Experimental	Treatment	Receives experimental treatment	Observation of the outcome being investigated
Control	No treatment	Receives existing treatment or none at all	

The distinguishing feature of a randomized experiment is that the units of analysis are assigned randomly to the treatment conditions. So, in the above example, a group of asthma sufferers would be randomly assigned to either the control or the treatment group and would be given the drugs appropriate for the group and their asthma symptoms observed over the duration of the experiment.

Variations on this design include more levels of the independent variable. The example given in Box 5.1 includes three levels of the independent variable – or more than one independent variable may be included.

Randomized field trials are claimed by some to be the 'gold standard' for evaluating programmes since random allocation is claimed to provide control over all other possible explanations for any differences found. But it is not always possible to randomly allocate participants, particularly in natural settings, so that randomized experiments are not always possible to conduct.

Other problems with randomized experiments include the following:

1. Attrition: attrition refers to participants leaving the experiment before it is concluded. If the attrition differs across groups, then the conclusions can be called into question.
2. Ethical issues: ethical issues have become important in the conduct of social research due to concerns that have been raised over early research. Participants are often deceived about the treatment they are receiving and this raises ethical issues if the treatment they are missing out on turns out to be beneficial.
3. Diffusion of treatment: this occurs when participants in different groups communicate with one another and members of, say, the control group adopt some of the treatments used in the experimental group, thereby invalidating the random assignment.

Quasi-experiments

Where random assignment is not feasible for ethical or practical reasons, rather than abandon experimental methods altogether, some researchers adopt what are called quasi-experiments. These designs have all the features of a randomized experiment but without the randomization.

An example of a quasi-experiment is the pre-test–post-test design where both the experimental and control groups are pre-tested on the outcome of interest and then again at the conclusion of the experiment and the changes in outcomes compared. If the change in the experimental group is greater than that of the control group, then this is regarded as evidence for the effect of the treatment.

The absence of random assignment in quasi-experiments creates problems for drawing conclusions as the lack of randomization means that differences between groups may be influenced by factors not controlled for.

Other problems which challenge the validity of quasi-experiments other than those already mentioned for randomized experiments include:

1. Selection: this refers to pre-existing differences between the groups that may be related to the experimental outcomes. In the randomized experiment, these are not related to the experimental conditions due to the randomization, but in quasi-experiments they can be important. Often, participants in the groups are matched on variables thought to influence outcomes. This is often done in health research and is called the case control method. But this matching procedure may miss out unknown important factors.
2. History: history effects come into play when there are before and after measures as in the pre-test–post-test design mentioned above. Changes may be due to events that occur between testing periods unrelated to the treatment.
3. Testing: a testing effect takes place when the process of making observations has an impact on later observations. This can be a factor in the pre-test–post-test design.
4. Maturation: maturation effects refer to changes that take place over time due to changes within participants such as ageing or learning effects. They can also be a factor in the pre-test–post-test design.

Two quasi-experimental designs that seek to overcome some of these problems are the Solomon four-group design and the replicated–interrupted time-series design.

The Solomon four-group design is shown in Table 5.2. It is basically the pre-test–post-test design with two additional groups that don't receive the pre-test. It is designed to control for testing effects.

Table 5.2 The Solomon four-group design

Group	Pre-test	Treatment	Post-test
Experimental with pre-test	Yes	Yes	Yes
Control with pre-test	Yes	No	Yes
Experimental without pre-test	No	Yes	Yes
Control without pre-test	No	No	Yes

The replicated–interrupted time-series design is shown in Table 5.3. In this design, a series of observations are made on the dependent variable before and after the introduction of the treatment. Trends in both the experimental group and the control group are compared. If changes take place in the experimental group over the post-treatment period but not in the control group, then there is some evidence that the treatment has brought about the changes. For example, the observations could be traffic accidents on two stretches of two highways of the same length in the same locality, and the treatment could be the placement of warning signs on one of the highways.

Table 5.3 The replicated–interrupted time-series design

Group	Pre-treatment observations			Treatment	Post-treatment observations		
Experimental	O_{e1}	O_{e2}	O_{e3}	Yes	O_{e4}	O_{e5}	O_{e6}
Control	O_{c1}	O_{c2}	O_{c3}	No	O_{c4}	O_{c5}	O_{c6}

Note: O_{ei} and O_{ci} stand for the observations of the experimental and control groups at time i respectively

The range of experimental methods outlined here give social scientists the opportunity to study a broad range of situations, but they are limited largely to interventions such as social programmes. Even then, the largely quantitative orientation of the design imposes limitations on what can be said about the programmes. The addition of qualitative methods through the use of mixed methods, as described in the next chapter, can address these limitations.

Survey research methods

A survey involves collecting information from a wide range of people, usually a random sample, about their attitudes, opinions, practices, knowledge and other views together with demographic information about themselves, usually by means of a questionnaire that has been delivered to them via mail, personal contact, email or more recently social media.

The **survey method** is used widely in the social sciences because it enables data to be collected about issues that characterize demographic groups in a society so as to draw comparisons. For example, a survey can be used to compare usage of social media across age groups in a geographical region such as a state or local government area.

Surveys are appropriate for collecting descriptive information, including correlational relationships. They are not useful for establishing cause–effect relationships as the direction of causation in relationships established by surveys is not known and cannot be established by this method. So, in the above example, differences in usage of social media may well differ across age groups but the explanation for this needs investigation by other methods.

Types of survey designs

There are two main types of survey research designs in use. These are *cross-sectional* and *longitudinal* surveys. The **cross-sectional survey** involves collecting data at a single point in time, whereas the **longitudinal survey** collects data at a number of different points in time.

Cross-sectional surveys

A cross-sectional survey is one that is administered at a single point in time. It aims to collect information on attitudes, practices and so on, from individuals, so as to compare variation in those variables across characteristics of the individuals, such as their age, gender, education level, religious affiliation, and so on. An example of a cross-sectional survey on young people's opinions about alcohol and other drugs in Australia is provided in Box 5.2. This survey is typical of a cross-sectional survey that explores opinions about a range of issues among a sample of a large population (in this case, young people in Australia) and examines differences in these opinions in sub-groups of the sample such as age and, in this case, drug and alcohol use.

━━━━━━━━ BOX 5.2 ━━━━━━━━

EXAMPLE OF A CROSS-SECTIONAL SURVEY OF YOUNG PEOPLE'S OPINIONS ABOUT ALCOHOL AND OTHER DRUGS IN AUSTRALIA

Lancaster, Ritter and Matthew-Simmons (2013) conducted an online cross-sectional survey of 2,335 young Australians aged between 16 and 25 years aimed at ascertaining opinions about drug and alcohol use and programmes and measures to control such use. Respondents were recruited through a variety of outlets including Facebook, career and youth-oriented websites and email lists. The questionnaire that respondents were asked to complete asked about drug and alcohol use, attitudes to drug use, the effectiveness of strategies to reduce problems associated with drug and alcohol use, and the extent of their support for harm-reduction interventions. The authors found strong support among respondents for treatment and rehabilitation programmes, drug law reform measures, including the legalization of personal use of drugs such as cannabis, and opposition to restrictions on alcohol availability and drug testing at work or school. More detailed findings can be found in the published report.

Source: Lancaster, Ritter and Matthew-Simmons (2013)

The major characteristics and limitations of a cross-sectional survey are summarized in Box 5.3.

━━━━━ BOX 5.3 ━━━━━

CHARACTERISTICS OF TYPICAL CROSS-SECTIONAL SURVEYS

Major characteristics of cross-sectional surveys

1. Aims to explore attitudes, opinions and practices about issues of social relevance such as drug use.
2. Typically administered to a large sample from a defined population, such as young people in Australia.
3. A questionnaire is usually used as the survey instrument and can be administered face to face, by mail, telephone or via the internet.
4. Demographic information such as age, gender and education level is usually obtained from the sample so as to enable comparisons among groups on the issues explored in the questionnaire.
5. Data obtained is mostly quantitative.

Limitations of cross-sectional surveys

1. They are not able to establish cause–effect relationships, only correlational ones.
2. They are limited in the amount and depth of information that can be obtained from respondents.
3. Information about changes over time are not able to be identified.
4. Non-responses can be a problem if they constitute a sizeable proportion of the sample.

There is little opportunity to ensure respondents have properly understood the questions, particularly when the questionnaire is self-administered.

There is, of course, considerable variability in cross-sectional surveys so that this summary is only indicative.

Longitudinal surveys

Longitudinal surveys are administered at more than one point in time and are designed to track changes over time.

There are two major types of longitudinal surveys, namely *panel* and *cohort* surveys. A panel survey is one in which the same group is surveyed at different times. The sample may be drawn randomly from a defined population and is then followed up, collecting the same or similar information at each point in time. An example of a panel study is outlined in Box 5.4.

━━━━━━━━ **BOX 5.4** ━━━━━━━━

AN EXAMPLE OF A PANEL STUDY – THE MRC NATIONAL SURVEY OF HEALTH AND DEVELOPMENT (UK)

This panel study follows up the health and well-being of a sample of 5,376 men and women born in the UK in March 1946. It collects data on a wide range of health and well-being issues of the sample, including cardiovascular ageing, physical capability, mental and musculoskeletal ageing. Details of the study can be found at www.nshd.mrc.ac.uk.

A cohort survey, sometimes called a repeated survey, is one in which different samples are drawn from the same cohort at different points in time. The cohort may consist of people sharing a particular characteristic, or, in the case of a repeated survey, the whole population of a country. An example of a cohort study is the General Social Survey conducted by the National Opinion Research Center at the University of Chicago, described in Box 5.5.

━━━━━━━━ **BOX 5.5** ━━━━━━━━

AN EXAMPLE OF A COHORT STUDY – THE NORC GENERAL SOCIAL SURVEY (USA)

The General Social Survey (GSS) has been conducted regularly since 1972 and collects information on a wide range of social and political issues from a random sample of adults living in households in the United States. It aims to provide information on trends in attitudes and behaviour, and to identify how these differ among various sub-groups. Details can be found at gss.norc.org.

Limitations of survey designs

A number of sources of survey design errors have been identified by Braverman (1996), which can weaken the validity of survey research if not carefully controlled. He divided these into two basic types: *errors of non-observation* and *errors of observation*.

Errors of non-observation refer to the non-inclusion of eligible participants either because of sampling bias, failure to include in the sampling important sub-sections of the population because of some characteristic that has been overlooked such as homelessness, or refusal to participate.

Errors of observation refer to poor question wording, misunderstanding or even deliberate misreporting by respondents.

In addition to these limitations, surveys rely on self-report data, that is, on what people report by answering questions about themselves. Such data is subject to the problem of **social desirability bias**. This refers to a tendency for people to present a more socially desirable image to the researcher rather than report their actual beliefs or behaviours.

Surveys collect information in isolation from the context in which that information actually exists. Where context is important, the survey is not the appropriate method to use.

Case study methods

The **case study method** investigates a situation in its real-life context. In this way, it differs from experiments and surveys which are removed from the context in which events take place. What makes a case study different from other methods is this focus on a real-life situation in which the researcher has no control over the events that constitute the situation.

Recognition of the case study as a research method owes much to the work of Robert Yin, whose book *Case Study Research* is now in its fifth edition (Yin, 2014). The first edition was published in 1984 and was the first text to systematically justify the case study method as a major research method in the social sciences. Subsequent editions, including the 2003 text, in providing examples of case studies, have further developed the method.

Yin set out to counter what he saw as the prevalent view that the case study method was an inferior method suitable only as an exploratory strategy designed to lead into more rigorous methods such as the experiment and the survey. Alleged weaknesses of the method include:

- There is a lack of rigour of case study research due to investigators not following systematic procedures.
- Case studies provide little basis for scientific generalization.
- Case studies take too long and generate too much information to form a viable research study.
- Causal relationships cannot be established by the case study method as it lacks a control over variables that can be achieved in the experimental method.

Yin (2014) goes on to argue that all these alleged weaknesses can be overcome by improved case study design, and sets out to develop these improvements throughout his book. He does, however, point out that the same weaknesses can apply to all research methods. The question 'How can you generalize from a single case?' can equally be applied to a single experiment. Just as experiments can be replicated, so too can multiple cases be included in a case study design, as outlined below.

Types of case study designs

Yin (2009) identifies four types of case study design in a 2 x 2 matrix. The two bases for classification are:

- single versus multiple cases
- single (holistic) versus multiple (embedded) units of analysis

These two bases generate four case study designs, as shown in Table 5.4.

Table 5.4 Designs for case studies

	Single-case designs	**Multiple-case designs**
Holistic	Single case with one unit of analysis	Multiple cases, each with one unit of analysis
Embedded	Single case with multiple units of analysis	Multiple cases, each with multiple units of analysis

Source: Yin (2009: 46)

Rationales for single-case designs

Single-case designs are appropriate in the following situations:

- critical case situation: the case is critical in testing a theory
- extreme or unique case situation: the case concerns a rare or extreme event such as the impact of an earthquake on a community
- representative or typical case: the case is designed to capture a typical situation such as a representative neighbourhood or school
- revelatory case: the case is designed to open up a new area of study
- the longitudinal case: this case study follows the same case at two or more points in time to establish how conditions might change over time.

A classic example of a critical single-case study is shown in Box 5.6 – Allison's (1971) analysis of the 1962 Cuban missile crisis. In this study, Allison compared three theories about decision making to explain the outcome of the crisis. This use of a case study to test theories is what makes the study a critical case situation and reinforces the value of the case study method as explanatory and not just a descriptive or exploratory method as many had claimed.

BOX 5.6

A CRITICAL SINGLE-CASE DESIGN EXAMPLE – ALLISON'S (1971) ANALYSIS OF THE CUBAN MISSILE CRISIS

Allison analysed the confrontation between the USA and the Soviet Union over the placement of missiles in Cuba in 1962. The USA mounted a blockade preventing Soviet ships from entering Cuba rather than a military strike, so the crisis ended peacefully with the Soviet Union removing the missiles. Allison compared three theories to explain the events that took place, using government documents and other sources.

The study has become a classic case study example. It is often cited to show that case study methods can be used to test theories and offer explanatory and not just descriptive analyses.

A representative or typical case design can be used to study an ongoing situation such as student behaviour in a school playground, or interactions at a social function. This design is often referred to as a **field study**. The data collection method used is observational. The observations may be qualitative or quantitative. An example of a quantitative field study would be observing motorists at an intersection and recording breaches of traffic rules to collect data on the frequency and nature of such breaches.

Rationales for multiple-case designs

Multiple-case study designs are appropriate when:

- the findings from one case study are tested using a similar case so as to provide additional support for them
- cases differ in some significant way and the effect of these differences is examined by comparing cases.

An example of a multiple case study is described in Box 5.7.

■ BOX 5.7 ■

AN EXAMPLE OF A MULTIPLE-CASE STUDY DESIGN – HICKSON ET AL.'S (1986) STUDY OF DECISION MAKING IN PUBLIC AND PRIVATE SECTOR ORGANIZATIONS

In this case study, types of decision-making strategies were examined with a view to comparing them in public and private sector, large and small and short-term versus long-term organizations; 40 organizations were included in the study to enable differences in strategies to be identified across these three dimensions.

A multiple-case study design has been used to identify factors leading to the successful implementation of a programme. Brinkerhoff (2003) has proposed a 'success case method', whereby successful examples of implementation are identified from preliminary research along with examples of implementation failure and a number of cases of each followed up to ascertain what differences in implementation of the programme have led to some being successful and others not.

Holistic versus embedded case study designs

The second basis for classification of case study designs, shown in Box 5.9 below, refers to the number of units of analysis in the study. Holistic designs have just one unit of analysis, whereas embedded designs have more than one.

In contrast to surveys and experiments which use just one unit of analysis, usually individuals, case studies often employ more than one unit of analysis. For example, a case study of psychiatric rehabilitation centres will most likely use several units of analysis. One such unit could be centres themselves which can vary in size, location (rural versus urban) and ownership (public versus private). A second unit could be the programmes offered by the centres (e.g. counselling, skills training, assertiveness training), and a third unit could be individual participants in the programmes offered by the centres.

Value of case studies

While the case study method is a useful method in its own right, it can also be used productively with other methods such as experiments or surveys in mixed-methods designs, as discussed in the next chapter.

One advantage of case studies lies in their flexibility of design. Their capacity to include multiple units of analysis and consequently multiple sources of data provide flexibility not available in other methods. This flexibility enables more complex research questions to be investigated.

Ethnographic research methods

Ethnography is a method of studying social groups through direct observation of the group over time. It places 'specific encounters, events, and understandings into a fuller, more meaningful context' (Tedlock, 2003: 165).

The ethnographic method was developed by anthropologists as a systematic way of studying cultures. The method was quickly adapted to the study of urban cultures and now forms a widely used method in sociology, human geography, education, psychology and many other areas.

Characteristics of ethnography

The major characteristics of the ethnographic method are as follows:

- Social groups are studied in their natural environment.
- The aim of ethnographic research is to gain an understanding of the culture of the group from the inside. This is referred to as the 'emic' perspective.
- The study usually takes place in the group environment over an extended period of time.
- The researcher adopts the role of 'participant observer'. That is, the researcher either joins the group as a member or participates in activities of the group but maintains an observer role.
- Ethnographers use a variety of data collection methods to gain an understanding of the social group they are studying. These include direct observation of the group in action and the recording of these observations in 'field notes', interviews with key group members ('informants') and the collection of artefacts representing group activity.

Ethnographic methods share many of the features of case studies, such as the focus on a 'real-life situation', as well as a similarity of the methods of data collection used. But the focus of ethnography on culture of the group or society being studied and the extended time period over which the study takes place warrant a separate research method category for it.

A variant of the ethnography is the 'Rapid Ethnographic Assessment Procedure (REAP)' (Low et al., 2005) where the research is conducted over a shorter time frame than traditional ethnographies and uses fewer sources of data. The method is used in social impact assessments and Low et al. used the method to study the impact of the 9/11 World Trade Center terrorist attack on residents of Battery Park City, a community located next to the Center. The authors argued that the REAP method enabled the community to articulate their concerns about the impact more clearly in an appropriate time frame.

Origins and examples of ethnographic research

Classic examples of ethnographies are found in the anthropological literature of the early 20th century. Malinowski pioneered the method in his study of the Trobriand Islanders, the inhabitants of a group of islands off the east coast of New Guinea from 1916 to 1918. He published his book recording his observations in 1922 (Malinowski, 1922). This study established **participant observation** as the key method of ethnography and is considered to be the founding of modern ethnography (see Box 5.8).

Other ethnographies followed, for example the study of adolescent development in Samoa by Margaret Mead (1928), in which she argued that the adolescent experience of Samoan females was not as stressful as it was in western societies due to the different cultural practices of the Samoans at the time of her study. The study attracted criticism and focused attention on the possible personal biases that ethnographers can unintentionally bring to their interpretations of the cultures they are studying.

━━━━━━━━━━ BOX 5.8 ━━━━━━━━━━

A CLASSIC ETHNOGRAPHIC STUDY PIONEERING THE METHOD – MALINOWSKI'S STUDY OF THE TROBRIAND ISLANDERS

Bronislaw Malinowski travelled to New Guinea in 1914 and from there to the Trobriand Islands in 1916 where he began his ethnographic study of the lifestyles, social systems, and in particular the method of exchange, used by the inhabitants. Malinowski developed the method of participant observation in this study by immersing himself in the culture of the islanders in order to gain an insider's perspective on their cultural practices.

(Continued)

Malinowski paid particular attention to the system of exchange, termed the Kula, in which armshells and necklaces form two commodities that are exchanged, accompanied by an elaborate ritual. Associated with this ritual are other secondary practices in which food and other commodities are traded. His detailed account of this practice and his interpretation of its significance to the islanders form a major part of the study.

The impact of Malinowski's detailed study has been said to redefine cultural anthropology.

The ethnographic method was soon adopted by sociology to study urban cultures. This research was pioneered by the Chicago School where the method was adapted to the study of urban society, in particular Chicago in the 1920s. Led by Robert Park and Ernest Burgess, the school used ethnographic methods to study crime gangs, adolescents, race relations and a host of other topics.

An example of a contemporary ethnography is the study by McDermott (2006) of working-class cultures in Boston and Atlanta in the 1990s (see Box 5.9).

■ BOX 5.9 ■

AN EXAMPLE OF A CONTEMPORARY URBAN ETHNOGRAPHY – MCDERMOTT'S STUDY OF WORKING-CLASS CULTURES IN TWO US CITIES

Monica McDermott studied race relations in two working-class neighbourhoods in Boston and Atlanta. She conducted her observations from the vantage point of working as a convenience store worker in both cities. This, she says, gave her the chance to observe interactions first hand through her participation in the daily activities of the communities.

Types of ethnographic research designs

Ethnographic research varies according to the role the researcher adopts in undertaking the study. These roles can be divided into two categories, in terms of whether the role adopted by the researcher is:

1. Overt or covert
2. Participant or observer.

An overt role is where the group being studied is aware of the research role of the ethnographer, whereas with a covert role there is no such awareness.

A researcher who adopts the role of participant joins the group and becomes a member, whereas in the observer role the researcher does not join the group but observes from the outside.

This categorization generates four researcher roles, as set out in Table 5.5.

Table 5.5   Roles of the researcher in ethnographic research

Extent to which research role is revealed to the group	Extent of involvement of researcher	
	Participant	**Observer**
Covert	Complete participant	Observer as participant
Overt	Participant as observer	Complete observer

A complete participant is a researcher who becomes a member of the group being studied and does not reveal the researcher role to the group. McDermott mostly adopted this role in the study described in Box 5.9.

A participant as observer is a researcher who becomes a member of the group but the group is aware of the research role of the researcher.

An observer as participant is a researcher whose primary role is that of researcher but does not actively become a member of the group but does not reveal the research role to the group. It should be noted, however, that the observer as participant may also adopt an overt role so the classification in Table 5.5 is not hard and fast.

The complete observer neither joins the group nor conceals the research role from group members. In this case, the researcher is detached from the group activities.

Problems with ethnographic research

Ethnographic research encounters problems less serious in other research methods. The major problems are as follows.

Access to the group or organization

Ethnographers need to gain access to the groups they wish to study. This can present a number of difficulties:

• If the group or organization is private, permission to conduct the research needs to be obtained from persons in authority, called *gatekeepers*. These gatekeepers may impose conditions on the way in which the research is conducted and these conditions may not suit the researcher. If the research is to be conducted within an organization, the gatekeepers may wish to ensure that the reputation of the organization is not harmed in any way by the research.

- If the setting is public, access needs to be negotiated with members of the group. This can produce problems, particularly if members of the group are suspicious about the motives of the researcher. Establishing rapport with the group on an ongoing basis is a challenge for the ethnographer.

Maintenance of a research perspective

Ethnographers can often become immersed in the culture of the group they are studying and lose their research perspective. The extreme form of this problem is referred to as 'going native'. In this case, the ethnographer adopts the perspective of the group and is unable to see the group culture from any other perspective.

Ethical issues

Ethnographic research can present ethical dilemmas not present in other methods. This is particularly the case in covert research where permission from group members to undertake the research is not possible due to the covert nature of the observations. Such research may encounter difficulties in getting ethics approval from ethics committees.

Value of ethnographic research

The examples presented here as well as many others testify to the importance of ethnographic methods in the social sciences. Although originating in anthropology, the method has been extended to many other social sciences with positive results.

It relies predominantly on observational field research (dealt with in Part 3), particularly participant observation. Such research yields predominantly qualitative data. This has led some critics to argue that findings from ethnographic research can't be validly generalized beyond the group included in the study. But generalization is not the purpose of the method. Rather, it is gaining an understanding of the culture of the group and this is not something that needs to be generalized.

One disadvantage of ethnographic methods is the time and detail required to collect sufficient information to arrive at conclusions about the culture of the group being studied. This makes it less attractive for a mixed-methods design unless a rapid assessment procedure is used. In this case, the ethnography often becomes indistinguishable from a case study.

In-depth interviews

The interview method can serve as a stand-alone research method or it can be a data collection method as part of a case study, an ethnography or a survey.

Types of interviews

There are three major types of individual interviews, namely structured, semi-structured and unstructured and these may involve individuals or groups. Interviews of groups can be either **focus group interviews** or group interviews.

Structured interviews

A **structured interview** is one in which the questions to be asked of the interviewee are predetermined with little scope for variation by the interviewer.

Structured interviews are frequently used in case studies where the researcher usually has a clear idea of what questions need to be asked. In mixed-methods research, structured interviews are often used in following up on respondents to a questionnaire in a survey. In the example provided in Box 9.1, students selected for interview were those who had indicated in a questionnaire completed in a survey that they were combining full-time study with part-time work.

Structured interviews are also used in surveys in place of self-completion questionnaires where the survey is conducted face to face. This tends to be an expensive way of conducting a survey compared with delivering self-completion questionnaires online or by mail. It does overcome some of the problems with self-completion questionnaires outlined in the previous chapter, such as misinterpretation of questions or incomplete questionnaires, but it does present other problems, as outlined later in this chapter.

Semi-structured interviews

Semi-structured interviews include predetermined questions as in structured interviews but permit the interviewer to ask follow-up questions on some topics for which additional information is considered necessary. Although the example given in Box 9.1 is a structured interview schedule, it might have been useful to turn it into a semi-structured interview by asking interviewers to follow up any problems identified in question 3 by asking interviewees how they dealt with these problems and whether they felt they had managed them adequately.

The semi-structured interview schedule would normally indicate where follow-up questions are appropriate and what issues can usefully be explored in more detail.

As with structured interviews, semi-structured interviews are often used in mixed-methods research in case studies following up on findings in a survey to gain additional information on survey respondents exhibiting particular characteristics.

Unstructured interviews

Unstructured interviews are those in which a general topic is specified but the questioning is left to the discretion of the interviewer. In such cases, the interview schedule would consist of an outline of the information needed from the interview and some suggested lines of questioning but would not include specific questions.

Unstructured interviews are widely used in ethnographic research where family or community issues are explored in depth. In mixed-methods research, unstructured interviews can be used in conjunction with surveys or even experiments where quantitative research is supplemented by in-depth experience by participants who satisfy particular criteria.

Interviewing groups

There are two major types of interviews involving more than one interviewee, namely the focus group and the group interview. In both forms, one or more interviewers interview a group of interviewees at the one time. Usually questions are put to the group as a whole and interviewees are invited to respond as they see fit. This procedure brings with it some advantages and disadvantages, as set out in Table 5.6.

Groups vary in size depending on the issue, but for practical purposes, more than around ten members may prove unwieldy.

Table 5.6 Advantages and disadvantages of group interviews

Advantages of group interviewing	Disadvantages of group interviewing
1. Participants may raise relevant issues of which the researcher is not aware or has overlooked.	1. Some topics are inappropriate for group discussion. They may be too personal or controversial for views to be expressed in a group context.
2. Participants may 'bounce' ideas off one another and as a result achieve a greater depth of understanding.	2. Some participants may not contribute to the discussion so that their views are not represented.
3. The dynamics of a group discussion enable issues to emerge that might not otherwise be considered.	3. Some participants may dominate discussion to the exclusion of others.
4. Insights can be gained about the nature of group interactions in discussions of social issues.	4. The group situation may inhibit the expression of views thought by participants to be unpopular by other members of the group.
5. Participants may feel 'empowered' by the group situation and take a greater role in initiating discussion.	5. Group discussions can veer off the topic of the research questions and be difficult to redirect.

Focus groups

The most common form of a group interview is the *focus group*. This is a form of group interview in which the interviewer, often referred to as the facilitator, directs questions to the group on a specific topic. Members of the group have usually been chosen because of their involvement with the topic being discussed.

The focus group interview schedule contains a set of questions to be asked of the group and provides a guide to the information to be gained on the topic of the interview. Suggestions for probing and follow-up questions may also be included.

Focus groups have been used extensively in market research where discussion focuses on reactions to the development and marketing of a new product. Social scientists have used the method to explore issues for which there are a range of often conflicting viewpoints. Examples are a proposed new government health policy, the treatment of refugees, or a renewable energy policy.

The aim of a focus group is not to achieve consensus about the issue being discussed but to gain an understanding of the range of viewpoints on the issue. To achieve this outcome, the focus group discussion needs to be conducted in a non-threatening environment where diverse viewpoints are able to be articulated without fear of ridicule or contempt.

Focus groups are designed to promote interaction among participants and to decrease the influence of the researcher over this interaction. Participants are encouraged to contribute openly to the group discussion in an environment designed to give them a 'voice'.

The main features of a focus group are:

1. It is focused on a specific topic as defined by the researcher.
2. It consists of up to ten individuals chosen because of their interest in or expertise on the topic of discussion.
3. A facilitator or moderator introduces the topic to the group and invites discussion.
4. Participants are encouraged by the facilitator to contribute to the discussion.
5. The environment is designed specifically to be non-threatening or intimidating so that participants feel free to express their views openly.
6. The aim of the discussion is to ascertain the diversity of viewpoints on the topic rather than to achieve any form of consensus in the group.
7. The outcome of a focus group is an in-depth understanding of the range of viewpoints on the topic of discussion.

Group interviews

Interviewees can be interviewed in groups in situations other than that of the focus group. Examples might be asking interviewees to report on an event such as a meeting or a function they had attended.

In a group interview, the researcher may be interested in observing the group interaction, whereas this is not normally the case with focus groups.

Otherwise, there are few differences between focus groups and other forms of group interviews, so that the advantages and disadvantages of group interviews, set out in Table 5.6, apply equally to both forms.

LINKING RESEARCH QUESTIONS TO RESEARCH METHODOLOGY

Research questions can be phrased in such a way that the data needed to answer them can be either quantitative or qualitative. Research questions giving rise to quantitative data usually ask 'how much' or 'how many' questions, whereas research questions giving rise to qualitative data ask about experiences or strategies. For example, in a study of paid work undertaken by full-time students (see Table 3.3 in Chapter 3), a quantitative question is 'How many hours per week do full-time students work in paid employment?', whereas a qualitative question is 'What coping strategies do full-time students who work more than 20 hours per week in paid employment adopt to balance their work and study?'. Clearly, the data needed to answer these two questions is going to be quite different. For the quantitative question, data will consist of the number of hours spent in paid employment by each student included in the study over a predetermined period of time, whereas for the qualitative question data will consist of reports by students about how they manage their time between work and study.

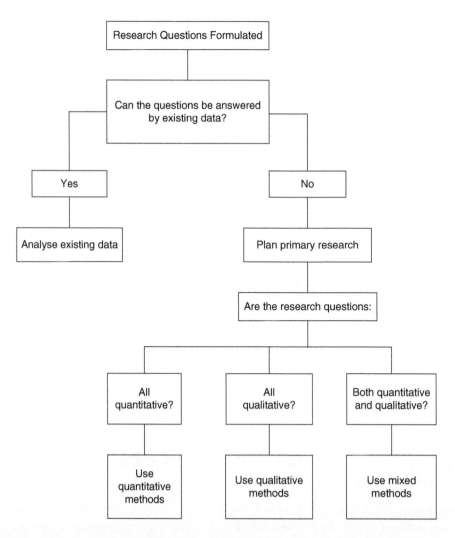

Figure 5.1 Flow chart for the relationship between research questions and methodology

It is at this point that a decision of whether to use mixed methods would normally be made. Mixed methods are appropriate when the research questions include both quantitative and qualitative components. The example given above would call for a mixed-methods design since both quantitative data and qualitative data are obtained. The relationship between research questions and the research methods chosen is summarized in Figure 5.1.

CONCLUSION

Research questions are the driving force behind choice of research methodology and the research methods to be employed. The formulation of research questions by researchers will depend, to a large extent, on the paradigm and the theoretical framework adopted by the researcher, as discussed in Chapter 4. A decision then to use a mixed-methods design will depend on whether the researcher is prepared to formulate both quantitative and qualitative questions to be answered in the same study.

It should be emphasized that the research methods included here are not intrinsically qualitative or quantitative, since this classification refers to the type of data collected. Experiments and surveys do, however, tend to be predominantly quantitative since generalization to a population is a usual aim of both. Ethnographies and in-depth interviews usually yield qualitative data as the focus of such methods is to gain understanding of the context of the subject of the research. Case studies often yield both quantitative and qualitative data. For example, a case study may include both an observational component, such as observing driver behaviour by counting the number of traffic violations, and in-depth interviews of drivers about their driving behaviour. In a mixed-methods study, the quantitative and qualitative components would be treated as separate methods.

CHAPTER SUMMARY

In this chapter, the major research methodologies and methods for undertaking primary research have been outlined and their strengths and weaknesses discussed. The methodologies included are qualitative, quantitative and mixed methods. The research methods are:

- Experimental methods: these include randomized field trials and quasi-experiments or case-control designs.
- Survey research: these include cross-sectional and longitudinal surveys.
- Case studies: these include holistic and embedded designs with single or multiple cases.
- Ethnographies: these include overt or covert methods with the researcher being either a participant or an observer.
- In-depth interviews: included here are individual and group interview techniques.

The randomized experiment is often referred to as the 'gold standard' of research methods due to its potential to identify cause–effect relationships. Critics of this claim point out that many of these experiments fall short of the standard required to make such claims due to methodological problems; that in many cases randomized control trials can't be conducted and lesser designs are employed, and that most social research does not seek to establish cause–effect relationships.

Survey research is probably the most widely used of the social scientific methods because of its capacity to generalize findings to a population, provided random samples are chosen. The survey method is limited in the depth of information that can be obtained on a topic as it mainly uses closed questions that are limited in the amount of information they provide.

Case studies and ethnographies yield mainly qualitative data and are limited in the extent to which findings can be generalized. They provide detailed information, however, on the event or group being researched, not available by other methods.

Mixed-methods research designs to be discussed in the next chapter enable the strengths of individual methods to be combined in a single study, providing greater scope for drawing conclusions. The predominantly quantitative methods, namely experiments and surveys, when used in combination with predominantly qualitative methods, namely case studies and ethnographies, potentially overcome the limitations of the methods in isolation and enable more complete information about the research topic to be gained.

FURTHER READING

Campbell, D. T. and Stanley, J. C. (1966) *Experimental and Quasi-Experimental Design for Research.* **Chicago: Rand McNally.**
This book is the classic statement on the use of experimental methods in social science. Donald Campbell was a pioneer of these methods.

deVaus, D. (2014) *Surveys in Social Research,* **6th edition. Sydney: Allen & Unwin.**
A comprehensive text on survey research, now in its sixth edition. The first edition was published in 1986 so this book has stood the test of time.

Hammersley, M. and Atkinson, P. (2007) *Ethnography: Principles in Practice,* **3rd edition. London and New York: Routledge.**
A thorough description of ethnography as a research method.

Yin, R. K. (2014) *Case Study Research: Design and Methods,* **5th edition. Thousand Oaks, CA: Sage Publications.**
A comprehensive account of the case study research method that has positioned case studies as a major social research method.

6

COMBINING METHODS IN MIXED-METHODS RESEARCH DESIGNS

INTRODUCTION

Mixed-methods research involves the use of two or more research methods in the one study where at least one method yields quantitative data and at least one yields qualitative data. As pointed out in Chapter 5, it is the nature of the research questions that is the main driver of the research design, including when to use mixed methods. What needs to be considered, however, are the rationales for including both qualitative and quantitative research questions in a research project and for deciding which of the wide range of possible mixed-methods designs to use that are available.

This chapter will deal with mixed-methods designs in common use along with the rationale for their use. A simplified classification of mixed-methods designs will also be presented.

RATIONALES FOR USING MIXED-METHODS DESIGNS

Using a mixed-methods design is going to be more time-consuming than using a single method. The reasons for choosing a mixed-methods design need to be carefully considered before going ahead with the choice. Greene, Caracelli and Graham (1989) compiled a set of purposes for mixed-methods designs from a review of 57 mixed-methods evaluation studies conducted during the 1980s. Although now over 30 years since this list was compiled, it still captures the major purposes for using mixed-methods designs. Greene et al.'s list of purposes is reproduced in Table 6.1.

Table 6.1   Purposes for choosing a mixed-methods design

Purpose	Description	Rationale
Triangulation	Aims to establish convergence, corroboration and correspondence of results from different methods	To increase validity of results by counteracting biases inherent in particular methods
Complementarity	Seeks elaboration, enhancement, illustration and clarification of results from one method with results from another method	To increase interpretability, meaningfulness and validity of results by capitalizing on method strengths and counteracting biases in sources
Development	Aims to use results from one source to assist development of other methods	To increase the validity of constructs and inquiry results by capitalizing on inherent method strengths
Initiation	Seeks the discovery of paradox and contradiction, new perspectives of frameworks, the recasting of questions or results from one method with questions or results from other methods	To increase the breadth and depth of inquiry results and interpretations by analysing them from the different perspectives of different methods and paradigms
Expansion	Seeks to extend the breadth and range of inquiry by using different methods for different inquiry components	To increase the scope of inquiry by selecting the methods most appropriate for multiple inquiry components

Source: adapted from Greene, Caracelli and Graham (1989)

Some additional purposes can be added to the list in Table 6.1, as outlined below.

Addressing a wider range of research questions

Mixed-methods designs enable a wider range of research questions to be answered. This is only an advantage if indeed a researcher formulates research questions that require both quantitative and qualitative data to answer them. But when it is recognized that research questions need not be restricted to those that need either qualitative or quantitative data, researchers are free to expand the range of questions they can answer in their research.

A survey of motorists, for example, can enable a researcher to find out the extent to which motorists admit to using their mobile (cell) phones while driving. It can also provide information on the characteristics of those users, such as age, gender, education level, and so on. But a researcher curious about the reasons heavy users give for their use would need to conduct a follow-up of heavy users and interview them about the reasons they give. So the quantitative data from the survey will enable the researcher to answer research questions about extent of use and the characteristics of users but will not provide information on the reasons heavy users give for their actions. This information is provided by the qualitative data from the follow-up interviews and enables the researcher to expand the range of research questions to be answered.

Facilitating more flexible paradigms

Mixed-methods research is not restricted to the narrow paradigms that have dominated quantitative and qualitative research, as discussed in Chapter 2. Instead, it is amenable to a range of alternative paradigmatic positions, including multiple paradigms or more flexible single paradigms.

MIXED-METHODS RESEARCH DESIGNS

Typologies for mixed-methods designs

There are a number of typologies of mixed-methods designs in the mixed-methods literature. Rather than describe all of these, as many of them overlap, two typologies from prominent writers in the field will be selected and a synthesis of these approaches suggested.

Teddlie and Tashakkori (2009) have developed a five 'family' typology, as shown below:

1. Parallel mixed designs: in these designs, the quantitative and qualitative components are implemented at the same time but relatively independent of each other.
2. Sequential mixed designs: in these designs, the quantitative and qualitative components occur chronologically. The order can be either quantitative following qualitative component or vice versa. The design of the second component can depend on the conclusions drawn from the first component.
3. Conversion mixed designs: parallel designs in which one type of data (qualitative or quantitative) is collected and transformed into the other and both forms are analysed.
4. Multilevel mixed designs: a multilevel design refers to a project that collects data from units of analysis at different levels. Data might be quantitative at, say, the individual level, qualitative at the family level and qualitative at the neighbourhood level.
5. Fully integrated mixed designs: parallel designs in which a mixing of qualitative and quantitative approaches takes place in an interactive manner, whereby each approach affects the formulation of the other.

This is a useful classification, although there is some overlap between the families – for example, 1, 3 and 5 are all parallel designs.

Creswell and Plano Clark (2011) identify six mixed-methods design types, as shown below:

1. The convergent parallel design: both quantitative and qualitative components are implemented independently during the same phase of the research process, with the results analysed separately and integrated only in the interpretation phase.
2. The explanatory sequential design: in this design, the quantitative and qualitative components are implemented sequentially with the quantitative component preceding the qualitative component. The qualitative component is designed to follow up findings from the quantitative component to assist in explaining these findings, hence the use of explanatory in the title.

3. The exploratory sequential design: in this design, both components are implemented sequentially but with the qualitative component preceding the quantitative component. The qualitative phase is seen as exploratory and the quantitative phase designed to generalize and build on the qualitative findings.
4. The embedded design: in an embedded design, a qualitative component is added within the framework of a quantitative research design, such as an experiment, or a quantitative component is added within the framework of a qualitative design such as a case study.
5. The transformative design: in this design, mixed methods are implemented within a transformative theoretical framework. It is the theoretical perspective that determines how the methods will be mixed.
6. The multiphase design: this design combines both parallel and sequential components over time. The parallel components may occur in the first phase followed by either a qualitative or quantitative component, which in turn may be followed by more components. Findings in each phase are then integrated in the final interpretation phase.

Unlike the classification by Teddlie and Tashakkori, this classification includes the purposes of the research, as in explanatory versus exploratory goals. A problem with this approach is that a particular design can serve either purpose. For example, the explanatory sequential design is one in which the quantitative component precedes the qualitative component, where the latter is said to 'explain' the quantitative findings. The use of the term 'explanatory' here is an inappropriate use of the term. The qualitative component can assist in exploring aspects of the quantitative findings in depth but to refer to this as explaining the findings is not consistent with common understandings of what constitutes explanation. Likewise, using the term 'exploratory' to refer to designs in which the qualitative component precedes the quantitative is limiting and leaves out projects in which the qualitative component is far from being exploratory. So research purpose will not be included in the typology developed here.

There are some overlaps between these two typologies as would be found with any comparison of typologies. The convergent parallel design by Creswell and Plano Clark is essentially the same as the parallel mixed design of Teddlie and Tashakkori, as are the multiphase design and fully integrated mixed design. The two sequential designs of Creswell and Plano Clark have been combined into the one sequential mixed design of Teddlie and Tashakkori. The conversion and multi-level mixed designs of Teddlie and Tashakkori and the embedded and transformative designs of Creswell and Plano Clark have no counterpart in the other's classification.

These two typologies have been outlined briefly to give the reader some appreciation of the attempts to classify mixed-methods designs in the growing literature on mixed-methods research.

More complex typologies have also been proposed (e.g. Leech and Onwuegbuzie, 2009; Nastasi, Hitchcock and Brown, 2010) incorporating more phases of the research process than the methods selection phase. Typologies for mixed-methods research are clearly in a state of flux. At a practical level, researchers need to know the basic designs available to them in order to plan their research. The following typology is aimed at achieving this purpose rather than providing a comprehensive typology.

A proposed typology

There is one major dimension in which mixed-methods research designs differ, namely whether the qualitative and quantitative methods are implemented concurrently or sequentially. Within this major dimension, the way in which the methods are implemented can differ. In parallel, (concurrent) designs, the methods can be implemented independently or one can be embedded in the other. In sequential designs, the order of the methods can be varied or more than two methods can be implemented, leading to an iterative or multiphase design. These combinations lead to the classification shown in Box 6.1.

BOX 6.1

A TYPOLOGY FOR MIXED-METHODS RESEARCH DESIGNS

Parallel designs

Parallel designs are mixed-methods designs in which the qualitative and quantitative methods are implemented concurrently. Variants of this design are:

1. Convergent parallel design: in this design, the qualitative and quantitative methods are of equal status and are implemented independently, with integration occurring at the interpretation phase of the research.
2. Embedded parallel design: in this design, one method (e.g. the qualitative) is embedded in the other (e.g. the quantitative). Usually, the embedded component plays a minor role in the design.

Sequential designs

Sequential designs are mixed-methods designs in which the qualitative and quantitative methods are implemented sequentially in time. Variants of this design are:

1. The elaboration sequential design: in this design, the quantitative method precedes the qualitative method. Usually, the qualitative method is designed to follow up some of the findings in the quantitative method to provide further understanding or explanation.
2. The developmental sequential design: in this design, the qualitative method precedes the quantitative method. Usually, the quantitative method is designed to examine the generalizability of the findings of the qualitative method or to develop concepts identified at the qualitative stage.
3. The iterative sequential design: in this design, more than two methods are implemented sequentially with subsequent methods designed to explore findings in preceding methods.

These designs will now be discussed, with examples provided of their use.

Parallel mixed-methods designs

Parallel designs involve qualitative and quantitative methods being implemented concurrently. There are two versions of this design: the **convergent parallel design** and the **embedded parallel design**.

The convergent parallel mixed-methods design

In this design, both quantitative and qualitative methods are implemented concurrently. Typically, in this design the quantitative method used is a survey and the qualitative component a multiple case study. These methods are conducted independently and the findings are compared and integrated at the final stage of interpretation.

This design will be illustrated using a hypothetical example shown in Box 6.2. The example involves a survey of aged care nursing homes in a state conducted in conjunction with a series of case studies of selected homes. The surveys provide quantitative information on size of homes, staff/resident ratios, number and qualifications of staff, and so on. The case studies provide more detailed information on activities provided for residents as well as in-depth information on satisfaction and concerns, if any, held by residents and their families. Integration of the findings from each method enables a comprehensive picture of the homes to be gained and provides for the possibility of concerns not necessarily gained from the survey to be identified in the case studies.

The mixed-methods design enabled three different units of analysis to be included. The survey obtained information about the aged care facilities while the case studies obtained information about the programmes offered (through the observational studies) and the individual residents and their family members (through the interviews).

━━━━━━━━━ BOX 6.2 ━━━━━━━━━

AN EXAMPLE OF A CONVERGENT PARALLEL MIXED-METHODS DESIGN

Aged care nursing homes are designed to provide services for the aged who are not able to care for themselves. The homes provide accommodation, meals, health care, social activities and entertainment for residents. Many of these will be publicly owned, while others are privately run. Following complaints about the treatment of residents in some of these homes, the state government has decided to commission a research project aimed at documenting the services provided by these homes and the level of satisfaction with these services of residents and their families.

The research project consists of a survey of all homes in the state to collect information about the number of residents, the number and qualifications of staff, the activities conducted for residents, and the fees charged.

In addition to the survey, case studies of 12 homes are to be conducted, six public and six private, four of each to be located in urban communities and two of each in rural communities. The case studies are to include interviews with staff, residents and their family members, where applicable, and observations of activities conducted with the residents.

The inclusion of the case studies was designed to provide in-depth information on the level of care provided by the homes to supplement the information derived from the surveys.

A potential problem with this design is the possible inconsistency between the quantitative and qualitative findings. This problem will be discussed in detail later in this book but at this point it should be noted that inconsistencies can be a result of poor choice of either quantitative or qualitative data collection, or it can mean that the methods are addressing different issues. So, rather than this being a problem, it is more likely a cross-check on the methods of data collection and analysis and can result in complexities being uncovered by the mixed-methods design that would not have been detected by either method separately.

The embedded parallel mixed-methods design

In this design, one method is embedded in the other and is conducted within the framework of the primary method. The embedded method plays a subordinate role in the design.

The primary method may either be quantitative or qualitative. The quantitative primary method may be either an experiment or a survey. Creswell, Fetters, Plano Clark and Morales (2009) show how embedding a qualitative method within an experiment can provide further understanding of the intervention included in the experiment. An example of a qualitative method embedded within a randomized control trial is provided in Box 6.3.

■■■ BOX 6.3 ■■■

AN EMBEDDED MIXED-METHODS DESIGN INVOLVING A RANDOMIZED CONTROL TRIAL

Victor, Ross and Axford (2004) reported a randomized control trial in which patients with knee osteoarthritis were randomly assigned to a health promotion intervention or a waiting list control group. The intervention did not produce significant benefits for the participants but the researchers also collected qualitative data during the intervention on patients' experience of living with arthritis and goals for care. Patients reported that living with osteoarthritis had a major impact on their lives, reducing their walking distance and limiting their daily activities. The authors concluded that the evidence from the combined quantitative and qualitative data provided insight into the patient's perspective.

In the embedded design, the embedded method addresses questions different from those of the primary method. In the example provided in Box 6.3, the randomized experiment was designed to determine whether the intervention improved patient outcomes, whereas the qualitative data was designed to provide evidence on the impact of osteoarthritis on patients' lives.

The primary method may also be qualitative, as in a multiple case study or an ethnography. The quantitative method embedded in these may take the form of secondary data, such as quantitative background information of the group being studied in the ethnography or the cases included in the case study.

The strengths of the embedded design are as follows:

- It can answer more questions than either the embedded or the primary method.
- It can, at times, provide an understanding of outcomes of the primary method not otherwise obtainable.

Sequential mixed-methods designs

In **sequential mixed-methods designs**, the methods are implemented at different times. Sequential designs are appropriate for a range of purposes, including that they can:

- generalize findings from qualitative research to a wider population by devising quantitative measures of the concepts established in the first qualitative phase
- elaborate and expand on the understanding of findings derived from a quantitative study by undertaking follow-up qualitative research on aspects of the quantitative findings
- develop theory from findings at an initial stage, either qualitative or quantitative, by designing a second stage to develop and test the theory.

Usually, the method implemented second follows up on some of the findings of the method implemented first. This feature is what makes the sequential design powerful. It enables new research questions to be included that were not envisaged at the outset of the research.

As included in Box 6.1, there are three versions of the sequential mixed-methods design, according to which method is implemented first or whether there are more than two phases to the research.

The elaboration sequential mixed-methods design

In this design, the quantitative method precedes the qualitative method. The aim of the qualitative method is to explore in greater depth some of the findings of the quantitative method. Creswell and Plano Clark (2011: 81) refer to this as the explanatory design as they argue that the purpose of qualitative method is to explain the findings of the quantitative method. While this may be the case in some instances, there will be many in which the qualitative method does not set out to explain but simply to explore the findings in more detail.

While any quantitative method may be used in this design, it is typically the survey that is used. In this case, the qualitative method, usually a case study, is designed to follow up on particular findings from the survey. Typical survey findings for follow-up are:

- extreme or atypical responses to survey questions, such as having been involved in a serious traffic accident in the past few weeks, or holding an extreme attitude position
- respondents who identify as supporting or belonging to political, social or other organizations of interest to the researcher
- respondents to the survey who satisfy particular demographic characteristics of interest to the researcher.

In the case of the quantitative method being an experiment, the qualitative follow-up can be that of participants who respond in particular ways to the experimental conditions.

There are many examples of this design in the literature. For example, Forrester et al. (2008) used this design to evaluate a family preservation service designed to improve the functioning of families in which parents engaged in substance misuse. The quantitative phase compared outcomes for an intervention group in which children were referred to the service with a comparison group in which no referral took place. The qualitative phase involved follow-up case studies of families who had participated in the programme within the previous 12 months. The aim of the qualitative phase was to identify components of the service that contributed to its effectiveness. In another example, Ivankova and Stick (2007) obtained quantitative data from an online survey of current and former students in a distributed doctoral programme in educational leadership. From the survey responses, the authors identified four sub-groups: a beginning group who had completed 30 or fewer credit hours; a matriculated group who had completed more than 30 credit hours; a graduated group of former students who had graduated from the programme; and a withdrawn/inactive group of former students who had either withdrawn from or terminated the programme or had been inactive for three terms prior to the survey administration. The qualitative phase used a multiple case study design in which one student/former student from each group was chosen on the basis of their being typical members of each group based on their responses to the survey questions. These students were then interviewed and information on their progress in the course collected. This data was used to elaborate on reasons for persistence in the programme.

These two examples show how the quantitative sequential design can provide comprehensive information on a programme or intervention not available from the use of a single method, either quantitative or qualitative.

The developmental sequential mixed-methods design

In this design, the qualitative method precedes the quantitative. The aim of the quantitative method is usually to identify the extent to which the concepts developed in the qualitative method are present in a target population. The qualitative method can be a multiple case study design, although it could also be an ethnography. The follow-up quantitative method may be a survey or it can involve the collection of secondary quantitative data.

The qualitative phase may be used to form groups based on themes emerging from interviews or focus group discussions. For example, focus groups conducted with sports coaches could be aimed at identifying effective coaching strategies. A follow-up quantitative phase could be to conduct a survey of coaches and athletes in which coaches are allocated to an effectiveness category determined in the qualitative phase and achievements of the athletes coached by them compared on quantitative data collected from events in which the athletes participated.

An example of this design is shown in Box 6.4, involving a study of teacher preparation by Mertens and colleagues.

▬▬▬ BOX 6.4 ▬▬▬

THE QUALITATIVE SEQUENTIAL MIXED-METHODS DESIGN IN PRACTICE

Mertens, Bledsoe, Sullivan and Wilson (2010) describe the evaluation of a teacher preparation programme designed to prepare teachers for students who are deaf or hard of hearing and who have an additional disability. The study commenced with a qualitative data strategy of document review, observation of a seminar attended by graduates of the programme, and interviews of the participants.

The quantitative method which followed was a web-based survey sent to all the graduates of the programme, dealing with issues identified at the qualitative stage.

The iterative sequential mixed-methods design

The iterative sequential design involves three or more phases in which quantitative and qualitative methods are employed sequentially, with one method providing input into a follow-up method which in turn provides input into a further method.

This design is less common in the literature than the two-phase designs discussed above due to the complexity of the design and the time and expense needed to conduct it.

A hypothetical example of how an iterative sequential mixed-methods design can be conducted is shown in Box 6.5. This example illustrates a quantitative–quantitative–qualitative iterative design.

There are of course many possibilities for iterative designs in both the number and sequencing of methods. The example in Box 6.5 is meant to illustrate how such designs can be constructed and used to answer more complex research questions.

━━━━━━ BOX 6.5 ━━━━━━

A HYPOTHETICAL EXAMPLE OF AN ITERATIVE SEQUENTIAL MIXED-METHODS DESIGN

The use of handheld mobile (cell) phones whilst driving is illegal in most countries. Yet drivers persist in using their phones for texting or speaking with callers while they are driving. Perhaps one reason for this is the apparent unlikely event of them actually being caught by police while using their phone. Yet some drivers are convicted for this offence so that the perception by drivers that they are not likely to be caught may not be well founded.

To ascertain the likelihood of getting caught, a valid indicator of phone use while driving needs to be established. Phase one of an iterative design could be aimed at ascertaining this. A quantitative field study would be suitable for this purpose. Observers are stationed at intersections in a randomly chosen set of locations in a city to record handheld mobile phone use by drivers approaching the intersection. The percentage of drivers observed using their phone under these circumstances can be used as an estimate of the incidence of mobile phone use while driving, although this will be an underestimate as not all drivers will be carrying their phones.

In phase two of the study to examine the frequency and impact of convictions for the use of mobile phones while driving, quantitative data is to be collected through a survey of drivers.

A suitable survey design needs first to be established. A convenient method for doing this would be to select car parks randomly in shopping malls or sporting venues and approach drivers as they leave or enter their cars and ask them to participate in the survey by completing a questionnaire addressing their use of mobile phones and whether any convictions had been found against them for such use. The percentage of admitted use can then be compared with the incidence of use observed in phase one, and the percentage of convictions admitted could be an estimate of the likelihood of being caught using a mobile phone while driving.

In phase three of the study, follow-up qualitative data could be obtained through interviews of drivers who have had convictions recorded against them and who agree to a follow-up interview.

The survey would yield quantitative data on the incidence of convictions and the impact of such convictions, while the follow-up qualitative data from the interviews would yield more detailed information on the effects and experience of being caught and convicted of such mobile phone use.

CONCLUSION

A researcher choosing to use a mixed-methods design needs to be clear about the reasons for choosing such a design and to link this choice to the particular design chosen. Green, Caracelli and Graham (1989) link the purposes they identify (Table 6.1) to design characteristics derived from their review of mixed-methods evaluations. They proposed a constrained-wide hierarchy of designs appropriate to specified purposes, with **triangulation** as the most constrained and expansion as the most open. The recommended design for triangulation as a purpose is what has here been called the convergent parallel design, while a range of alternative designs were considered appropriate for expansion as a purpose.

Mixed-methods designs have been used in a far greater range of fields since the publication of the Greene, Caracelli and Graham journal article, so that the linking of purpose to design choice has become more complex. No single set of recommendations would seem appropriate as each study will need to consider the most suitable design for its purpose and the nature of the research questions.

CHAPTER SUMMARY

In this chapter, rationales for using mixed-methods research designs have been outlined and the major designs in use described.

Mixed-methods designs enable a wider and more complex set of research questions to be answered, can overcome the weaknesses of single methods and provide more flexibility in the paradigms adopted to guide the research.

There is a wide range of mixed-methods designs in the literature. Two have been described and compared in this chapter and an alternative typology developed. In this typology, designs have been differentiated on the basis of whether the qualitative and quantitative methods have been implemented concurrently or sequentially. Research purpose and theoretical orientation have not been included since these are matters that transcend design characteristics and are best dealt with separately.

The major mixed-methods designs outlined here are:

- parallel mixed-methods designs:
  - o the convergent parallel design
  - o the embedded parallel design.

- sequential mixed-methods designs:
  - o the elaboration sequential design
  - o the developmental sequential design
  - o the iterative sequential design.

These designs are now being used extensively in mixed-methods research. They encompass a wide range of research aims and purposes and enable many more research questions to be answered than by any single method.

FURTHER READING

Creswell, J. W. and Plano Clark, V. L. (2017) *Designing and Conducting Mixed Methods Research*, **3rd edition. Thousand Oaks, CA: Sage Publications.**
Chapter 3 of this book develops the design typology described in the text.

Nastasi, B. K., Hitchcock, J. H. and Brown, L. M. (2010) An inclusive framework for conceptualizing mixed method design typologies. In A. Tashakkori and C. Teddlie (eds), *Sage Handbook of Mixed Methods in Social and Behavioral Research*, **2nd edition. Thousand Oaks, CA: Sage Publications.**
A summary of existing typologies for mixed-methods research and the development of an inclusive framework for design typologies.

Teddlie, C. and Tashakkori, A. (2009) *Foundations of Mixed Methods Research*. **Thousand Oaks, CA: Sage Publications.**
Chapter 7 of this book sets out a design typology that includes single methods which involve collecting both quantitative and qualitative data and converting the data to one form, mostly quantitative.

CONDUCTING SOCIAL RESEARCH

Part 3 deals with the stages of research where data collection instruments are designed and data is collected. Where a researcher is using mixed methods, both the instruments used and the data collection procedures adopted need to be carefully integrated. Methods for doing this will be discussed throughout this part since it is assumed that the researcher is most likely going to use mixed methods.

The data collected is either *primary data*, that is, data that has not previously been collected, or *secondary data*, that is, data that has been collected by others and is available for use in your research.

Primary data can be self-report, or where participants provide the researcher with information about themselves through completing questionnaires or answering interview questions, either as individuals or in groups. Secondary data is that provided by other researchers or information collected by agencies such as government statistical bodies.

This part is organized according to the methods used to collect data.

Chapter 7 deals with the process of choosing research participants, otherwise called sampling methods. Differences in sampling in quantitative and qualitative research and how these are combined in mixed-methods research will be discussed.

Chapter 8 deals with self-completion questionnaires administered by mail or through the internet. These are the major instruments used in survey research and are widely used to collect the quantitative data in mixed-methods research.

Chapter 9 deals with interview techniques. Interviews can be structured or unstructured or a combination of both. Unstructured interviews are essentially qualitative and are used in ethnographic or case study research. They regularly form the qualitative component in mixed-methods research.

Observational methods are covered in Chapter 10. Observational methods are used in both case studies and ethnographic research. Their use in mixed-methods research will be discussed.

The collection of secondary data will be dealt with in Chapter 11.

7

SAMPLING METHODS: CHOOSING RESEARCH PARTICIPANTS

INTRODUCTION

Decisions about how participants in the research project are to be recruited and the location/s of the research, need to be made before any data can be collected. These decisions are based on the nature of the research design, and more specifically on the research questions.

Choosing research participants is often referred to as sampling. The method of sampling differs for quantitative and qualitative research methods. In qualitative research, participants are chosen because they meet certain criteria derived from the research questions. An example is women CEOs of telecommunications companies who are chosen as interviewees to explore the problems women experience in managing a company in a traditionally male-dominated industry. Another example is choosing pre-schools in low socio-economic areas to explore their policies about providing educational experiences for the children attending the centres.

Sampling in qualitative research is often purposive sampling, since, as the above two examples illustrate, participants or sites are chosen because of their relevance to the research questions.

In quantitative research, sampling may also be purposive but more often it is random since in many quantitative methods the aim of the research is to generalize findings to a wider population.

The term 'population' is used in sampling to refer to the totality of elements from which samples are chosen. These elements may be individuals, such as all students enrolled at a university, organizations such as all hospitals in a state, groups such as families or sporting clubs, or any other entities of interest to the researcher.

The term **sampling frame** refers to the listing of population units from which a sample is drawn. Once a population is defined, it is necessary to be able to determine how to access elements of the population from which to draw a sample. This is the job of the sampling frame. It must include all elements of the population and identify means for accessing them.

In mixed-methods research, both purposive and random sampling are common, the random sampling used in the quantitative component to generalize findings and the purposive sampling used to explore issues raised in the quantitative component in greater depth, often by choosing participants identified as exhibiting particular characteristics during the quantitative phase. Examples of such practices will be provided in Chapters 9 and 10.

In this chapter, sampling methods in both qualitative and quantitative research will be outlined and discussed, and the combination of these in mixed-methods designs considered.

The chapter will conclude with a discussion of problems encountered in accessing research participants as well as the ethical issues involved in conducting research on humans.

Before considering sampling methods in detail, the major types of sampling strategies will be outlined and their basic features discussed.

SAMPLING STRATEGIES IN RESEARCH

Sampling strategies fall into two major categories, namely **probability sampling** and **non-probability sampling**. These are defined in Box 7.1.

Probability sampling is used almost exclusively in quantitative research, particularly in surveys and randomized field trials, where it is considered important to be able to generalize findings to a wider population.

Non-probability sampling can be used in both qualitative and quantitative research when it is not intended that the findings are to be generalized beyond the sample. Most qualitative research is of this kind.

━━━━━━ BOX 7.1 ━━━━━━

MAJOR SAMPLING STRATEGIES

Probability sampling

Probability sampling is a method where all members of a defined population have a known probability of selection in the sample. What constitutes a population is defined by the researcher and will depend on the research aims. It could be all students enrolled in courses at a university, or all hospitals in a state. Whatever the population samples are chosen from, it is a random manner as described later in this chapter, so that all members of the population have a chance of being selected, usually an equal chance.

Probability sampling enables a researcher to use statistical inference procedures to generalize findings from the sample to the population. In order to use such procedures, data needs to be quantitative.

Non-probability sampling

Non-probability sampling refers to a variety of methods where sampled elements are chosen in a non-random manner, usually based on criteria set by the researcher. Such sampling procedures do not use random procedures for choosing sample elements so that no generalization to a population is warranted.

Non-probability sampling is used when a researcher is interested in particular individuals or organizations because of some special characteristics attributable to them, such as individuals who have particular roles in an organization, like managers, or organizations headed by a female CEO. In such cases, the sampled elements are studied because of their particular characteristics and not because they are representative of a population.

Non-probability sampling is used predominantly in qualitative research methods such as ethnographic or case-study methods where there is no intention to generalize to a population.

PROBABILITY SAMPLING METHODS

Probability sampling is used when generalizations to a population are a feature of the research. To generalize to a population, a measurement of some kind is needed, even though this might only be a simple presence or absence of a characteristic, such as a response of yes or no. So probability sampling methods require quantitative data.

Research methods in which probability sampling methods are applicable are the survey and randomized control trials. In these methods, generalization to a population is often intended.

Probability sampling methods include simple random sampling, systematic sampling, cluster sampling and stratified sampling. These will now be described and the conditions under which they are used outlined.

Simple random sampling

A **simple random sample** is one in which all members of the population from which the sample is chosen have a known, usually equal, probability of selection. This requires all elements of the population to be identified in some way so that they can be eligible for choice in a sample. The simplest way to choose a simple random sample is to number each element of the population and use a random number generator to choose the sample. So, if the population of interest is all hospitals in a state, then each hospital is assigned a number and a random number generator used to select hospitals in the sample.

In most research, simple random sampling is not feasible since populations of interest are too diverse to be enumerated, as in the above example. If, for example, a researcher wishes to draw a sample from the population of all residents of a city, then identifying each resident and assigning them a number is clearly implausible so that alternative sampling methods would be needed.

Systematic sampling

The simplest variation on simple random sampling is **systematic sampling**. In this case, one element of the population is chosen at random and then every kth member, where k is a whole number, is chosen thereafter until the sample size is reached. For this to be achieved, the population needs to be ordered in some way. The number k is referred to as the sampling fraction.

An example of systematic sampling is provided in Box 7.2. It is, however, limited to such cases where the population of interest can be accessed sequentially, such as in a queue or where elements of the population form some sort of sequence. Most populations don't correspond to such simple structures.

━━━ BOX 7.2 ━━━

EXAMPLES OF SYSTEMATIC SAMPLING

1. A researcher interested in studying attitudes to drug-taking in sport among fans attending a major sporting fixture chooses a sample consisting of every twentieth person arriving at the sporting stadium. This sample would qualify as a systematic sample provided that all persons attending the event must pass through admission gates at which researchers are located. The sampling fraction in this case is 20 so that a 5% sample of the population would be obtained.

2. In a study of attitudes of students at the University of New South Wales to a requirement to complete units of general education as part of their degree requirements, every tenth student attending the enrolment centre was interviewed (Hall, 1978). At the time of this study, the sampling method qualified as a systematic sampling method since it preceded online enrolment. Clearly, such a method would no longer be appropriate.

Cluster sampling

Cluster sampling is a much more realistic random sampling method where populations are difficult to enumerate than either simple random sampling or systematic sampling. In cluster sampling, the population is divided into clusters. Such clusters are convenient ways of subdividing the population for easier access. If the population consists of residents of a city, then clusters could be suburbs of that city.

Clusters themselves can be further subdivided into smaller clusters. Suburbs, for example, can be divided into local areas and these even further divided into streets.

Multistage cluster sampling is a method of random sampling where clusters are successively divided into smaller clusters, and at each cluster level clusters are chosen at random, and at each of the smallest cluster levels, all elements of the cluster are chosen in the sample. An example will help to make this sampling strategy clear. Suppose we wish to obtain a statewide random sample of school students. Natural clusters for students would be schools and classes within schools. So, a two-stage cluster sample could consist of a random sample of schools followed by a random sample of classes in the schools chosen in the first stage. The sample would then consist of all students enrolled in the classes chosen.

An advantage of cluster sampling is that it enables samples to be easily obtained where populations are located in clusters such as streets, schools, hospitals, and so on. Attempting to obtain a simple random sample in such situations would be difficult and time-consuming. Researchers can take advantage of the existence of clusters.

Stratified sampling

A stratified random sample is one in which elements are chosen from strata within the population. That is, the population is divided into a number of strata and a sample is drawn randomly within each stratum.

It is important that the strata are mutually exclusive. That is, a given population element can fall into only one stratum. Otherwise, population elements will have different chances of selection in a sample if they fall into more than one stratum.

Populations often fall into convenient strata such as gender and age of individuals, private or public schools, or hospitals and many others. It is often easier to sample from within strata than to sample from a population as a whole.

Strata may have different sizes so that researchers may need to choose their sample sizes from each stratum in accordance with its size. This strategy is referred to as *proportional stratified sampling*. In this case, the same sampling fraction is applied to all strata. If, for example, the sampling fraction is 1/10, then sample sizes from each stratum will be one tenth of the size of the stratum.

Choosing among probability sampling methods

Deciding which probability sampling method to use in a research project depends on the nature of the research project and on the population to be sampled. Randomized control trials tend to be conducted on samples drawn from quite specific populations where simple random sampling or systematic sampling are most appropriate. An example of a randomized control trial would be where clients of a psychiatric rehabilitation clinic are assigned randomly to either a skills training group or a control group by a simple randomized procedure. In this case, the randomization takes place at the level of assignment to the groups rather than selection from a population. This form of randomization is referred to as *random assignment*. The clients themselves are not randomly sampled but are assigned randomly to the groups to avoid any systematic bias in group membership.

Surveys of large or diverse populations, on the other hand, are more likely to use stratified or cluster sampling methods since simple random or systematic sampling are not feasible. For example, residents of a city are more readily sampled using a cluster sampling method involving local areas and streets.

NON-PROBABILITY SAMPLING METHODS

Non-probability sampling is particularly appropriate for use in qualitative research, although it can also be used in some quantitative research.

Research in which non-probability sampling methods are used depends on the nature of the research method used and the type of data to be acquired. As mentioned above, most situations involve the collection of qualitative data. Qualitative data can take many forms, including textual data from interview transcripts, visual images as in photos or product advertisements appearing in magazines, video clips of events and many others.

As outlined in Chapter 5, the main research methods used to obtain qualitative data are the case study, ethnography and in-depth interview methods. Qualitative data may also be obtained from surveys where open-ended questions are included in questionnaires, but, in such cases, it is the quantitative design that determines the sampling procedure.

The main non-probability sampling methods are purposive sampling, theoretical sampling, convenience sampling and snowball sampling. Descriptions of these methods are outlined below.

Purposive sampling

Purposive sampling involves choosing sample elements on the basis of their relevance to the research questions. These elements may be research sites in a multiple case study or particular individuals to be interviewed. The basis of choice is how well the sampled unit is likely to provide information that answers the research questions.

Types of purposive sampling include:

1. Extreme cases where sampled units are extreme or deviant in some respects relevant to the research, such as programmes to assist disadvantaged students that have been extremely successful.

2. Critical cases where the sampled units are considered to be critical to the research aims, such as parents of children accessing disability services in a study of the adequacy of such services.

3. Typical cases where sampled units are judged to be typical of those for which the research project is concerned.

Theoretical sampling

Theoretical sampling involves choosing sampling units that can be used to test a theory. In this form of sampling, the researcher derives predictions from a theory and then chooses a sample unit that satisfies the conditions for a test of the theory.

While this form of sampling can be conducted in the context of any appropriate theory, it has traditionally been developed in the context of grounded theory, as developed by Glaser and Strauss (1967). In this approach, theory is generated by the data collected rather than the other way around. Grounded theory is dealt with in Chapter 16.

Convenience sampling

A convenience sample is one chosen by a researcher because of its ready accessibility. **Convenience sampling** involves including sample elements available to the researcher, either due to their being located in the proximity of the researcher or their being easily contacted, such as through Facebook.

Students form a convenience sample for many academic researchers since they are often required to serve as research subjects as part of their undergraduate requirements, notably on psychology courses.

Shoppers can also form a convenience sample as researchers can approach them at a shopping mall.

Convenience samples aren't confined to people. Locations can also form a convenience sample such as schools in a particular area.

A limitation of convenience sampling is that the sample may not be appropriate for the research questions.

Snowball sampling

A snowball sample is one where subsequent sampled elements depend on previously chosen elements, often through a referral process. The analogy is to a snowball gathering more snow and getting larger as it rolls downhill.

Snowball sampling is used when participants are difficult to find because of particular characteristics they possess that are either rare or hidden in a population. Illegal drug users are such a hidden population. Contacting such users can be difficult so that a researcher may well need to use social networks of users to put together a sample. Gaining access to this network can be a delicate process as the cooperation of network members would be based on trust.

A problem with snowball sampling is that it can produce biased samples. Relying on social networks to gain sample members can narrow down the potential range of participants, omitting those not part of the network but nevertheless highly appropriate as informants.

SAMPLING METHODS IN MIXED-METHODS RESEARCH

Most mixed-methods research projects will involve both probability and non-probability sampling methods. The probability sampling method will apply to the quantitative component and the non-probability method to the qualitative component. But, in mixed-methods research, the sampling methods adopted are not usually independent of one another. In a quantitative sequential design, for example, the sample used in the qualitative component is often derived from the probability sample chosen in the quantitative component. So, for example, in a survey of residents of a rural community about their attitudes to the establishment of a new coal mine in the area, the researcher may be interested in follow-up interviews of residents opposed to the mine. In this case, a multi-stage cluster sampling technique would be most appropriate for generating the survey sample, while a purposive sampling technique using responses to the survey questionnaire would be used for the qualitative component, namely the follow-up interviews.

In **parallel mixed-methods designs**, where the quantitative and qualitative components are conducted simultaneously, the samples are usually closely related, often with the qualitative sample being a subset of the quantitative sample.

DETERMINING SAMPLE SIZE

Once the sampling method or methods have been decided, the sample size needs to be considered. The considerations in deciding sample size are different in probability and non-probability sampling. In probability sampling, where generalization to a population is intended, the sample size determines the level of precision with which such generalizations are made. In general, the larger the sample size, the greater the precision; but with large samples, further increases in precision are small.

With simple generalizations, for example average differences between two groups, such as males and females, the level of precision of a generalization to a population about such differences can be estimated (see statisticshowto.com). Most research projects are far more complicated than just testing for differences between two groups, so the sample size determination is not so simple. Factors that need to be taken into account in deciding on the size of a sample in quantitative research are:

- Size of the population: for small populations that are reasonably accessible, a relatively large sample size may be practicable. As the population size increases, the sample size will need to increase to achieve a given level of precision, although the size of the sample will level off as population size increases beyond around 100,000.
- Margin of error: when a researcher draws a sample from a population, there will always be a margin of error associated with any generalizations made. The researcher can reduce this margin of error by increasing sample size.
- Variability in the population: in general, the more variability associated with the measures being taken, the larger the sample is needed to achieve a given level of precision.
- Costs of sampling: the costs associated with sampling need to be balanced against the increase in precision obtained from large samples.

In non-probability sampling, there are no simple formulae for determining sample size, so that other considerations need to be made. Morse (2000) lists a number of factors that need to be taken into account in deciding on sample size in qualitative research. These include:

- The scope of the study: the broader the scope of the research, the greater the amount of information needed to answer the research questions. This can be achieved by either increasing the sample size if one data collection method is used, such as interviews, or by employing diverse data collection methods.
- The nature of the topic: the greater the complexity of the topic being researched, the greater the amount of information needed to answer the research questions, so that sample size needs to be higher with more complex topics.
- Quality of data: high quality data can be achieved from well-designed interviews or focus group discussions and this can result in smaller sample sizes being needed to answer research questions than if the data is of lesser quality.
- Study design: the design of the research project will impact on the sample size needed to answer research questions. A study involving follow-up interviews of individuals, or one in which group dynamics are the focus, will most likely involve smaller samples as more information is obtained from each individual or group. As Morse (2000: 5) argues: 'There is an inverse relationship between the amount of useable data obtained from each participant and the number of participants. The greater the amount of useable data obtained from each person (as number of interviews and so forth), the fewer the number of participants.'

While in probability sampling the notion of precision of estimation of population characteristics is a guiding principle in determining sample size, in non-probability sampling the notion of *saturation* becomes the major criterion. Saturation is achieved when information derived from additional sources does not add to the information already obtained.

SAMPLING ERROR

Errors that may occur in sampling can impact on the validity of all research. Both probability and non-probability sampling methods are prone to sampling errors. The major kinds of sampling errors are:

- Sampling frame errors: sampling frame errors can include *missing elements* where *some elements* of the population are not included in the sampling frame, or *multiple listings*, where *some elements* of the population are listed more than once, thereby increasing their chance of being sampled. These errors are important in both probability and non-probability sampling.
- Non-response errors: non-response errors occur when the sampled element cannot be contacted, such as when sampling households the residents are not at home, or when the sampled element does not provide information, as when an interviewee refuses to answer questions in a questionnaire. Such errors are common in survey research and can cause significant bias in the sample if the non-response rate is high. Mail surveys often experience non-response rates of over 70%. The researcher in such cases has no way of knowing whether those that do not return survey questionnaires might have different views to those that do.
- Random errors: any sample that does not include the whole population of interest can be subject to error. Probability sampling seeks to minimize this error, and in general the larger the sample size, the less the random sampling error.

Minimizing such errors is not always easy, particularly non-response errors. If, for example, an interviewee refuses to answer questions, there is little the researcher can do to address this problem.

A researcher can, however, address possible sources of error in setting up the sampling frame by taking steps to ensure there are no missing elements or multiple listings.

ACCESSING RESEARCH PARTICIPANTS

There are both practical and ethical issues associated with the conduct of research involving human participants. Practical problems include locating, recruiting and gaining the cooperation of participants, and ethical issues include informed consent to participation, privacy, risk and benefits to participants.

Practical issues

A well-designed sampling scheme can be rendered ineffective if the recruitment of participants is poorly implemented. Non-response rates need to be minimized to ensure the sample satisfies the criteria under which it was chosen. Steps that can be taken to minimize non-response include:

- Gaining support for the study by organizations with credibility in the field in which the study is conducted and communicating this support to potential participants. This can be in the form of letters, advertisements in local newspapers, emails or social media posts. Such support should stress the potential benefits of the study to the community.
- Taking steps to locate the individuals chosen as participants by using a variety of channels.

CONCLUSION

The sampling strategy adopted for a research project sets limits on the conclusions that can be drawn from the findings. In a survey, for example, findings cannot be generalized to a population if the sample has not been drawn by an appropriate random sampling procedure. Likewise, in a focus group, useful information will not be obtained if the criteria for choosing participants are not carefully formulated and group membership chosen using these criteria.

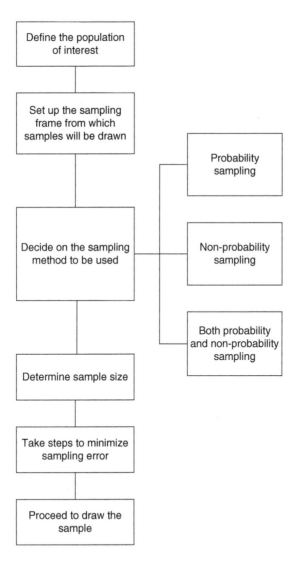

Figure 7.1 A summary of the steps involved in sampling

These considerations are even more important in mixed-methods research, since, as outlined above, the samples for qualitative and quantitative components are often closely related. A deficiency in one component will impact on the other.

Deciding on a sampling strategy is an important first step in the conduct of the research project once the aims and research questions have been formulated. The steps involved in doing this are set out in Figure 7.1.

Determining sample size and minimizing sampling error need to be addressed. Increasing sample size in both probability and non-probability sampling will help to minimize error, but this comes at a cost. Research funding available for the project and the time involved in obtaining samples, set limits to the size of the sample that can practically be obtained.

CHAPTER SUMMARY

This chapter has dealt with sampling procedures in research. These procedures are classified into two major types: probability sampling and non-probability sampling. Probability sampling is used in quantitative research, such as surveys, where the generalization of findings to a population is intended. Non-probability sampling methods are used mainly in qualitative research where detailed information on particular issues is required. This information can be used to generate new theory through the application of grounded theory, as described in Box 7.2, or to test existing theory. These differences between probability and non-probability sampling methods are described in Box 7.1.

In mixed-methods research, both probability and non-probability methods are used and, in most cases, the methods are closely related. The sample for qualitative research is often a subset of the sample for the quantitative component.

Once the sampling method is decided on, the sample size needs to be determined. Factors influencing sample size differ for probability and non-probability methods. In probability sampling, the level of precision with which generalizations can be made increases with increasing sample size. In non-probability sampling, the degree of saturation increases with increasing sample size. That is, new information is less likely to be added to the existing information as sample size increases.

In both cases, however, the sample size is limited by the available time and resources for the research.

FURTHER READING

Bryman, A. (2015) *Social Research Methods*, 5th edition. Oxford: Oxford University Press.
Contains a chapter on sampling covering much of the material discussed here and some information on sampling in interviewing.

Henry, G. T. (1998) Practical sampling. In L. Bickman and D. J. Rog (eds), *Handbook of Applied Social Research.* **Thousand Oaks, CA: Sage Publications.**
A good account of the practical problems in sampling methods, particularly in applied research.

Kemper, E. A., Stringfield, S. and Teddlie, C. (2003) Mixed methods sampling strategies in social science research. In A. Tashakkori and C. Teddlie (eds), *Handbook of Mixed Methods in the Social and Behavioral Sciences.* **Thousand Oaks, CA: Sage Publications.**
A discussion of sampling methods in mixed-methods research.

8

COLLECTING DATA USING SELF-COMPLETION QUESTIONNAIRES

INTRODUCTION

This chapter deals with the use of self-completion questionnaires to collect information mostly about individuals. Questionnaires are used predominantly in survey research and can be delivered by mail, in person or, as is more commonly the case, via the internet.

Questionnaires are useful for collecting information about attitudes, opinions, intentions, experiences, reported activities and demographic information. The latter is used to compare attitudes and so on, across characteristics of individuals such as age, gender, level of education, to establish whether differences in attitudes exist among these characteristics.

In this chapter, the structure and design of questionnaires will be outlined and methods of collecting questionnaire data discussed.

In mixed-methods research, the questionnaire is usually used in the quantitative component of the research and is either followed by, preceded by or collected simultaneously with the qualitative component. Where the questionnaire data is preceded by the qualitative research, the researcher will aim to quantify important concepts established during the qualitative phase and seek to establish the extent to which they are present in defined populations, as discussed in the qualitative sequential mixed-methods design in Chapter 6. Where the questionnaire data precedes the qualitative research, the researcher often seeks to explore some of the findings from the questionnaire in more detail in a subset of the population surveyed, as discussed in the quantitative sequential mixed-methods design in Chapter 6.

STRUCTURE OF A QUESTIONNAIRE

A questionnaire consists of the following components:

- Introductory section: this section explains the purpose of the questionnaire and the use to be made of the findings. It should also address matters of confidentiality. An explanation of the importance of the information being sought in the questionnaire can help to motivate respondents to complete it and so increase the response rate.
- Instructions for completing the questionnaire: instructions are necessary to avoid misinterpretations of questions and to assist respondents in choosing which questions to answer if there is a choice. The instructions need to be clear and unambiguous.
- Content questions: these questions address the main topic of the questionnaire. They may be closed- or open-ended questions or a combination of the two. An example of some closed-ended questions is given in Box 8.1.
- Demographic questions: these questions normally come at the end of the questionnaire and cover any personal information needed such as gender, age, education level, and so on.

━━━━ BOX 8.1 ━━━━

AN EXAMPLE OF SOME CLOSED-ENDED QUESTIONS FROM A QUESTIONNAIRE ON STUDENT EXPERIENCE OF COPING WITH UNIVERSITY STUDY

Please indicate your level of agreement/disagreement with the following statements:

	Strongly disagree	Disagree	Neutral	Agree	Strongly agree
I often find myself doing things that interfere with my study because I can't seem to say 'NO' to people.	1	2	3	4	5
I have a clear idea of what I want to accomplish during the next week.	1	2	3	4	5
I often feel overwhelmed by the number of tasks I have to complete.	1	2	3	4	5
I feel that I am in control of my time.	1	2	3	4	5
I tend to take on more tasks than I can handle well.	1	2	3	4	5

	Strongly disagree	Disagree	Neutral	Agree	Strongly agree
I often find myself doing unimportant things instead of my assignments.	1	2	3	4	5
I am good at setting priorities and keeping to them.	1	2	3	4	5
I have difficulties in finding the motivation to study for my courses.	1	2	3	4	5

TYPES OF QUESTIONS

As indicated above, content questions may be either closed or open.

Closed questions

In a closed question, respondents are presented with a fixed set of response alternatives from which they are to choose one that is most appropriate to them. The examples in Box 8.1 are typical of closed questions. The alternatives may range from a simple yes/no dichotomy to a wide range of alternatives such as a 10-point scale. Providing a large number of alternatives may not result in the researcher being able to make finer discriminations. In a classic journal article, Miller (1956) presented evidence that people were only capable of discriminating around seven categories along a continuum, even when presented with sounds varying in intensity. Subsequent evidence suggests that Miller may have underestimated the capacity of individuals to discriminate among alternatives, and Cummins and Gullone (2000) have proposed that 10-point scales are appropriate for measuring subjective quality of life. It is unlikely, though, that providing more than 10 alternatives will improve discrimination.

Closed questions are used in quantitative research since they can be readily converted to a numerical scale if the alternatives are not already numerical.

Care needs to be taken in formulating the response alternatives in closed questions. The main principles for deciding which alternatives to use are the following:

1. Response categories should be appropriate to the question: having a standard set of response categories can sometimes result in them being inappropriate for some questions. For example, a set of response alternatives commonly used is the 'strongly agree, agree, neutral, disagree, strongly disagree' set. This set may be useful for many questions but there are those for which they are not. For example, if information about the extent or amount of some experience is required, it is better to get respondents to rate their extent on a scale rather than simply indicate their level of agreement. So, instead of indicating level

of agreement with the statement 'I have difficulty managing my time', more information will be gained if the question is rephrased as 'Please rate the level of difficulty you have with managing your time', with the alternatives being, say, '1 – great difficulty' through to '7 – no difficulty at all'.

2. Response categories need to be mutually exclusive and exhaustive: a common problem with response categories is that some might overlap (not mutually exclusive) as in age – for example, 20–30, 30–40, 40–50, and so on, instead of 20–30, 31–40, 41–50, and so on. Another problem is that the categories are not exhaustive, that is, they leave out options that are relevant to the question. So, if the question is 'What mode of transport do you use to travel to work?' and the only options presented are car, train and bus, then clearly walking has been left out, as has cycling, and indeed respondents may use more than one mode. Researchers may not always be aware of the range of response categories to include in a closed question. If time is available, an open-ended question can be trialled to identify the categories supplied by respondents and then these can be listed in a closed question in the main study. Schuman and Presser (1981) found that this produced a higher level of agreement between the open and closed formats.

3. Response categories need to be balanced: the number of positive and negative categories need to be the same and preferably a neutral category in most cases should be provided – for example, strongly agree, agree, neutral, disagree, strongly disagree. It should be mentioned though that in some research forcing respondents to adopt a position is favoured.

Open questions

In an open question, respondents are asked to answer the question in whatever way they choose. This can vary from a simple yes or no to a long explanation. The researcher has little control over the length and content of the response.

Open questions are designed to elicit detailed information from a respondent, as in their views about an issue. They are particularly useful when the issue being investigated is complex and the researcher does not want to limit the nature and amount of information provided by respondents.

Open questions provide qualitative data, which can be analysed by one or more of the qualitative data analysis techniques to be discussed in Part 4.

Deciding question type

Whether to choose all closed, all open or a mixture of closed and open questions in a questionnaire depends on the aims and nature of the research. The strengths and weaknesses of each are set out in Table 8.1.

Table 8.1 Strengths and weaknesses of open and closed questions

	Open questions	Closed questions
Strengths	1. Respondents are given the opportunity to answer in their own terms rather than those forced on them by the researcher. 2. Respondents may provide information not anticipated by the researcher.	1. Closed questions easily enable comparisons to be made across respondents. 2. The questionnaire is likely to be less time-consuming to complete if respondents are not asked to produce lengthy answers.
Weaknesses	1. Respondents may vary widely in the depth of information they are prepared to provide in their answers. 2. Respondents may provide answers that have little to do with the question.	1. Response alternatives provided may not adequately reflect the views of the respondents. 2. By limiting response options, researchers may forgo information important to the topic.

In a single method design such as a survey, the researcher may well wish to use both types of questions, particularly when the researcher does not want to limit respondents to predetermined options on some issues explored in the questionnaire.

In mixed-methods research, qualitative data will most likely be left to the research method focusing on qualitative information so that the questionnaire can focus on the quantitative information provided by closed questions.

DESIGNING QUESTIONS

A questionnaire can only yield high quality data if the questions are well constructed. Although constructing questions may seem to be simple, there are many pitfalls that even experienced researchers can fall into, thereby rendering their data of little value. Some of the pitfalls in designing questions that need to be considered in constructing a questionnaire are set out in Table 8.2.

There are many guides to question design in the literature and most of these are available on the internet (e.g. Siniscalco and Auriat, 2005). Most research methods texts also include detailed guidance on question design (e.g. Bryman, 2015; Neuman, 2011).

DECIDING QUESTIONNAIRE LENGTH

As a general principle, questionnaires should be kept as short as possible to avoid respondent fatigue and impatience with the seemingly never-ending questions. Although there is no clear evidence relating questionnaire length to response rate, most texts on research methods claim that shorter questionnaires achieve a better response rate (e.g. Bryman, 2015; Neuman, 2011).

Table 8.2   Some pitfalls to be avoided in designing questions

Principle	Description	Example
Ambiguity	Ambiguous questions are those that can have more than one meaning or for which the meaning is unclear	Do you often shop at your local supermarket? Both 'often' and 'local' are ambiguous
Double-barrelled questions	Questions that include more than one issue	Should science and maths be compulsory subjects in high school?
Leading or loaded questions	Questions that lead the respondent towards a particular answer	No responsible parent would feed their children junk food
Negative questions	Questions stated in the negative	The government should not introduce taxes on home-owners
Technical language	Questions that include material likely to be unfamiliar to respondents	Should the government adopt the UNESCO policy on childcare?
General questions	Questions that lack specificity	Do you support feminism?

DEALING WITH SOCIAL DESIRABILITY BIAS

Social desirability bias is the tendency for respondents to questions to seek to portray themselves in a socially acceptable way rather than answering questions truthfully. This bias is more likely to be present in questions about sensitive or emotional issues such as drug use, sexual activity or areas that are seen to have potentially socially unacceptable options.

Strategies for dealing with social desirability bias include careful phrasing of questions to avoid triggering socially acceptable responses, or pre-testing questions by administering them along with a measure of social desirability bias and ascertaining whether any relationship exists between the questionnaire and the measure used. There are a number of measures of social desirability bias in the literature, the most widely used being the Marlowe-Crowne Social Desirability Scale (MCSDS), although this measure has been shown to consist of two factors, namely *self-deception*, the tendency to see oneself in a favourable light, and *impression management*, which is the tendency to answer questions in such a way as to create a favourable impression (Zerbe and Paulhus, 1987). It is this latter concept that is seen to be a potential contaminant of questionnaire responses. Methods for identifying and correcting for social desirability bias are discussed by King and Bruner (2000) to which the reader is referred should it be considered a potential problem in a questionnaire.

LIMITATIONS OF SELF-COMPLETION QUESTIONNAIRES

In addition to the problem of social desirability bias discussed above, there are a number of other limitations of self-completion questionnaires. These are:

1. Misinterpretation of questions: respondents may misinterpret questions, particularly those dealing with sensitive issues. There is no control over the way in which questions are interpreted as respondents are left to their own devices in filling out the questionnaire.
2. Incomplete questionnaires: respondents may fail to complete the questionnaire, either accidentally by missing pages or deliberately. Again, there is no control over how respondents answer the questions.
3. Poor response rates: response rates to self-completion questionnaires tend to be poor, particularly if they are sent by mail. Response rates of around 50% are quite common, and the extent to which this results in a biased sample of respondents can be a serious problem.

These limitations can be addressed to some extent by careful wording of questions, trialling the questionnaire and following up on participants to encourage them to complete the questionnaire. Enlisting credible individuals to support the questionnaire and providing plausible reasons for encouraging participants to complete it, may help to increase the response rate.

ADMINISTERING QUESTIONNAIRES

Questionnaires can be administered by mail, by personal contact or by means of the internet. These methods of administration will now be discussed.

Mail-out

Sending questionnaires to potential respondents by mail is a method that precedes widespread use of the internet. It was widely used at a time when home computers and email addresses were a rarity. Sending questionnaires through the mail has a number of drawbacks in addition to those outlined above. Addresses may be out of date so that questionnaires may not even reach the intended participants, and the added task of returning the questionnaire, even when self-addressed return envelopes are provided, may result in poor response rates.

Collecting completed questionnaires can address this problem but this is an expensive alternative to returning the questionnaire in the mail.

Personal contact

In some situations, questionnaires can be delivered personally and either posted back after completion or collected at the time. A typical such situation would be at the end of a group workshop or meeting where a questionnaire could be administered to all those present.

Advantages of this mode of delivery are that the researcher, being present, can answer any questions about the questionnaire to clarify any misunderstandings, and response rates tend to be high, particularly if the researcher remains to collect the completed questionnaires.

A disadvantage of this method of delivery is the possibility of biased samples in situations where the groups are not randomly selected but rely on individuals attending a particular class or function. Those attending may not be representative of those potential respondents who don't happen to be at the gathering.

The internet

The rapid growth of internet usage over the past 25 years has facilitated the delivery of questionnaires, either online or by email. The high level of internet usage in developed countries makes it a viable option for distributing questionnaires. An advantage of this method of delivery is that the questionnaire can easily be tailored to a respondent's characteristics. That is, questions can be presented depending on the answer to a previous question. Although this can be achieved in paper questionnaires, it is often confusing with expressions like 'if you answered x to question 2 then go straight to question 8, otherwise answer question 3'.

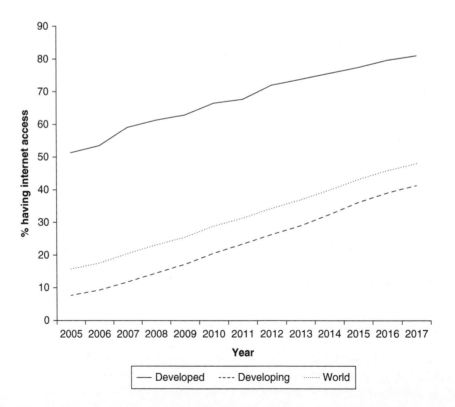

Figure 8.1 Growth in internet access in developed and developing countries since 2005 (*Source:* Statista.com)

The relatively low level of internet access in developing countries means that, at this stage, samples are likely to be biased in the direction of the characteristics of internet users, namely professionals earning high incomes and living in affluent areas. These characteristics are also present in developed countries but to a much lesser extent.

Telephone

The administration of questionnaires over the landline telephone was a common practice before the advent of the internet. While it is still in use, the rapid expansion of mobile phone ownership has rendered this approach of less use. Landlines are rapidly being replaced by mobile phones so that many households no longer even have landlines. One of the advantages of landlines was that area codes could be used to generate stratified samples, but as mobile phones don't have area codes this method is no longer useful.

USE OF QUESTIONNAIRES IN MIXED-METHODS RESEARCH

Questionnaires are widely used in mixed-methods research, usually as the data collection instrument in a survey designed to find out the incidence of the subject matter of the questions in a population. For example, a questionnaire dealing with the quality of teaching may be administered to university students at a number of universities with a view to finding out differences among universities on ratings of teaching quality. In such a case, the questionnaire will contain mostly, if not all, closed questions that can be converted into a measure of quality.

A mixed-methods researcher will most likely want to follow up on students in universities that have received either very high or very low ratings of quality, using interviews or focus groups to collect qualitative data on what it is about the teaching that received the high or low ratings. This approach would correspond to the quantitative, sequential, mixed-methods design discussed in Chapter 6.

CONCLUSION

Self-completion questionnaires are a key data collection instrument in survey research, and as such form the quantitative component in many mixed-methods research projects. They are easily administered and provide information on a wide variety of characteristics of individuals such as their attitudes, intentions, experiences, values, and so on.

Closed questions provide quantitative data that can be related to the demographic characteristics of the respondents. Open questions provide qualitative data that can be used to provide more in-depth information on specific topics.

Self-completion questionnaires are extremely useful in mixed-methods research since they are able to provide quantitative data across a large sample, so as to provide a basis for the exploration of findings in greater depth through qualitative research.

CHAPTER SUMMARY

This chapter has dealt with the collection of data using self-completion questionnaires. They form the most common instrument in survey research and yield mostly quantitative data on attitudes, intentions, opinions and experiences, along with the demographic characteristics of respondents.

Questionnaires consist of either closed or open questions. Closed questions specify a set of response categories from which the respondent chooses one, or, in some cases, more than one, to represent their view. Open questions require respondents to provide a written response.

Closed questions provide quantitative data, while open questions provide qualitative data.

Self-completion questionnaires suffer from limitations due to the absence of any oversight in their completion and can result in the misinterpretation of questions or failure to complete the questionnaire. Response rates can often be unacceptably low.

Self-completion questionnaires can be administered through the mail, via the internet or by personal contact. Internet administration is now widely used due to its convenience and capacity to tailor delivery to individual respondents.

Mixed-methods researchers use self-completion questionnaires in the quantitative phase of the study to explore relationships among concepts tapped by the questionnaire, and these often form the basis for follow-up qualitative research to explore findings in greater depth.

FURTHER READING

Bulmer, M. (ed.) (2003) *Questionnaires*. London: Sage Publications.
A four-volume set covering all aspects of questionnaire design and administration.

Converse, J. M. and Presser, S. (1986) *Survey Questions: Handcrafting the Standardized Questionnaire*. Thousand Oaks, CA: Sage Publications.
Although now over 30 years old, this book contains a lot of useful information on questionnaire design.

Fowler, F. J. (1995) *Improving Survey Questions*. Thousand Oaks, CA: Sage Publications.
Contains excellent information on designing questions in surveys.

Lavrakas, P. (ed.) (2008) *Encyclopedia of Survey Research Methods*. London: Sage Publications.
Contains a detailed account of questionnaire design.

9

COLLECTING DATA USING INTERVIEWS

INTRODUCTION

Interviews are a data collection procedure used extensively in social research, particularly in case studies and ethnographic research, but also as a research method in its own right. Interviews are used predominantly to collect qualitative data, although some interviews can be highly structured to include at least some quantitative data. Structured interviews can be used to collect survey data.

The interview as a research method was outlined in Chapter 5. This chapter will deal more specifically with the conduct of interviews as a means of collecting data.

The instrument used in the conduct of interviews is the interview schedule, in which the questions to be asked and the way the interview is to be conducted are set out for the interviewer. The features of interview schedules will be outlined below.

Interviews can be structured or unstructured and can be conducted with individuals or with groups. The process of conducting interviews differs both for structured and unstructured interviews as well as for individual and group interviews. These differences will be discussed in this chapter.

Mixed-methods research makes extensive use of interviewing, primarily as a qualitative method. This chapter will conclude with a discussion of the role of interviewing in mixed-methods research designs.

THE INTERVIEW SCHEDULE

The instrument used to collect interview data is referred to as the interview schedule. It contains the sequence of questions to be asked by the interviewer. A sample structured interview schedule is provided in Box 9.1, taken from a research project on experiences of full-time students engaged in part-time work conducted at the University of New South Wales in 2006 (Hall, 2010).

The interview schedule for a structured interview contains a series of specific questions that need to be asked in the order contained in the schedule. There is little room for improvisation on the part of the interviewer, except perhaps to prompt interviewees if they are not providing much detail in their responses.

The interview schedule for unstructured interviews is much less specific, giving the interviewer much more scope to ask follow-up questions. The schedule usually contains a few broad questions with suggestions for further exploration of the topic, as considered relevant by the interviewer, to gain more in-depth information from the interviewee.

━━━━ BOX 9.1 ━━━━

AN EXAMPLE OF A STRUCTURED INTERVIEW SCHEDULE ON WORK EXPERIENCE OF FULL-TIME STUDENTS (HALL, 2010)

Work experience interview schedule

Thank you for agreeing to answer these questions about the effect of your employment on your study at this University. Your participation will help the University provide a better learning environment for students. Your answers will be strictly confidential.

Question 1

Do you work because you need the money to cover your expenses or do you have other reasons for working?

Question 2

Please tell us about your job and how it relates, if at all, to your study at university.

Question 3

We would like to know what problems you have experienced around fitting work and study into your schedule.

Question 4

What improvements do you suggest might be made to make it easier for you to combine work and study?

Question 5

Finally, we would like some details about you for our research:

Your gender: Male/Female

Your age: _____years

Your first language: English/Other

Your faculty: Arts/Built Environment/COFA/Commerce/Engineering/Law/Medicine/Science (or faculties if combined degree)

Your programme of study: _____

Your year of study: 1st/2nd/3rd/4th year or higher

Your enrolment category: Local HECS/Local full-fee/International

Your enrolment type: Full time/Part time

Hours of employed work per week during session time: _____ hours

Thank you for your time in this interview.

Source: Hall (2010)

CONDUCTING INTERVIEWS

Interviewing individuals

An interview is a two-way relationship between interviewer and interviewee and this relationship needs to be established on a firm footing for the interview to be a success. While this relationship is important for both structured and unstructured interviews, it is essential for the latter. This is because in unstructured interviews there is much more flexibility in the line of questioning to be followed.

Some key features of the conduct of interviews are set out in Box 9.2.

BOX 9.2

CONSIDERATIONS IN CONDUCTING INTERVIEWS

1. Establishing rapport: an interviewer needs to gain the confidence of the interviewee. This can be achieved by relaxing them through friendly conversation preceding the interview.
2. Establishing credibility: an interviewee will be more likely to provide useful information if she or he understands the purpose of the interview, the nature of the organization sponsoring the research project and the use to which the information gained will be put.
3. Ensuring confidentiality and privacy: confidentiality and privacy are key features of all interviews, particularly unstructured ones. Interviewees will be more likely to provide sensitive information if they are convinced the information will remain confidential.

(Continued)

4. Adapting the question format to the interview situation, particularly in unstructured inter-
    views. Flexibility of the interview process enables use of a range of questioning strategies.
    Some useful such strategies are:

    - follow-up questions: these are questions asked by the interviewer to obtain further
      information or elaboration of a previous answer. They are aimed at exploring issues in
      greater depth than that provided by the interviewee in their initial response.
    - probing questions: these are questions designed to delve deeper into a situation by
      asking for more reasons or examples.

5. Concluding the interview: interviewers need to be sure to thank their interviewees for their
    time and provide an opportunity for them to ask questions about the interview or to add any
    additional information.

Unstructured interviews are more flexible than either structured or semi-structured interviews,
but this brings with it a need for skills in interviewing techniques. The interviewer will need
to gain the confidence of the interviewee and be able to put them at ease so as to extract the
required information from the interview.

Although unstructured interviews can be used in a wide variety of situations, one special
form is the *life history interview*. This is an unstructured interview in which the interviewee
reflects back on their entire life. It can have a particular focus such as experience of discrimination, or experience of a particular traumatic event, in which case it is sometimes referred to
as an *oral history interview* to distinguish it from a life history.

Group interviews

For a group interview to be successful, the interviewer will need to be highly skilled in conducting such interviews. Some of these skills are set out in Table 9.1. Many of these skills also
apply to individual interviews.

Table 9.1 Skills needed for group interviewing

Skill	Detail
Facilitation skills	An interviewer needs to be skilled in facilitating group interactions. These involve: 1. Body language: the interviewer needs to adopt a relaxed and informal posture to put interviewees at their ease. 2. Attention: interviewers need to pay attention to interviewees and maintain a positive expression.
Communication skills	Interviewers need good communication skills. These include the following: 1. Interviewers need to encourage participants to contribute to discussion. 2. Interviewers need to be non-judgemental and to acknowledge a participant's contribution to discussion without conveying agreement or disagreement with them.

Skill	Detail
Management skills	1. Maintain relevance: interviewers need to ensure that discussion does not drift too far away from the topic of the interview.
	2. Manage individual contributions: to ensure all participants contribute, interviewers need to ensure that discussion is not dominated by particular members.

Conducting focus group interviews

Facilitation skills are particularly important in conducting focus groups (see Chapter 5), since the interviewer needs to ensure that the group discussion keeps to the specified topic and that all participants are given the opportunity to contribute.

One of the key features of a focus group is that participants are able to take some control of the discussion and contribute to the content in ways they are not likely to do in other forms of interview. This can result in more issues relevant to the topic being raised as participants gain more confidence in expressing their views. A good facilitator needs to encourage such input in order to maximize the benefits of the format. As pointed out by Madriz (2003: 368):

> Focus groups minimize the control the researcher has during the data gathering process by decreasing the power of the researcher over research participants. The collective nature of the group interview empowers the participants and validates their voices and experiences.

Focus groups can work effectively with marginalized or vulnerable groups whose views are not generally available in the wider community. Madriz (2003) has argued that the focus group method is particularly suited for low-socioeconomic status women of colour; and Porcellato, Dughill and Springett (2002) reported successfully using focus groups with children as young as 7.

THE ROLE OF INTERVIEWS IN MIXED-METHODS RESEARCH

Interviews usually form the qualitative component in mixed-methods research. They can be used in any of the mixed-methods designs outlined in Chapter 6.

In parallel mixed-methods designs, the interviews are conducted at the same time as the quantitative data is collected. Box 6.3 provided an example where the quantitative data was obtained through a randomized control trial of patients with knee osteoarthritis where some were assigned to a health promotion intervention and others to a control group (see Box 6.3 in Chapter 6 for more detail), and quantitative outcomes of lifestyle measured. During the trial, the patients were interviewed about their experience of living with arthritis. The interviews provided far more detailed information on the impact of osteoarthritis and daily activities.

In sequential mixed-methods designs, interviews are conducted either before or after the quantitative data is collected. When interviews are conducted first, they are designed to explore an issue in depth, with the information gained being used to either design a new questionnaire or to use an existing questionnaire, to be administered in a survey to determine the incidence of the characteristics found in a population.

An example of this design was provided in Box 6.4 (in Chapter 6), in which participants in a teacher preparation programme for students who have a hearing impairment were interviewed about their experiences of the programme. The quantitative method involved a web-based survey of graduates of the programme, canvassing issues raised during the qualitative phase.

When interviews follow the quantitative phase, they often involve choosing some respondents to a questionnaire administered in a survey and following up on these respondents with in-depth interviews, expanding on their questionnaire responses. In this way, the quantitative research identifies the distribution of responses to the questionnaire in the population under consideration, and the qualitative interviews provide greater depth of understanding of the individual experiences that led to particular questionnaire responses.

An example of this use of interviewing is provided by research by the author (not yet published) on first-year undergraduate students participating in a peer-mentoring programme. These participants completed a questionnaire on their experience of the programme. One of the questions dealt with whether they had considered discontinuing their studies and, if so, what impact the peer-mentoring programme had on their decision to continue in their course. Those students who reported that they had considered discontinuing were followed up with in-depth interviews, exploring their reasons for considering discontinuation and the role of the mentoring programme in their decision to continue. In this way, interviews can add depth to a survey finding that is not readily available from questionnaire data.

A further example is provided in Box 9.3 from a study by Thorgersen-Ntoumani and Fox (2005) of physical activity and mental well-being among employees of an organization.

■■■■■ BOX 9.3 ■■■■■

A MIXED-METHODS STUDY OF PHYSICAL ACTIVITY AND MENTAL WELL-BEING AMONG EMPLOYEES OF AN ORGANIZATION

Thorgersen-Ntoumani and Fox (2005) used a sequential mixed-methods design to study physical activity and mental well-being in an organization. The first stage involved an online survey of employees, and from the results of the questionnaire they classified employees into four groups: self-assured, exercising happy, mentally unhappy and physically unhappy employees. The second stage involved interviewing a purposeful sample of 10 participants with at least two from each of the four groups. The interviews explored aspects of their experiences relating to group membership to provide what the authors call a 'richer source of data on group membership'. They concluded that the qualitative phase provided insights into the characteristics of group membership that added value to the quantitative phase.

These examples show that in-depth interviewing plays an important role in many mixed-methods research designs.

Focus groups are also playing an increasing role in mixed-methods research. Cyr (2017) has argued that focus groups are particularly suited for mixed-methods research, in particular with large-sample quantitative research. She gives two reasons for this:

1. They can be used in advance of the quantitative research to access diverse perspectives on the issues that are being researched in the survey. This enables researchers to design their questionnaires to be used in the survey with confidence that the questions take into account viewpoints brought forward in the focus group.
2. They can be used to follow-up findings in a survey to pursue issues in greater depth in a group discussion situation. As Cyr (2017: 1040) points out: 'focus groups reveal why and how individuals think as they do – something that surveys and other large-N methods cannot easily accomplish.'

Although the examples given by Cyr (2017) apply to sequential mixed-methods designs, focus groups can readily be used in parallel designs along with any quantitative method.

RECORDING INTERVIEWS

To analyse interview data, the interview needs to be recorded using one of the available techniques. These include notetaking by the interviewer or a co-researcher, aural recording by a phone or tape recorder, or videotaping by a video camera.

Permission must be obtained from the interviewee before any form of record of the interview is obtained.

Videotaping of interviews provides by far the most detailed information since it not only includes all responses of the interviewee, but also the body language of both the interviewer and the interviewee. Analysing videotapes of interviews is more time-consuming than audio or written notes of the interview since it permits more detail to be recorded.

CONCLUSION

Interviews constitute a key data collection method in social research through their use in case studies, ethnographic research or surveys. They can be quantitative or qualitative in the data they collect but their main advantage is in collecting qualitative data.

Use of interviews in mixed-methods research provides a source of information that complements quantitative data. Interviews can be used in both parallel and sequential mixed-methods designs and, in both cases, yield data that provides in-depth information on some aspects of the quantitative findings.

For similar reasons, focus groups have been used in both parallel and sequential mixed-methods designs to provide qualitative data to supplement quantitative data.

CHAPTER SUMMARY

This chapter has dealt with interviewing as a data collection method in the social sciences. Interviews can be individual or group. In both cases, the interview process enables in-depth information to be collected on the topic of the interview that is not able to be gained from questionnaires.

Interviews can be structured, semi-structured or unstructured. A structured interview contains a fixed series of questions where there is little opportunity to vary the question format, whereas an unstructured interview specifies a topic of the interview and guidance to the interviewer about the information required but allows the interviewer scope to decide on the sequence and content of the questions asked. A semi-structured interview includes components of both forms.

Instructions for conducting the interview are contained in an instrument termed an interview schedule.

Group interviews, including focus groups, provide data involving participant interactions not available with individual interviews. Such data can reveal group dynamics and interactions, leading to consensus (or lack thereof) over the issue being discussed.

Both individual and group interviews are used extensively in mixed-methods research.

FURTHER READING

Bryman, A. (2015) *Social Research Methods*, **5th edition. Oxford: Oxford University Press.**
Contains chapters on interviewing and focus groups.

Fielding, N. G. (2003) *Interviewing*. **London: Sage Publications.**
A comprehensive four-volume set covering all aspects of interviewing.

Madriz, E. (2003) Focus groups in feminist research. In N. K. Denzin and Y. S. Lincoln (eds), *Collecting and Interpreting Qualitative Materials*, **2nd edition. Thousand Oaks, CA: Sage Publications.**
A discussion of the use of focus groups with minority populations.

Stewart, C. J. (2014) *Interviewing: Principles and Practices*, **14th edition. London: McGraw-Hill.**
A thorough treatment of interviewing, including interview settings, communication theory and the structuring of interviews.

10

COLLECTING DATA USING OBSERVATIONAL METHODS

INTRODUCTION

Observational research, often referred to as field research, involves observing events or situations as they occur. The events observed may be natural events as they occur in the real world, such as children interacting in a playground, or events set up by the researcher such as a group discussion.

Observational research is a data collection procedure used in case studies, ethnographic research and experimental research. In case studies, observational research is often conducted along with interviews of people having some special relationship to the subject of the case study. In ethnographic research, observational study of interactions among members of the family, group or community being the subject of the ethnography can be used to provide an alternative perspective to data obtained from documents or interviews, and in experimental research observations can form the major data collection method. In these cases, the observations form one or more of the data collection procedures, whereas the case study, ethnography or experiment are the research methods employed as outlined in Part 2 of this book.

Observational methods can be contrasted with self-report methods. In observational research, the researchers observe situations as they occur, whereas in self-report methods, such as self-completion questionnaires or interviews, the researcher asks the participants to report their experiences or describe events as they perceive them.

An advantage claimed for observational research is that it does not rely on participants telling us what has happened, since we observe what is happening directly. In this way, we avoid potential biases being introduced by relying on the honesty or accuracy of the perceptions of the participants. This advantage does not apply if the information being sought from participants is their attitudes, opinions or knowledge since these are matters that cannot be observed.

A problem with observational research is that it relies on the skill of the observer to record and report on the events being observed accurately and without bias.

In this chapter, observational methods will be outlined and discussed and their use in mixed-methods research considered.

TYPES OF OBSERVATIONAL RESEARCH

While there are various ways of classifying observational methods, four categories will be used here. They are:

1. The observational situation: situations can be classified according to whether they occur naturally or whether they are constructed by the researcher. Examples of the former situation are children playing in a school playground, a committee meeting or traffic flowing through an intersection. These situations are those that take place in the real world. Observational research in such situations is usually referred to as *field research*. Examples of the latter situation are placing children in a room with a limited number of toys to observe how they interact, or staging a mock accident to observe how bystanders respond. In these cases, the researcher sets up a contrived situation to explore the specific responses of the participants.
2. The role of the observer: the observer can either be a participant in the situation being observed or a non-participant. A participant observer is either a member of the group being observed or joins it at the time the observation takes place, whereas a non-participant remains outside the group and makes observations from an outsider position. Differences between participant and non-participant observation are set out in Table 10.1.

Table 10.1   Differences between participant and non-participant observation

	Participant observation	Non-participant observation
Role of the observer	The observer is a member of the group being observed.	The observer is not a member of the group being observed.
Observational stance	Observations are made from within the group.	Observations are made from the outside of group membership.
Relationship to aims of the group	The observer usually identifies with the aims of the group.	The observer has no particular relationship to the aims of the group.

3. The observational structure: observational techniques can vary from being highly structured at one extreme to unstructured at the other. A *structured observation* involves recording observations according to a detailed set of instructions as set out in an *observational protocol* (see later in this chapter). Unstructured observation leaves the detail

of what to observe up to the observer who is free to decide what observations best further the aims of the research.

4. Participant awareness: participants may either be aware that they are being observed or not. In most cases, it is a condition for ethics approval of the research project that participants not only are informed that they are being observed but that they agree to the observations. This has not always been the case, though, as the example in Box 10.1 shows.

━━ BOX 10.1 ━━

A CLASSIC EXAMPLE OF PARTICIPANT OBSERVATION RESEARCH

Humphreys (1970) reported a study of what he called impersonal sex, which involved recording homosexual encounters in public toilets. Humphreys took on the role of 'watchqueen', a person who keeps lookout for possible intruders or police so as to protect the participants. He did not reveal his research role to the participants and even collected information about them in order to follow them up at a later stage to interview them about their lifestyles. This research by Humphreys has been instrumental in raising ethical issues concerning the deception of participants and the role of informed consent.

Research in the 1970s and earlier was not subject to ethical scrutiny so that studies were conducted that would not now meet ethical guidelines. The study reported in Box 10.1 is clearly an example of such research. It was conducted without the awareness of participants and at a time when ethical approval was not required.

There are situations, however, where the participants being observed cannot be identified nor contacted so that prior approval is impractical. An example is the observation of pedestrian behaviour at an intersection (see Box 10.2). Such situations are referred to as unobtrusive observation. In these cases, the ethical issues that arose in the Humphreys example do not apply – deception is not involved as the individuals being observed cannot be identified.

━━ BOX 10.2 ━━

AN EXAMPLE OF UNOBTRUSIVE OBSERVATION RESEARCH

Bungum, Day and Henry (2005) reported a study of observations of pedestrians at a crosswalk in Las Vegas, Nevada. Researchers unobtrusively observed and recorded pedestrian characteristics

(Continued)

and the extent of distracted walking they exhibited while crossing the road. Distraction was defined as talking on a phone, wearing headphones, eating, drinking or talking as they crossed the street. The researchers aimed to assess the relationship between distracted walking and cautionary behaviour by pedestrians as they crossed the road. They found that only 13.5% of pedestrians exhibited cautionary behaviour at the crossing and that this lack of respect for road rules placed pedestrians at increased risk of death or injury.

A second example of unobtrusive observation, involving the observation of traffic movements in school zones in Sydney, Australia, is provided in Box 10.3. The aim of the study was to document the extent to which drivers and pedestrians observed road rules devised specifically to protect children arriving at and leaving school. The study used a mixed-methods design, involving a survey of drivers and multiple case studies of the behaviour of drivers and pedestrians in school zones.

■■■■■■ BOX 10.3 ■■■■■■

AN EXAMPLE OF AN OBSERVATIONAL PROTOCOL IN A STUDY OF SCHOOL CROSSINGS

The observational component of a multiple case study design involved researchers observing traffic flow in school zones during arrival and departure times at selected schools in Sydney, Australia in 2006. The researchers observed both pedestrian (adults as well as children) and driver activity during designated school zone times.

Two researchers were located at pedestrian crossings to observe and record vehicle movements across the crossing and pedestrian behaviour using the crossing. During school arrival and departure times, the crossing was manned by a crossing guard who directed traffic and pedestrians. The researchers recorded details of any breaches of directions by the crossing guard by either pedestrians or vehicles.

Two further researchers were located at school access gates and observed vehicle drop-off of children at arrival times and pick-up at departure times, and recorded any breaches of school regulations concerning traffic movements as well as pedestrian behaviour.

The observations were recorded in space provided in the observational protocol for both quantitative (number of violations) and qualitative (nature of violations) elements.

Observational research is recorded using an **observational protocol**, an instrument that sets out the observations to be made and how they should be recorded. Observational protocols are discussed in the next section.

OBSERVATIONAL PROTOCOLS

An observational protocol is a guide to observers, detailing what it is they should be observing and how to record their observations. They are used in field research where researchers observe events as they occur in 'real world' situations. An example is an observation of children interacting in a playground during a school lunchtime recess where the researcher may be interested in detailing gender differences in the types of interactions in which the children engage.

The format of an observational protocol depends on the nature of the observations being made so that it is not feasible to set out any clear guidelines on its construction. In general terms, a protocol should specify clearly what is to be observed and how the observations should be recorded. Only where the situation being observed is very specific can a standardized observational protocol be devised. Bales (1950) constructed such a protocol for observing social interactions using a procedure he called 'Interaction Process Analysis'.

Observational protocols are used widely in field studies. One example is provided by a study of observations of smoking bans in bars in a Californian city after the introduction of statewide bans on smoking inside restaurants and bars (Lee, Moore and Martin, 2003). In the study, observers used a structured observational protocol to record the extent of compliance with the bans and found significant levels of breaches of the laws.

CHARACTERISTICS OF OBSERVATIONAL METHODS

Observational research involves the observation of people engaged in their everyday lives, such as in social or sporting activities, neighbourhoods and many other situations.

Observational research methodology was initially developed by anthropologists to study traditional societies. It was adapted to the study of urban groups in the early 20th century by the Chicago School of Sociology led by Robert Park and William I. Thomas. It led to observations of marginalized groups in society such as street gangs. Since then, it has been diversified to a range of other situations and is now widely used in all areas of social research including mixed methods.

The main characteristics of observational methods are the following.

Selecting the observational site

The observational site is the location at which observations are to be made. This site, or sites, will be determined by the research questions and the nature of the research project. It may be a single location, such as a traffic intersection, or a classroom, or it may consist of multiple locations, such as sporting venues or shopping malls. If the observations are of a group of people the site may change as the members of the group move from one location to another.

Accessing the observational site

Gaining access to observational sites can be difficult. Sites may be closed or open (see Box 10.4). Access to a closed setting requires permission from those in authority over the site, often referred to as *gatekeepers*. This may be a manager of an organization if the site is to be a workplace, or a principal of a school if the site is to be a classroom or playground. To gain the cooperation of such gatekeepers, they will need to approve the research project and the nature of the observations being made. They will also most likely be concerned about the amount of time that participants are expected to devote to the study, particularly if staff members of an organization are involved.

━━━━━━━━ BOX 10.4 ━━━━━━━━

TYPES OF OBSERVATIONAL SITES

Observational sites can be divided into two main categories: open versus closed sites.

Open sites

Open sites, often referred to as public settings (Hammersley and Atkinson, 2007), are those for which no permission is needed to gain access. They include public streets, parks, beaches and public land. They do not include public amenities such as libraries, hospitals, schools and public swimming centres, which are under the control of government agencies.

Closed sites

These are sites which are either privately owned, such as people's homes, private workplaces or shops, or are publicly owned but under the control of a government agency such as public schools or hospitals. In these sites, permission to conduct research is needed from the owner of the site or the appropriate government agency.

Access to open sites is less problematical but still may require negotiations with participants to gain agreement to the observations to be made.

Role of the observer

As outlined above, the observer can either be a participant or non-participant observer. There are, however, gradations of this distinction. Gold (1958) set out four roles of an observer on a continuum ranging from involvement to detachment, as shown in Figure 10.1.

1. Complete participant: the complete participant is a fully functioning member of the group being observed and as such plays an active role in the activities of the group. The group members may not be aware of the research role of the observer, or the observer may only become a researcher after having left the group.
2. Participant as observer: the participant as observer is also a fully functioning member of the group but makes the research role clear to members.
3. Observer as participant: the observer as participant is primarily a researcher and only secondarily a participant in group activities.
4. Complete observer: the complete observer is detached from the group, plays no role in the activities of the group, and only interacts with the group insofar as it is necessary to observe its activities.

There are, of course, limitations to the role a researcher can play. For example, an adult cannot be a participant observer in groups consisting of children. But, apart from these structural limitations, the degree of group involvement is a matter for the researcher. A participant may gain access to key information not available to an outsider, but runs the risk of identifying too closely with the group and losing a research perspective.

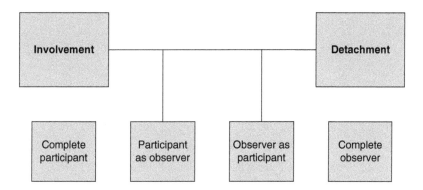

Figure 10.1   Gold's (1958) classification of participant observation roles

COLLECTING AND RECORDING OBSERVATIONAL DATA

Observational methods vary from highly structured to unstructured observations, which means that there is a wide variety of procedures available to collect data. Highly structured observations are usually quantitative, involving counting occurrences of an event or rating activities on a scale. In such cases, the observer is provided with detailed instructions in the observational protocol on what to record.

Unstructured observations are more likely to be qualitative and may involve taping or filming events as they take place. Observers record their observations in *field notes*. These are records not only of observations made but also of reflections on those observations by the observer. They provide information on the context of the observations that may be overlooked in the recording process. A guide to recording field notes has been developed by Phillippi and Lauderdale (2018). They argue that field notes can improve the depth of qualitative findings by situating observations within a larger social and temporal context.

Types of field notes are listed in Table 10.2. These serve different functions in field research, as described in the table.

Table 10.2   Types of field notes in observational research

Type	Description
Jotted notes	These are brief notes made in the field to record observations to serve as memory joggers to be developed into more comprehensive notes later.
Analytic notes	Notes written as commentary on the progress of the research which may include theoretical insights gained during observations or methodological issues that arise unexpectedly. They are generally made while reflecting on the research rather than during observations.
Personal notes	Notes that describe your personal reactions to observations made, written much in the way of a diary. They are a source of information about reflections on your observations.
Descriptive notes	These are the detailed descriptions of what you have observed to help you understand the context and nuances of the observational situation.

A researcher working in the field must decide what to record and how to record it. As Wolfinger (2002: 85) points out, 'Decisions made at this juncture of the research process may have a profound impact on the final ethnographic report.'

THE ROLE OF OBSERVATIONAL RESEARCH IN MIXED-METHODS DESIGNS

Because of their flexibility, observational methods can serve either as the quantitative or the qualitative component in mixed-methods designs. They can also be used in either sequential or parallel designs.

Where observational methods form the quantitative component, they most likely would either precede or be simultaneous with the qualitative component. As an example, the Bungum et al. (2005) observational study reported in Box 10.2 could easily be extended to a mixed-methods design by the researchers conducting interviews with pedestrians who displayed distracted behaviour while crossing the road, either at the time of the crossing or as a follow-up study. This research would then become either a sequential mixed-methods design using quantitative observation methods followed by qualitative interviews, or a parallel mixed-methods design if the interviews were to be conducted on the spot.

Where observational methods form the qualitative component, they could follow a survey in which, say, schoolteachers complete a questionnaire on the handling of bullying behaviour in school playgrounds to be followed by observation of play behaviour in the playgrounds being supervised by those teachers.

In either case, the observational research forms an important part of the mixed-methods design.

CONCLUSION

Observational methods play an important role in social research generally and mixed-methods research in particular. They have the advantage that researchers can observe situations directly without having to rely on reports by participants, which may be subject to social desirability bias. They have the disadvantage of relying heavily on the skill of the observer to make accurate observations and avoid potential sources of bias.

Observational research can form a useful role in mixed-methods research as either the quantitative or qualitative component, as detailed above.

CHAPTER SUMMARY

In this chapter, observational methods of data collection have been outlined. They are used in a variety of research methods, including case studies, experiments and ethnographies.

Observational methods can involve either quantitative, qualitative observations or both. They can be classified as to whether they are situations that occur naturally, as in case studies or ethnographies, or are situations constructed by the researcher, as in experimental research.

The researcher may be a participant in the activities being observed, in which case the role is that of a participant observer, or may be a detached observer. The participants themselves may either be aware of the role of the researcher or not.

The recording of observational research is usually made in accordance with an observational protocol which sets out instructions about what is to be observed and how it is to be recorded.

The major characteristics of observational research include choosing and accessing the research site and adopting an observational role.

Observational methods are useful in mixed-methods designs either as the quantitative or qualitative components.

FURTHER READING

Angrosino, M. V. and de Perez, M. (2003) Rethinking observation. In N. K. Denzin and Y. S. Lincoln (eds), *Collecting and Interpreting Qualitative Materials*. Thousand Oaks, CA: Sage Publications.
A good discussion of the role of observation in qualitative research.

Bryman, A. (2015) *Social Research Methods,* **5th edition. Oxford: Oxford University Press, Chapters 12 and 19.**
Chapter 12 contains a discussion of quantitative observations, and Chapter 19 qualitative observations.

Teddlie, C. and Tashakkori, A. (2009) *Foundations of Mixed Methods Research.* **Thousand Oaks, CA: Sage Publications.**
Chapter 10 contains a discussion of the role of observations in mixed-methods research.

Wolfinger, N. H. (2002) On writing fieldnotes: Collection strategies and background expectancies. *Qualitative Research,* **2 (1), 85–95.**
A useful guide to the role of field notes in qualitative research.

11

COLLECTING SECONDARY DATA

INTRODUCTION

Secondary data is data that exists prior to the research being undertaken. It can be data from previous studies, data collected by government agencies such as statistical information, or information held by organizations such as employment records, meeting records, and so on. It can either be publicly available, as is the case for most government agency data, or private, owned by individuals or organizations. It can also be either quantitative, such as government statistical data, or qualitative, such as minutes of meetings or diary entries.

Such data may also take a variety of forms such as photographs, video clips or films, as well as written text or statistical data. It can also take the form of *physical traces*, that is, signs left as a consequence of social activity. Examples are rubbish left at a concert arena as an indicator of what is consumed by patrons of the concert, or empty alcohol containers in waste or recycling bins as a measure of household alcohol consumption.

In this chapter, the use of secondary data in social research will be discussed and its application in mixed-methods research outlined.

TYPES OF SECONDARY DATA

Secondary data can be classified on the basis of the following criteria:

1. Private or public availability: private sources of secondary data include information that is owned by individuals or organizations that is not made available to the general public. It also includes data that has been published in academic journals which are subject to copyright and data sets produced by research centres that require a subscription payment

to access. Publicly available sources include most government statistical publications, open access journals, newspapers and magazines, information contained on websites accessible to the public, television programmes, films and documents stored in public libraries.

2. Qualitative or quantitative structure: secondary data may be in either quantitative or qualitative form. Quantitative data includes government statistics, survey data held by research centres or by government agencies, as well as many records held by organizations, such as employment records. Qualitative data includes textual data such as minutes of meetings, photographs, films and videos, diaries and reports published in journals. Although the structure of such data is qualitative, it can be quantified by such techniques as **content analysis** or other forms of coding. These techniques will be discussed in Part 4 of this book.

3. Pictorial or written form: secondary data may be written text, such as diary entries, minutes of meetings or statistical data, or it may be in pictorial form, such as photographs, videos or films, or even cartoons or paintings.

4. Size of the data set: secondary data can vary from a single item such as a photo or diary entry to very large data sets, as in the relatively new concept of 'big data'. Small data sets are not difficult to manage since computers have the speed and storage capacity to handle reasonably large data sets. Big data, however, comprises data sets beyond the capacity of most software programs to process. The term is generally thought to have originated in the late 1990s in a talk by John Massey (Lohr, 2013). The characteristics and applications of big data are described in Box 11.1.

■■■■ BOX 11.1 ■■■■

CHARACTERISTICS AND APPLICATIONS OF BIG DATA

Big data has been widely characterized by reference to the following 'V's':

- Volume: the quantity of data. This is expressed in petabytes where a petabyte is 1×10^{15} bytes. A byte is a unit of data storage in a computer consisting of eight binary digits. Clearly, a petabyte is a very large data set.
- Variety: this characteristic refers to the type of data in the data set. Data can be structured, semi-structured or unstructured.
- Velocity: the rate at which data is generated.

These three Vs are the initial characteristics said to be devised by Doug Laney in 2001. Subsequently, several more have been added, namely:

- Veracity: the trustworthiness of the data.
- Variability: the ways in which data can be used.

Health care is an area where big data has been applied. The introduction of electronic health records in hospitals and government health departments produces big data that can be used to expedite the diagnosis of health problems far more rapidly than by using traditional means.

In the USA, the Food and Drug Administration (FDA) uses big data to track occurrences of food-based infections.

Researchers dealing with national characteristics may find accessing big data sets necessary to identify trends. To do this, they will need to update computer capabilities and install the appropriate software to deal with such data. An alternative is to engage an organization with such capabilities.

SOURCES OF SECONDARY DATA

Secondary data is located in a variety of public and private sources. Public sources include government statistical agencies such as the Office of National Statistics in the UK or the United States Census Bureau in the USA. Private sources include non-government agencies involved in health care, employment and other services, as well as business organizations which may make information available to researchers conducting case studies on areas in which those businesses are involved.

Examples of some of these sources are given in Box 11.2.

▬▬▬ BOX 11.2 ▬▬▬

SOME EXAMPLES OF SECONDARY DATA

Example 1: The General Social Survey

The General Social Survey (GSS) is conducted in even-numbered years (since 1994) in the USA by the National Opinion Research Center (NORC) at the University of Chicago. It was first conducted in 1972. The survey questionnaire is administered to randomly selected individuals in the USA. It includes a wide range of social and behavioural issues. Researchers can access data to track changes in attitudes and values over time as well as examine current beliefs from the most recently (2016) published results. The GSS is widely reported in social research. It can be accessed through the NORC website (http://gss.norc.org).

Example 2: Newspaper editorials

Alireza and Samuel (2012) compared headlines in newspaper editorials in two newspapers in different countries, namely *The New York Times* and *The Tehran Times*. They compared the

(Continued)

rhetorical devices used to convey the prevailing ideologies in each newspaper. They show that use of headlines in editorials is a useful area for research.

Example 3: Facebook use

Facebook has become a widely used means of social communication, attracting millions of users worldwide. Facebook posts provide a contemporary source of data on social communication. Wilson, Gosling and Graham (2012) reviewed 412 articles on research on Facebook and argued that they provide a foundation for future research on social networks.

Example 4: The Living Costs and Food Survey (LCF)

This survey of UK residents is conducted annually and collects information on household budgets. According to the Office of National Statistics (www.ons.gov.uk), the results are 'an important source of economic and social data for a range of government and other research agencies'.

USE OF SECONDARY DATA IN RESEARCH

Secondary data can be a useful source for research, either on its own or in conjunction with the collection of primary data. It can be used to portray social attitudes as they are presented in media outlets such as television or newspapers, or in social networking such as Facebook, or to track changes in attitudes and behaviour over time using longitudinal data, such as that collected in the General Social Survey.

Historical-comparative research is one field where secondary data is used extensively. Neuman (2011: 465) argues that historical-comparative research 'is a powerful tool for addressing many of the central issues in social theory'. This is because it examines patterns in societies that change over time, and so addresses the many 'big' questions about entire societies or cultures.

Historical-comparative research examines society and culture, either within nations or across nations and either at a single point in time or across different time periods, as set out in Table 11.1.

For example, Viterna and Fallon (2008) examined the relationship between gendered outcomes and democratic transitions in four countries, namely Argentina, El Salvador, Ghana and South Africa. These countries were chosen because of their different outcomes for women's movements. They found that the effectiveness of women's movements depended on a number of factors, including the history of women's activism in the country, the nature of the transition process and the extent to which the ideology behind the transition supported gender equality.

Table 11.1 Types of historical-comparative research

Entities compared	Time dimension	
	One point in time	**Two or more points in time**
Groups within one nation	Examines differences among social/cultural groups	Examines changes in social/cultural patterns over time
Nations	Cross-cultural research across nations	Changes in cultural patterns over time across nations

Historical-comparative researchers use sources available in the groups or nations being compared. These sources are classified into primary and secondary sources. A **primary source** is a first-hand account of an event or situation as it occurred, whereas a **secondary source** is an analysis or reconstruction of that situation. Primary sources include diaries, autobiographies, legislation, government publications and original documents, such as birth or death certificates. Secondary sources include newspaper reports of events, books reporting on events, and biographies. Both the primary and secondary sources here are, however, secondary data in that they have been produced by others and not by the researcher.

Researchers undertaking historical-comparative research need to address the problems encountered in comparing documents across time periods or cultures. Meanings often change over time so that the same terms may not convey the same meaning in different historical epochs, and documents in different languages may not be able to be translated into equivalent concepts. This is known as the problem of equivalence (Przeworski and Teune, 1973). Addressing this problem is a priority in conducting historical-comparative research. Strategies for doing this are set out in Przeworski and Teune (1973).

USE OF SECONDARY DATA IN MIXED-METHODS RESEARCH

Secondary data can serve as either the quantitative or qualitative component in mixed-methods research. As the qualitative component, it would most likely be part of a case study conducted either in conjunction with or following a survey providing the quantitative component. As the quantitative component, it may include survey results obtained from data sets such as the GSS (see Box 11.2) and be supplemented by a qualitative follow-up through interviews or case studies of events identified in the survey as relevant to the research aims.

In either of the above cases, secondary data can form part of a mixed-methods design.

LIMITATIONS OF SECONDARY DATA

Some difficulties with using secondary data are the following:

1. Appropriateness for the research questions: a disadvantage of secondary data is that since it has been collected for a purpose quite different from that of the research project, it may not be adequate to answer the questions posed. The data may be incomplete or address issues not relevant to the current research.
2. Access problems: access to public documents is usually not a problem but access to private documents can present difficulties. Permission to use the documents will need to be obtained and in some cases this may be denied. Such denial may be motivated by the intention to conceal information and this cannot easily be overcome, except perhaps by an appeal to a higher authority.
3. Document quality: because secondary data is not necessarily produced for the purpose of research, it may be incomplete or inadequate in many respects. Its quality may also suffer because of assumptions or biases in its production due to the values of the organization or individual responsible. Even official government publications are not immune to such biases, as Miles and Irvine (1979) have pointed out. They claimed that the method of calculating unemployment statistics is changed frequently so as to make the unemployment rate appear to be lower and so as not to embarrass governments. There is little researchers can do to overcome these limitations of document quality, but an awareness of them is necessary to avoid reaching inadequate conclusions.

Despite these difficulties, the attraction of secondary data is in its status as evidence about the way society functions produced by institutions or individuals in the course of daily activities. It is the interpretation of this data that is a challenge to researchers.

CONCLUSION

The use of secondary data plays an important role in social research due to its availability and relevance to the research aims. Documents produced by individuals and organizations can provide data for case studies, giving insights into the beliefs and values of the individual or mode of operation of the organization. Statistical data produced by government agencies or research centres can provide quantitative data for analysis. Longitudinal data is particularly useful for ascertaining trends such as changes in unemployment over time, or changes in attitudes among segments of the population, as revealed by longitudinal survey data.

Mixed-methods research can make use of secondary data by combining it with the primary data collected to supplement the secondary data.

CHAPTER SUMMARY

The use of secondary data in social research has been the focus of this chapter. Such data can be obtained from prior research studies, personal or organizational documents or statistical information collected by government agencies or research centres attached to universities. The data may be publicly available, as with most government agencies and some research centres, or it may be privately owned, requiring permission to access.

Secondary data may be either qualitative or quantitative in form. Qualitative data includes documents such as minutes of meetings, diaries or social media postings, or pictorial material such as photos, videos or films. Quantitative data includes government statistical data such as unemployment statistics, or survey data collected by research centres such as the NORC at the University of Chicago.

While secondary data is widely used in research, it does suffer from limitations, including its inappropriateness to answer research questions due to it having been collected for an entirely different purpose, problems accessing data, particularly from private sources, and problems with document quality.

Secondary data can be used as either the quantitative or qualitative component in mixed-methods research. As the quantitative component, government statistical data or survey data collected by research centres can be supplemented by the interview or case study data collected to explore findings from the quantitative data. As the qualitative component, it can form part of a case study following up on a survey or experimental study.

FURTHER READING

General Social Survey: http://gss.norc.org
Contains information about the survey, its history and a bibliography of publications using the data.

Bryman, A. (2015) *Social Research Methods*, 5th edition. Oxford: Oxford University Press.
Chapter 21 deals with documents as qualitative data sources.

Neuman, W. L. (2011) *Social Research Methods: Quantitative and Qualitative Approaches*, 7th edition. Boston, MA: Pearson Education.
Chapter 11 contains a discussion of quantitative secondary data, and Chapter 14 sets out the basics of historical-comparative research. Note that Chapter 14 has been omitted from subsequent editions of this book.

Teddlie, C. and Tashakkori, A. (2009) *Foundations of Mixed Methods Research*. Thousand Oaks, CA: Sage Publications.
Chapter 10 contains a discussion of the role of unobtrusive observations in mixed-methods research.

ORGANIZING AND ANALYSING RESEARCH DATA

Part 4 deals with the analysis of data from quantitative, qualitative and mixed-methods designs. Problems in combining qualitative and quantitative data in mixed-methods designs are discussed.

Chapter 12 deals with the processing of raw data into a form suitable for analysis. This process is different for quantitative and qualitative data. Often, quantitative data needs to be converted into a measurement scale, so procedures for doing this are described as are the requirements for reliability and validity of the scales so constructed.

Chapter 13 describes methods for the analysis of quantitative data. In this chapter, it is assumed that readers are familiar with basic statistical procedures so that some of the more advanced methods of statistical inference commonly used in quantitative research are outlined.

Chapter 14 deals with methods of analysing qualitative data. In this chapter, a distinction is drawn between holistic and classificatory methods of analysis. Holistic methods seek to preserve the context of any section of the data by limiting its reduction into smaller components. This approach includes narrative, discourse and conversation analysis and is usually favoured by those supporting an interpretivist or a constructivist paradigm. Classificatory methods break down the text into codes designed to extract the meaning from it, while enabling comparisons across different individuals or groups.

Chapter 15 combines these methods in mixed-methods designs. Various options for conducting analysis of mixed-methods data are outlined and discussed.

12

PREPARING DATA FOR ANALYSIS

INTRODUCTION

When data is collected, it is in a raw form and generally not suitable for analysis. Some processing of this data is usually needed to prepare it for analysis. This further processing applies to both quantitative and qualitative data.

In doing this, it is crucial to ensure that the key characteristics of the data are not lost in the process. Steps to ensure the integrity of the data is retained are necessary.

In this chapter, ways in which data collected by any of the data collection methods discussed in this part are further modified, for the purpose of analysis will be outlined.

This further processing differs for quantitative and qualitative data so these will be discussed separately.

PROCESSING QUANTITATIVE DATA: CONSTRUCTING MEASURES

In constructing data collection instruments to collect quantitative data such as questionnaires or observational protocols, researchers are seeking to identify social concepts that can be turned into measures. The steps involved in doing this are outlined below.

Measurement of social concepts

In order to construct a measure of a social concept, whether it relates to individuals or organizations, a number of steps need to be followed:

1. Conceptualization: conceptualization is the process of defining the concept to be measured. This may be developed from previous literature on the topic or from a theoretical framework. It should lead to a clear, unambiguous and systematic definition of the concept.
2. Operationalization: operationalization is the process of developing a set of procedures to construct a measure of the concept as defined. This process involves choosing a measuring instrument, such as a questionnaire or rating scale, and constructing a measure using this instrument.
3. Determining reliability and validity of the measure: reliability and validity were introduced in Chapter 3. When applied to quantitative measures, reliability refers to the extent to which the measures are reproducible, and validity refers to the extent to which the measure accurately reflects the conceptual definition.

These steps will now be discussed in more detail.

Conceptualization

The first step in measuring a concept is to define it clearly and unambiguously. Quantitative concepts are referred to as variables since they can take on a number of values on a measurement scale. Quantitative variables can be independent, intervening or dependent variables, as illustrated in Figure 4.2 (see discussion in Chapter 4).

Most social concepts will already have been defined in previous studies so a thorough search of the literature is a necessary step in locating such definitions. Once located, a concept may need to be refined or updated for the purposes of current research. A theoretical framework may well be useful in any such modification of a conceptual definition.

Operationalization

Once an adequate conceptual definition is arrived at, the concept needs to be operationalized. This involves developing the measuring instrument to construct a measure of the concept. The process entails:

* Choosing the measuring instrument: social scientists have a range of measuring instruments available, as discussed in Part 3. These are questionnaires, rating scales, structured interviews, observational protocols and secondary quantitative data. The choice of a suitable instrument will depend on the research questions, and in particular on whether data or instruments exist that are suitable for use.
* Specifying the measurement level: in the social sciences, measurement can take different forms, unlike measurement in the physical sciences. In a pioneering paper, Stevens (1946) identified a range of measurement scales appropriate for the social sciences and these have been widely adopted since. They are set out in Box 12.1. Most measurements in the social sciences are nominal or ordinal scales, although some scales constructed to measure such concepts as ability or attitude are claimed to have interval scale properties.

━━━━━━━━ BOX 12.1 ━━━━━━━━

MEASUREMENT SCALES

Measurement scales identified by Stevens (1946) are as follows:

Nominal scale: a nominal scale is one in which the concept is divided into categories that are mutually exclusive and exhaustive, such as gender, marital status or nationality. Nominal scales are the weakest form of measurement.

Ordinal scale: an ordinal scale is one in which an order relationship exists among the values assigned to the concept. Level of education is an example of an ordinal scale.

Interval scale: in an interval scale, the distance between levels of the measurement are preserved. The classic example of an interval scale is temperature, as measured by the Fahrenheit or Celsius scales. In an interval scale, there is no absolute zero.

Ratio scale: a ratio scale is one that preserves intervals, as in an interval scale, but in addition has an absolute zero. Height and weight are examples of ratio scales. The only arbitrary component in a ratio scale is the unit of measurement, such as centimetres or inches.

- Constructing the measure: there is a range of options for choosing an appropriate measure for the concept. These include rates, **indexes**, single- and multiple-item scales. They are set out in Box 12.2.

━━━━━━━━ BOX 12.2 ━━━━━━━━

TYPES OF MEASURES

Measurement types include the following:

Rates: a rate is a measure obtained by converting a number to a percentage or other ratio for comparison purposes. Examples of rates are the unemployment rate, the rate of population growth or the literacy rate in a country. Rates are a type of standardization that adjusts for the different sizes of the populations from which the measures are drawn.

Indexes: an index combines a number of distinct measures of a concept into a single score. Indexes are usually constructed from secondary data such as country statistical information. An example of an index is the Human Development Index (HDI), which combines life expectancy at birth, education level and income of a country to provide a measure of well-being in a country.

Single-item scale: **a single-item scale** is one constructed from a rating scale or a single question providing a range of options from one extreme to the other. An example is a rating of job satisfaction:

(Continued)

Please rate your job satisfaction on the following seven-point scale:

| 1 | 2 | 3 | 4 | 5 | 6 | 7 |

Most satisfying   Least satisfying

Multiple-item scale: a **multiple-item scale** combines a number of separate questions into a single scale. Examples in common use are **Likert scales** and **Rasch scales** (see Box 12.3).

Multiple-item scales are widely used to measure attitudes as well as in ability measurement. They are designed to obtain a single measure of the degree of favourableness towards the object of an attitude or the level of ability in the case of an ability scale. Two techniques for doing this are described in Box 12.3.

━━━━ BOX 12.3 ━━━━

METHODS FOR CONSTRUCTING MULTIPLE-ITEM SCALES

Multiple-item scales in current use are the following:

- Likert scales: this technique for constructing a scale from multiple items was originally developed by Rensis Likert in 1932 and has survived to still be widely used in developing attitude scales. Items are chosen to represent levels of agreement and are rated on a scale from strongly agree to strongly disagree. Scores are assigned to each category and a total score is obtained by adding the score on each item in the scale. Items that discriminate between high and low scorers on the scale are retained in the final version and items that don't discriminate are deleted, leaving a scale consisting of items that are considered to measure the attitude well.
- Rasch scales: this technique was introduced by Rasch in 1960 (see Rasch, 1980) in which he proposed a model for measuring both items and individuals on the one measurement scale. The technique is widely used in educational measurement.

Determining reliability and validity of measures

Measurements need to meet criteria of reliability and validity to be useful in research. There are several notions of both reliability and validity that apply to measurements of social concepts. These will now be outlined:

Meanings of reliability

- Stability: **stability** refers to the extent to which the measure does not change over time. It is measured by the *test–retest method*. This involves taking the measure at two time periods and calculating the correlation between the two measures. A high correlation means that the test–retest reliability is high.
- Equivalence: **equivalence** refers to the extent to which the measure yields similar results to alternative measures of the same concept. It is also used to refer to the extent to which multiple items in a scale correlate with one another. For a multiple-item scale to measure a single concept such as an attitude, items need to correlate highly with one another and with the total score on the scale. The measure of equivalence used in such cases is Cronbach's alpha, described in Box 12.4.

Meanings of validity

- Face validity: **face validity** refers to the judgement by users of the measure that it is a valid measure. That is, a measure has face validity if there is consensus among users that it is a valid measure of the concept. It is not a particularly useful notion of validity as there are many situations where wide agreement over a concept has turned out to be false.
- Content validity: a measure has **content validity** if it includes all aspects of the concept being measured. For some concepts, areas in which the concept applies are not always obvious so that care needs to be taken in defining the concept to ensure such areas are included.
- Construct validity: **construct validity** refers to the extent to which a measure of a concept does in fact measure the concept accurately. Construct validity is often inferred from a theory from which the concept is derived.
- Criterion validity: a measure is said to have **criterion validity** if it correlates with a pre-existing criterion or predicts some future event regarded as a consequence of the concept being measured.

━━━ BOX 12.4 ━━━

MEASURING EQUIVALENCE USING CRONBACH'S ALPHA

Equivalence reliability of a multiple-item scale can be measured using Cronbach's alpha. It can be interpreted as the average correlation of all possible subscales derived from items in the scale with one another. A subscale is a score derived from choosing a subset of items from the total set and constructing a score from that subscale. If all subscales correlate highly with one another, the measure is said to have high equivalence reliability. Alpha measures of more than .7 are considered to be satisfactory.

Cronbach's alpha can be computed using any of the available statistical packages for the social sciences, such as SPSS or SAS.

PROCESSING QUALITATIVE DATA

Qualitative data is collected through both primary and secondary research methods. Primary research methods include in-depth interviews, ethnography and case studies, and secondary research includes the collection of existing documents that are qualitative in nature. Open-ended questions in survey research can also be a source of qualitative data.

In-depth interviews can be recorded in transcripts of the interviews or videos, if the interview is videotaped. In this case, not only is the interview recorded but also the body language of both interviewer and interviewee is included, which can be used to supplement the interview text.

Ethnographic and case study research commonly include observations of events recorded in field notes or video recordings of these events. Observational methods, particularly participant observation, are major sources of qualitative data. An example of the generation of qualitative data by participant observation is provided in Box 12.5.

BOX 12.5

AN EXAMPLE OF QUALITATIVE DATA PRODUCED BY PARTICIPANT OBSERVATION

In a study of gambling behaviour by slot-machine gamblers, researchers Parke and Griffiths (2008) adopted the role of patrons in gambling establishments which enabled them to study the behaviour of gamblers, in most cases without revealing their role as researchers. They argued that concealment of the researcher role in this case avoided what they called the 'researcher effect', which involved gamblers providing more contrived and inhibited responses than if they thought they were having a conversation with a peer.

Data from this study included observations of patrons of slot machines, discussions with these patrons and, where possible, discussions with staff.

Secondary research also produces a wide variety of qualitative data, including organizational documents relevant to case studies, videos, films and photos collected as part of an ethnographic study.

How qualitative data is processed will depend on the kind of data collected as well as on the paradigmatic assumptions adopted by the researcher. Participant observation, for example, will produce quite different data to an in-depth interview or a focus group so will need to be processed differently.

Ryan and Bernard (2003) distinguish between two traditions in approaching qualitative data analysis which they call the linguistic and the sociological traditions. The linguistic tradition treats text as an object to be analysed in itself, whereas the sociological tradition treats text as 'a window into human experience' (p. 259). Methods of analysis to be outlined in

Chapter 14 that fall into the linguistic tradition include narrative analysis and discourse analysis, while those that fall into the sociological tradition include coding, qualitative comparison analysis and content analysis.

Processing data for analysis in the sociological tradition includes the strategies of mental maps, word counts, constructing codes and trustworthiness of qualitative concepts, which will be looked at next.

Mental maps

These include strategies that involve grouping words or phrases into categories that reflect similarities among those included in a category.

Mental maps are diagrams that represent relationships among ideas or concepts. They are often referred to as 'mind maps' or 'concept maps', although the latter are viewed by some as a distinct type of mapping process.

A hypothetical example of a mind map relating to the experience of 'good parenting' is shown in Figure 12.1.

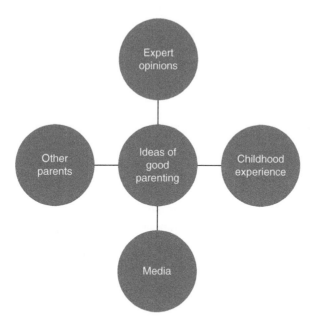

Figure 12.1   Simplified mind map for ideas about good parenting

Mind maps can be constructed by researchers from information included in interviews, observations or focus groups. For example, Burgess-Allen and Owen-Smith (2010) constructed mind maps from focus group discussions on alcohol service use to summarize the results of the discussions.

Alternatively, participants in research can be asked to construct their own mind maps based on their own experience. For example, Wheeldon and Faubert (2009) asked trainers in a legal reform project to construct maps of their experience and their role in training.

As Wheeldon and Faubert (2009: 72) point out, researchers can use mind maps 'to help guide more in-depth analysis'.

Word counts

Word counts can be used to ascertain patterns in qualitative data derived from interviews or focus groups. Ryan and Bernard (2003) provide an example of word counts of descriptions of children by their parents and noted that mothers were more likely to use emotional and interpersonal words, while fathers were more likely to use achievement-related words. They conclude that this approach can identify important constructs and facilitate group comparisons in further analysis.

Constructing codes

Coding qualitative data involves extracting from text, photographs, videos, and so on, codes which are designed to capture ideas in the data by summarizing blocks of text with a single code. This process is discussed in more detail in Chapter 14 since it is closer to an analysis of the data than a preparation for analysis.

Trustworthiness of qualitative concepts

While quantitative concepts are assessed for their reliability and validity, qualitative concepts are assessed for their trustworthiness, although this distinction is not universally supported by qualitative researchers. It was proposed by Guba and Lincoln (1989), who argued that concepts such as validity and reliability are not appropriate to qualitative research, and proposed they be replaced by trustworthiness, consisting of credibility, transferability, dependability and confirmability.

Morse (2015), on the other hand, does not support this move, arguing that validity and reliability apply to qualitative research as much as they do to quantitative research.

Whether the concepts of reliability and validity are replaced or not, the processes required for assessing trustworthiness (or reliability and validity) are not the same as those for quantitative research. Some of the main methods for assessing trustworthiness in qualitative research are member checking, data triangulation and multiple coding of data.

Member checking

This strategy refers to providing a transcript of the interview or a mental map of a group discussion and having the participant(s) comment on the accuracy of the transcription or analysis. This strategy is intended to provide a means for identifying any misrepresentation by the researcher. But Morse (2015) does not support this strategy, arguing that the view of the participant is not necessarily an informed view, and that the researcher is a better judge of the analysis. Nevertheless, gaining feedback from participants would seem to be a useful exercise and the researcher can interpret this feedback as he or she sees fit.

Data triangulation

Data triangulation refers to analysing the data by two different and independent methods to ascertain whether the same or similar conclusions are reached.

Multiple coding of data

Where data is coded having more than one researcher code, the same data can be used to establish agreement about the coding system.

CONCLUSION

The processing of raw data for further analysis is an important strategy in research. It enables concepts to be identified for comparison purposes as well as theory development. There is often a fine line between the processing of data and analysis with the two merging into each other. The distinction is however useful in the methods considered in this chapter, particularly in the construction of measures, since these form the data for the next stage of quantitative analysis to be discussed in the next chapter.

CHAPTER SUMMARY

Methods for processing or transforming raw data for further analysis have been the subject of this chapter. These methods differ for quantitative and qualitative data.

Processing quantitative data can involve the construction of measures of social concepts such as attitudes. These measures take the form of rates, indexes and single- or multiple-item scales. They need to be reliable and valid to be used for analysis purposes.

Processing qualitative data involves extracting concepts, relationships among ideas and codes from textual data. This process of reduction enables large volumes of unstructured data to be prepared for analysis and interpretation, but runs the risk of losing context and possibly overlooking important detail.

FURTHER READING

Blaikie, N. (2003) *Analyzing Quantitative Data*. London: Sage Publications.
Chapter 8 on data reduction provides additional information on the measurement issues discussed in this chapter.

Ryan, G. W. and Bernard, R. (2003) Data management and analysis methods. In N. K. Denzin and Y. S. Lincoln (eds), *Collecting and Interpreting Qualitative Materials*, 2nd edition. Thousand Oaks, CA: Sage Publications.
A useful discussion of data handling in qualitative research.

13

ANALYSING QUANTITATIVE DATA

INTRODUCTION

In this chapter, the features of quantitative data are outlined and methods of analysis of such data described. Quantitative data is derived from questionnaires, rating scales, secondary statistical data and measurements such as age, weight, time and height.

Quantitative data take the form of measurements. Measurement is the assignment of numbers to represent characteristics of concepts. These concepts may refer to characteristics of individuals, organizations or societies. There are differences in the way these characteristics are measured and these differences will be discussed in this chapter.

There has been a long-running debate over whether social concepts are measureable. Opponents to measurement argue that social concepts are complex and nuanced and cannot be reduced to measurements that trivialize the concept. Supporters of measurement argue that measurement is the basis of all scientific research and that to exclude social concepts from measurement would be to deny scientific status to any study of the social.

Mixed-methods researchers concede that some social concepts defy measurement but that there are many such concepts that are capable of measurement. One of the attractions of mixed methods is that it takes a less dogmatic approach to the debate by supplementing measurement of some social concepts with qualitative elaboration of the complexities of the concepts.

The nature of measurement of social concepts will be outlined before examining how these measurements are analysed in social research.

ANALYSING QUANTITATIVE DATA

Purposes

There are three main purposes in analysing quantitative data:

1. To provide a descriptive account of the research findings: a descriptive account involves presenting summaries of the data in graphs or tables. This is common with exploratory research or in comparative research where, for example, countries are compared on social indicators such as health or education.
2. To generalize to a population from which a sample has been drawn: in much quantitative research, samples are drawn randomly from populations for the purpose of generalizing to the populations from which these samples are drawn. In such cases, the findings are not limited to the particular sample drawn but are relevant to a much wider group. Procedures for doing this are called *inferential statistics*.
3. To test a theory about the nature of the relationships among the variables being measured: a theory may predict specific relationships among variables included in the research and the data may be used to test whether these relationships hold either in the sample or in the population from which the samples are drawn.

Describing quantitative data

Descriptive methods for analysing quantitative data are referred to as *descriptive statistics*. This involves calculating measures of central tendency and dispersion and presenting the findings in graphic or tabulated forms.

Measures of central tendency and dispersion appropriate for each of the measurement scale types outlined in Chapter 4 are shown in Table 13.1.

Table 13.1 Measures of central tendency and dispersion appropriate for measurement scale types

Scale type	Appropriate measures	
	Central tendency	**Dispersion**
Nominal	Mode	Range
Ordinal	Median	Interquartile range
Interval/ratio	Mean	Standard deviation

For a nominal scale, the lowest level of measurement, it makes no sense to calculate means or medians as there is no order or metric information contained in the scale. It is no more than a classification.

For an ordinal scale, the mode or median can be used as a measure of central tendency, although the median contains more information as it uses the ordering properties of the scale.

For an interval or ratio scale, all three measures of central tendency are appropriate but the mean is the most appropriate as it uses the metric (interval and/or ratio properties) of the scale.

Similar arguments hold for the measures of dispersion.

Methods of calculating these measures can be found in any introductory text on statistics so will not be reproduced here.

Likewise, table and graph design can be found in introductory statistics texts as well as in examples of tables in Chapter 5 (e.g. Tables 5.1 and 5.2) and in graphs in this book.

Inferential statistics

Inferential statistics are the procedures used to generalize from a sample to a population. As outlined in Chapter 7, samples need to be randomly chosen from a population for these methods to be used.

The logic of inferential statistics is that it enables a generalization to be made to a population with a known level of confidence. The types of generalizations mostly of interest to researchers are whether differences among groups or relationships among variables found in a sample reflect real differences in the populations from which the samples are drawn. Since the populations themselves cannot be observed in their entirety, the inferences drawn from the samples can only be made within a specified level of confidence, expressed as a probability. The most common level of confidence used in the research literature is 95%, although, in some instances, where more certainty is needed, the level is set at 99%. Another way of expressing this is to say that if the level of confidence is set at 95% the likelihood that any differences or relationships obtained in the samples are due only to chance rather than to any real differences or relationships existing in the population(s), is less than .05.

When inferences are made on a probabilistic basis, they are open to possible error. The hypothesis being tested in each case is that there are no differences or that the relationships are zero in the population(s). This hypothesis is referred to as a null hypothesis (H_0). It can either be accepted or rejected on the basis of the findings of the statistical test. This means that there are two possible kinds of error, as shown in Table 13.2. A type I error is rejecting a null hypothesis when it is true and a type II error is accepting a null hypothesis when it is false. The aim of inferential statistics is to minimize, as far as possible, both kinds of errors.

Table 13.2   Type I and type II errors in statistical inference

	State of affairs in the population	
Decision based on statistical test	**H_0 true**	**H_0 false**
Accept H_0	Correct decision	Type II error
Reject H_0	Type I error	Correct decision

Theory testing

The third purpose of analysing quantitative data is to test theories about social processes. In most cases, social theories specify relationships holding in a population so that inferential statistics are required to conduct such tests.

An example of theory testing using inferential statistics is provided in Box 13.1.

BOX 13.1

AN EXAMPLE OF THE USE OF STATISTICAL INFERENCE TO TEST A THEORY

Roh and Choo (2008) tested predictions from social disorganization theory in four suburban cities in Texas. The hypotheses they derived from the theory and tested using inferential statistics were as follows:

Crime, disturbance, and the demands of civil service are positively related in suburban areas with:

1. Poverty
2. Racial/ethnic heterogeneity
3. Residential mobility
4. Family disruption.

The authors found that social disorganization theory was only partially supported in the suburban areas studied, with family disruption overshadowing poverty and racial/ethnic heterogeneity and residential mobility having the opposite effect to that predicted.

Studies like the Roh and Choo example in Box 13.1 use inferential statistical methods to test theories.

Methods of analysis

The kinds of statistical inferences most commonly made in social research fall into three categories:

1. Establishing differences among groups
2. Examining relationships among variables
3. Predicting one variable from one or more other variables.

Some common methods of analysis for each of these categories will now be outlined. These methods are normally applied using statistical software such as R, SAS or SPSS.

Establishing differences among groups

Appropriate methods for testing for group differences will depend on the level of measurement of the dependent variable(s). Each dependent variable can be measured on an interval/ratio, ordinal or nominal scale.

Analysis of variance

For dependent variables measured on interval/ratio scales, **analysis of variance** is the most common method used. It tests the hypothesis that there are no differences in the populations from which the samples are drawn among the means of each dependent variable.

Readers not familiar with this method may be familiar with the t-test which compares two groups. The analysis of variance is an extension of the t-test to compare two or more groups, so it subsumes the t-test as a special case.

The simplest case is one independent variable and one dependent variable. A hypothetical example of such a case is provided in Box 13.2. In this example, the independent variable is skills training and the dependent variable is time spent in paid employment following completion of the programme.

BOX 13.2

A HYPOTHETICAL EXAMPLE OF A ONE-WAY ANALYSIS OF VARIANCE

A study of the effectiveness of skills training on the subsequent employment of unemployed youth involved assigning youths attending a job training centre (chosen at random from a range of such centres) randomly to one of three groups: Group 1 received instruction in job application procedures, Group 2 received counselling in self-confidence and Group 3 received neither but were told to wait until places in training were available. Thus, Group 3 acts as a control group for Groups 1 and 2. Twenty youths were assigned to each group.

Three months after programme completion (for Groups 1 and 2), all participants were followed up to obtain the number of hours spent in paid employment over this period by the youths.

The hypothesis to be tested is whether the mean number of hours worked by youths in each of the three groups is equal in the populations from which the youths have been sampled.

(Continued)

To apply the analysis of variance, the data is entered into a spreadsheet for analysis by a computer package such as SPSS. Three columns have data entered, with column 1 being the ID number of the youth, column 2 being the group number to which the youth was assigned and column 3 being the number of hours in paid employment.

Two conditions need to be satisfied for the analysis to be appropriate:

1. The samples must be randomly selected.
2. The group variances must be equal in the populations from which the samples are chosen.

Condition 1 is satisfied by the procedure used by the researcher. Condition 2 can be tested as part of the analysis. This is the Levene test for homogeneity of variance. Output of the analysis is as follows:

Levene statistic	df1	df2	Sig.
.061	2	57	.351

df1 and df2 are referred to as degrees of freedom; df1 is one less than the number of groups and df2 is the number of groups times one less than the number of youths in each group. Sig. is the level of significance of the test. Since it is greater than .05, the hypothesis of equal variances can be accepted so the analysis can proceed.

Output for the test of significance for the equality of means is as follows:

	Sum of squares	df	Mean square	F	Sig.
Between groups	52.250	2	26.125	17.244	.000
Within groups	86.342	57	1.515		
Total	138.592	59			

The mean square between groups is the sum of squares divided by the degrees of freedom and is an estimate of the variability. If the variability between the groups is much greater than the variability within groups, this is an indication that the means are most likely not equal. The F value is the mean square between groups divided by the mean square within groups and is the basis for the test of significance. The computer package used includes tables of F values and can look up the significance level. In this case, the significance is .000, which is less than .05, so the hypothesis that all means are equal is rejected.

To interpret this finding, the mean hours of paid employment in each group need to be examined. This will be done in the following discussion.

Conclusions drawn from the analysis of variance in Box 13.2 were that significant differences did occur among the group means, but these did not indicate where the differences lay. To establish this, a further test is needed. Such a test is referred to as a **post-hoc comparison**. The term 'post-hoc' means after the event. The event in this case is finding that a significant difference exists in the analysis of variance. Were the analysis of variance to find no significant differences, there would be no point in conducting post-hoc comparisons, as all population means would be presumed to be equal.

There are a number of post-hoc comparison methods available. When multiple tests are performed on the one set of data, the likelihood of making a type I error increases. Post-hoc methods attempt to control for this. The Scheffe technique is the most stringent of these methods by setting the type I error rate for the whole set of tests. This means that the type I error rate for any particular comparison is much lower than the overall error rate, usually set at .05.

Results of applying the Scheffe technique to the data in Box 13.2 are shown in Table 13.3. In this analysis, the means for Groups 1 and 2 are found to be not significantly different but both are significantly different from the mean for Group 3. This can be interpreted as showing that both forms of instruction provided were equally effective in improving employment among the youth completing the programme, since youths in both these groups were employed on average for more hours than those in Group 3 who did not receive either programme.

Table 13.3   Results of post-hoc comparisons

Group	Mean hours worked	Comparison group	Mean difference	Significance
1	45.83	2	3.27	.852
		3	27.05	.000
2	42.56	1	−3.27	.852
		3	23.78	.000
3	18.78	1	−27.05	.000
		2	−23.78	.000

The analysis of variance can be extended to two or more independent variables and to two or more dependent variables. In the former case, it is referred to as a *factorial analysis of variance*, and in the latter case as a *multivariate analysis of variance*. Both methods can be found in books on statistical methods and will not be dealt with here.

The analysis of variance can only be used for dependent variables measured on interval or ratio scales and then only if the variances of the distribution of values for each level of the independent variable are equal.

Where this equal variance assumption is not satisfied or the dependent variables are measured on an ordinal scale, alternative methods are required. These are referred to as *non-parametric methods*.

Non-parametric methods

Non-parametric methods are useful for analysing group differences when the dependent variable is measured on an ordinal scale or on an interval or ratio scale where the equal variance assumption is not satisfied. These methods use only the ordinal properties of the data.

The Kruskal-Wallis test is a non-parametric method that uses ranking data rather than measures. It is only suitable for data for which there is a wide range of measures of the dependent variable, such as interval/ratio scale measures or ordinal scale data with a large number of values such as a rating on a 100-point scale.

The values of the dependent variable are ranked from highest to lowest and the mean ranks of each group compared. The test statistic used is the chi-square which provides a significance level for the differences among the groups.

Applying the **Kruskal-Wallis test** to the data in Box 13.2 results in a chi-square value of 18.75 with 2 degrees of freedom, resulting in a significance level of .000, which agrees with the findings of the analysis of variance. The conclusion from this is that the groups are not equal but there are no post-hoc comparison methods available, as in the analysis of variance to find out where the differences lie. Inspection of the mean rank for each group and comparing them is the only method for deciding which group (or groups) differs from the others. This comparison is less precise than the post-hoc comparison methods available for the analysis of variance.

Other, non-parametric methods for examining group differences include the Mann-Whitney U test (for two groups only), Mood's Median test and the Wilcoxon signed rank test.

Examining relationships among variables

In some research, a measure of the extent to which the relationships holding among variables is needed. If all variables are measured on interval or ratio scales, the method used is correlation.

Correlation analysis

A **correlation coefficient** measures the extent to which two variables are related. The most common measure used is the *Pearson product moment correlation coefficient, r.* To use this measure, the variables need to be approximately normally distributed and the relationship needs to be linear.

Correlation coefficients vary between +1 and –1. Interpretation of correlation values is shown in Table 13.4.

In many cases, it is useful to know if the correlation coefficient obtained in the sample is significantly different from zero. That is, does a relationship between the variables exist at all? This can be tested using a t-test with N-2 degrees of freedom.

Statistical packages calculate the correlation coefficient as well as the t-test of significance and report these in a table.

Table 13.4 Interpreting the correlation coefficient, r

Correlation coefficient r	Interpretation
1	A perfect linear relationship: all values lie on a straight line with positive slope
0.5	A moderate positive relationship: high values of one variable tend to go with high values on the other
0.2	A weak positive relationship: a very slight tendency for high values on one variable to go with high values on the other
0	No relationship at all between the variables
−0.2	A weak negative relationship: a very slight tendency for high values on one variable to go with low values on the other
−0.5	A moderate negative relationship: high values on one variable tend to go with low values on the other
−1	A perfect negative linear relationship: all values lie on a straight line with negative slope

Where there are more than two variables, the correlations are reported in a correlation matrix. This is a table showing the correlations between each pair of variables. An example using hypothetical data is shown in Box 13.3.

Where the assumptions underlying the use of the Pearson r measure of correlation are not satisfied, a non-parametric alternative termed Spearman's rho can be used in its place. Spearman's rho is a version of the correlation coefficient that does not assume the measures are normally distributed. It was developed by Charles Spearman to provide an alternative to Pearson's r where the variables are measured on ordinal scales. For example, in Box 13.3 the relationship between health status and BMI is not likely to be linear since both very high and very low levels of BMI are indications of health problems. So the Spearman rho may have been a better choice for this example.

━━━━━━━━━━ BOX 13.3 ━━━━━━━━━━

A SAMPLE CORRELATION MATRIX BASED ON A HYPOTHETICAL HEALTH STATUS STUDY

A (hypothetical) study examined the relationships between health status, exercise level, body mass index and hours of sleep in a random sample of 400 individuals over 50 years of age, to investigate the correlates of health in the aged population. Health status was measured by the SF-6D scale (Brazier et al., 2002), exercise level by reported hours of physical exercise per

(Continued)

week, body mass index by calculating the index from height and weight, and hours of sleep by reported average hours of sleep per night. Correlations are shown in the following table:

	Heath status	Exercise	BMI	Sleep
Health status	1			
Exercise	0.74*	1		
BMI	-0.43**	-0.34**	1	
Sleep	0.08	0.15	-0.06	1

*Significant at p<.01

** Significant at p<.05

The table shows that health status is significantly related to exercise level and negatively related to BMI, with no significant relationship to hours of sleep.

The asterisks are shown to indicate the level of significance of the correlations, as is usual in studies involving correlations.

Measures of association for nominal and ordinal scale data

The measures of correlation discussed above are not applicable to nominal and ordinal scales. In such cases, measures of association derived from cross-tabulation of variables are used. An example of a cross-tabulation is shown in Table 13.5. This table is taken from volunteers for a peer-mentoring programme in the first year at the Faculty of Arts and Social Sciences at the University of New South Wales in 2015–17. Mentees were asked to rate their success in making the transition to university on a four-point scale from poor to excellent. The table shows males and females separately. The association between gender and rating of transition to university is tested by using a **chi-square test** with 3 degrees of freedom (rows-1 x columns-1). This distribution is commonly used for testing for significance in such cross-tabulations (referred to as contingency tables). The value of chi-squared obtained is 8.14 and for 3 df the p value is greater than .05 so the relationship is not significant. Hence, the conclusion is that there is no relationship between gender and ratings of transition to university among mentees. It does not follow that this finding applies to students in general since many did not join the peer-mentoring programme.

Were the chi-square test in Table 13.5 to be significant, a measure of association could be calculated to measure the strength of association. Several such measures are available. For nominal scales, the contingency coefficient is an appropriate measure. The contingency coefficient cannot take on negative values as there is no sense in which a correlation between nominal scales can be negative as there is no direction in the scales. It can only vary between 0 and 1.

Table 13.5 Cross-tabulation of mentee ratings of transition to university by gender, 2015–17

Rating of transition to university	Gender				
	Males	%	Females	%	Total
Poor	0	0.0	6	3.5	6
Fair	8	22.2	34	19.6	42
Good	10	27.8	83	48.0	93
Excellent	18	50.0	50	28.9	68
Total	36		173		209

For ordinal scales, the strength of the relationship can be measured by Somer's d or by gamma. Both measures can take on negative values, reflecting the directional properties of an ordinal scale. So, the values of both measures can vary between –1 and 1, with 0 indicating no relationship.

For three or more variables, relationships can be tested using log-linear analysis. An exposition of this method can be found in Anderton and Cheney (2004).

Predicting a variable from one or more other variables

Predicting a dependent variable from one or more independent variables is a strategy for answering research questions that seek to identify factors that account for particular outcomes. For example, the problem in Box 13.3 can be reformulated to ask whether health status can be predicted from level of exercise, hours of sleep and body mass index. In this example, health status is the dependent variable and level of exercise, hours of sleep and body mass index are the independent variables or predictors.

Another example would be predicting first-year university grade point averages from university admission scores, IQ score, family socio-economic status and a measure of motivation to succeed.

Multiple regression is the most commonly used statistical inference technique to identify predictors of a dependent variable. This method expresses the dependent variable as a linear combination of the independent variables. Expressing this as an equation, where y is the dependent variable, and $x_1, x_2, \ldots x_k$ are the independent variables, the regression equation is:

$$y = \beta_1 x_1 + \beta_2 x_2 + \beta_3 x_3 + \ldots\ldots\ldots\ldots + \beta_k x_k + \varepsilon$$

Where the β_1 are the regression coefficients, k is the number of independent variables, and ε is an error term.

For the regression model to be used, the following assumptions need to be satisfied:

- The sample is an independent random sample from a population.
- The relationship between the dependent and each of the independent variables is linear.
- The distribution of the dependent variable is normal.
- The variance of the dependent variable for each independent variable is equal (homoscedasticity).

These assumptions sound quite restrictive but minor breaches of them are not usually considered to be crucial.

In the usual regression model, all variables are measured on interval/ratio scales, but there are alternative models for ordinal and even nominal scales. Also, it is not unusual for some independent variables to be dichotomous (take on values 0 or 1). These are referred to as *dummy variables*. An example is gender, where, say, female would be assigned the value 1 and male the value 0 (or vice versa).

Regression involves calculating a best-fitting linear model to the data and tests for goodness of fit. Statistical software packages include a variety of regression models as well as the linear model presented above.

An example of **regression analysis** is provided in Box 13.4 and taken from a study of relationship preferences (McGill, 1997). In this study, data was collected from introduction agencies on the preferred characteristics of an ideal partner. One of these characteristics was preferred age of the ideal partner. The questions relating to ideal age enabled calculation of an average preferred age and it is this age that is the subject of the regression analysis. The analysis has been conducted for males and females separately, rather than including gender as a dummy variable in order to show the differences in the regression lines for males and females.

In Box 13.4, R is the correlation between observed and predicted values of the dependent variable and its square is an estimate of the percentage of variance of the dependent variable explained by the regression equation. Adjusted R square is a correction made to adjust for departures from assumptions underlying the model. Note that in this case the adjustment is very small.

The adjusted R square values are very high for both males and females, indicating a good fit of the model. Also note that the regression coefficients (slope of the regression lines) show a significant difference.

The actual regression lines for males and females are shown in Figure 13.1. Note that the slope of the lines is steeper for females than males, which explains the significant differences found in the regression coefficients.

The graph in Figure 13.1 shows that females prefer male partners older than themselves, but this difference declines up until age 60 when it reaches zero. Males, on the other hand, prefer partners younger than themselves after around age 30 and this difference increases with increasing age.

Although the example in Box 13.4 and Figure 13.1 contained only one predictor, namely actual age, the analysis can include any number of independent variables and each can be tested for significance in terms of its contribution to the overall equation.

Regression models can be extended to data in which the dependent variable is measured on a nominal scale (logistic regression) or an ordinal scale (ordered logit) or to data where the relationships are non-linear (nonlinear regression}.

━━━━━━━ BOX 13.4 ━━━━━━━

A LINEAR REGRESSION ANALYSIS OF RELATIONSHIP PREFERENCES FOR AGE OF PARTNER (MCGILL, 1997)

In this example of a regression analysis involving clients of introduction agencies, the dependent variable is average preferred age of partner and the independent variable is actual age of the client.

The regression results are as follows:

Gender	R	R square	Adjusted R square	Standard error of estimate
Males	.834	.696	.694	4.1912
Females	.840	.705	.704	4.1504

t = 3.538; df = 407 p<.01

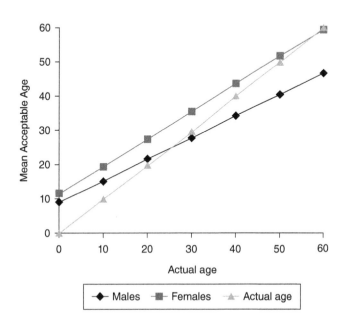

Figure 13.1   Regression lines for relationship preference data

SOFTWARE PACKAGES FOR QUANTITATIVE DATA ANALYSIS

The analyses of quantitative data reported in this chapter have all been conducted using the data analysis software package Statistical Package for the Social Sciences (SPSS). This is just one of many software packages available for the analysis of data. Other examples are Statistical Analysis Systems (SAS) and R.

Both SPSS and SAS date back to the 1960s and have undergone many revisions. R was first developed in 1993 and is available free of charge (go to www.r-project.org).

CONCLUSION

Establishing measures of social concepts is the first step in quantitative data analysis. These measures should satisfy the criteria for reliability and validity before they can be usefully included in research projects.

Statistical inference procedures can then be used with these measures to test hypotheses about group differences or relationships among variables, providing sampling has been random.

A summary of the statistical inference procedures appropriate to various combinations of independent and dependent variables is provided in Table 13.6.

Table 13.6 Appropriate statistical procedures for various combinations of one dependent variable and one or more independent variables

	Independent variables					
	Nominal scales		**Ordinal scales**		**Interval/ratio scales**	
Dependent variable	**One**	**Two or more**	**One**	**Two or more**	**One**	**Two or more**
Nominal scale	Chi-square	Loglinear analysis	Chi-square	Loglinear analysis	Logistic regression	Logistic regression
Ordinal scale – few values	Chi-square	Loglinear analysis	Chi-square	Loglinear analysis	Ordered logit analysis	Ordered logit analysis
Ordinal scale – many values	Kruskal-Wallis	Recode dv and use loglinear	Kruskal-Wallis	Recode dv and use loglinear	Spearman correlation	Spearman correlation
Interval/ratio scale	One-way analysis of variance	Two-or-more way analysis of variance	One-way analysis of variance	Two-or-more way analysis of variance	Simple regression or correlation	Multiple regression

Although statistical inference methods are widely used in the social sciences to test hypotheses, it should be recognized that these tests are not definitive since they are based on probabilities. Indeed, criticisms have been levelled at the widespread uncritical use of these procedures on the following grounds (Cohen, 1994):

- Null hypotheses are never likely to be true. There is always likely to be some differences or associations among variables. The most important question is whether these are sufficiently large to be meaningful.
- Tests are often conducted on very small samples so that meaningful differences are unlikely to be detected.
- The use of type I error rates of .05 or.01 is entirely arbitrary.
- With very large samples, even trivial differences are likely to be found to be significant.

For these reasons, critics such as Cohen advocate abandoning hypothesis testing and examining the size of effects, instead arguing that these can be interpreted scientifically.

The debate over the use of inferential statistics is ongoing, but until it is settled quantitative researchers will need to be able to use and interpret them.

CHAPTER SUMMARY

In this chapter, the process of constructing quantitative measures of social concepts and methods of analysing them have been outlined.

The types of social concepts that are considered to be measurable are:

- characteristics of individuals, such as age, abilities, physical capabilities, values and many others
- characteristics of organizations, such as outputs and outcomes
- characteristics of societies, such as unemployment rates, divorce rates, and so on.

To construct measures of social concepts, three main steps need to be followed:

1. Conceptualization
2. Operationalization
3. Determination of reliability and validity.

Social concepts are measured on either nominal, ordinal, interval or ratio scales.

Analysis of measurements of social concepts can be either descriptive or inferential. Descriptive statistics summarize the properties of the measurements in the sample, such as means, variances or frequency distributions. The descriptive statistics used depend on the type of scale involved, as set out in Table 13.1.

Inferential statistics are used to test hypotheses about differences between groups or relationships among variables in the populations from which the samples were drawn. To do this, the samples must have been drawn by a random procedure, as discussed in Chapter 7.

A range of widely used inferential statistical methods applicable to social scientific data have been outlined here. They are available in most statistical packages, such as SPSS, SAS, R and others.

Some criticisms of the uncritical use of inferential statistics have been outlined and the use of effect sizes has been suggested as an alternative to their use.

FURTHER READING

Hardy, M. and Bryman, A. (2004) *Handbook of Data Analysis*. London: Sage Publications.
A comprehensive account of quantitative data analysis in the social sciences.

Lynch, S. M. (2013) *Using Statistics in Social Research: A Concise Approach*. New York: Springer.
An exposition of the statistical inference procedures outlined in this book, with detailed explanations of their underlying assumptions.

Neuman, W. L. (2011) *Social Research Methods: Qualitative and Quantitative Approaches*. Boston, MA: Pearson Education.
Chapter 12 provides an account of the major methods for analysing quantitative data.

14

ANALYSING QUALITATIVE DATA

INTRODUCTION

In this chapter, the features of qualitative data are outlined and methods of analysis of such data described. Qualitative data can take on a wide variety of forms, from text, photos, film or video clips to social media, among many others.

This variety of forms distinguishes qualitative from quantitative data and underlies the range of approaches that have been taken to the analysis of such data. These approaches derive from alternative paradigms for research, some of which have been discussed in Chapter 2.

The approaches to qualitative data analysis can be classified into two categories:

1. Those that adopt a holistic approach to analysis in which the data is treated as a unified whole in the context in which it is obtained. In this approach, qualitative data is seen as more than the sum of its parts so that dividing the data into sub-categories loses overall meaning.
2. Those that classify qualitative data into codes and categories to facilitate comparison across units of analysis.

Data analysis proceeds quite differently under these two approaches, as will be discussed in this chapter.

In mixed-methods research, qualitative data and quantitative data need to be integrated in some way to derive the benefit from using mixed methods. This requirement does place some limitations on the analysis of each type of data, as will be discussed in the next chapter.

QUALITATIVE DATA AS TEXT

In many of the methods of analysis of qualitative data included here, the term 'text' is used to refer to data well beyond the usual meaning of the term as written documents. Non-linguistic material can be considered as text for the purpose of analysis if it provides information relevant to the research questions being answered. Visual images such as photographs, advertisements, videos and films can all be considered as text in the sense that they convey meaning and are embedded in social and cultural contexts.

Likewise, events such as concerts, theatrical productions and sporting fixtures can be seen as text that can be 'read' to extract meaning and to exemplify social and cultural values.

The term 'text' in qualitative data analysis should be seen in the widest sense to include all material that conveys meaning.

ANALYSIS OF QUALITATIVE DATA

As mentioned above, the analysis of qualitative data will be divided into two major categories – those that treat data holistically and those that classify the data into components through coding.

Holistic methods of analysis

Three holistic methods that have many adherents in the qualitative research literature will be outlined here. These are **discourse analysis**, **conversation analysis** and **narrative analysis**.

Discourse analysis

Discourse analysis is an approach to the analysis of text that situates the text within the context in which it was produced. It seeks to interpret the text by examining the assumptions underlying its production. These assumptions are often hidden and require a critical analysis of the ways in which meaning is constructed by the linguistic formations that give rise to them. Social realities are seen as being constructed by language in the form of discourses. This viewpoint sees language as 'organized into discourses which are culturally specific and whose availability depends upon social, historical and cultural contexts' (Willig, 2014: 342).

The origins of discourse analysis derive from early works by Michel Foucault in the 1960s. Foucault wrote in French and his works were fairly quickly translated into English when the importance of his contribution to political and social analysis was recognized. In *The Order of Things* (Foucault, 1970), and in *The Archaeology of Knowledge* (Foucault, 1972), Foucault sets out a form of discourse analysis to analyse text.

Modern versions of discourse analysis have diverged from Foucault's approach and incorporated developments from recent social and political theory (Wodak and Meyer, 2016).

Conducting a discourse analysis of text involves focusing on language. It is the way in which language is used to construct social realities that is the subject matter of analysis. This involves:

- identifying the assumptions about social realities that have given rise to the text
- analysing how meaning has been constructed by the discursive formations that have produced the text
- examining the effects of discursive formations on the ways in which social realities are constructed.

Box 14.1 provides an example of the use of discourse analysis in a study of the experience of a participant in extreme sport.

Discourse analysis can be applied to texts in the more general sense, as described in the previous section of this chapter.

The important contribution of discourse analysis is its recognition of the role of language in understanding how people construct their social realities. Although, as Willig (2014) points out, there are many different versions of discourse analysis – they have in common this focus on language, which is easily overlooked in other approaches to qualitative data analysis.

BOX 14.1

AN EXAMPLE OF THE USE OF DISCOURSE ANALYSIS IN AN INTERVIEW WITH A PARTICIPANT IN EXTREME SPORT

A participant in extreme sports was interviewed about her involvement in such sports, such as white-water rafting, bungee jumping and sky diving. The interview took the form of a conversation that focused on her experiences of engaging in such activities and the reasons she gave for doing so.

A discursive analysis of the interview identified two discursive resources that were used to provide insight into her experiences. These were:

- discourse of addiction
- dualistic construction of self.

The discourse of addiction was invoked to understand the compulsion to seek out dangerous situations because of the adrenaline surge experienced in undertaking such activities, not dissimilar to the experience of taking addictive drugs.

The dualistic construction of self involves seeing the self as being constructed of separate parts with little or no communication among them, in such a way that actions by one part, such as taking part in extreme sport, are not accessible to another part, such as conscious experience.

Through this discursive analysis, it is argued that an understanding of extreme sport participation is enhanced.

Source: Willig (2008)

Conversation analysis

Conversation analysis focuses on human interaction as it occurs naturally through talk. It involves a detailed analysis of conversations to provide an account of what happens in social interactions. It is based on the assumption that conversation is central to human interaction and is 'the primary means by which we manage and negotiate our mutual roles, identities and relationships with one another' (Toerien, 2014: 328).

Conversation analysis was developed in the 1960s due largely to the work of Sacks and his co-workers (see Sacks, Schegloff and Jefferson, 1974). It was developed in order to provide a framework for the analysis of human interaction through talk.

Undertaking a conversation analysis requires a detailed examination of the interactions among the speakers, including pauses, intakes of breath, emphasis and turn taking, among others. This requires a detailed transcript of the conversation and either a video or audio recording of it. A video recording enables additional components of the conversation to be included such as body movements.

Some of the key characteristics of conversation analysis are as follows:

- formality of the conversation: conversations can be formal or informal. Formal conversations include those between professionals and their clients such as doctor–patient, counsellor–client, supervisor–worker conversations. Informal conversations are those among friends, colleagues, and so on, where there are no formal relationships involved. The structure of the conversation differs between formal and informal due to the status of one member in a formal conversation.
- turn design: taking turns at speaking is a central characteristic of conversation analysis. It refers to the ways in which a speaker initiates a turn at talking in a conversation. How this is done affects the flow of the conversation. Turns can be initiated as a question or as a declaration. Intonation can reflect claims to authority by the speaker and this can have an impact on the subsequent conversation.
- sequence organization: sequence organization refers to the relationships between turns at conversation. Turns at talk are structured. As Toerien (2014: 331) points out, '*linked turns* are the *basic building blocks* of meaningful interaction'. Linked turns include question and answer, offer and acceptance, greeting and return greeting, and so on.
- repair mechanisms: repair mechanisms refer to attempts to bring a conversation back on track when it has been interrupted in some way, such as by someone speaking before the previous speaker has completed their turn, or someone does not respond to a question. Repair mechanisms are an important component of conversation analysis as they are instrumental in normalizing the conversation.

These are just a few of the basic features of conversation analysis. Further detail can be found in texts devoted to conversation analysis, such as Sidnell and Stivers (2012).

Narrative analysis

Another approach to analysing text is narrative analysis. It refers to the ways in which people construct stories to make sense of their lives and events. According to Polkinghorne (1988), a narrative is 'a meaning structure that organises events and human actions into a whole' (p. 18).

Many narrative researchers adopt a constructionist approach to their analyses (Esin, Fathi and Squire, 2014) because of the focus on how individuals construct reality rather than on how they interpret an external reality. (See Chapter 1 for an outline of social constructionism.)

Bamberg (2012) distinguishes between two forms of narrative research: (i) research *with* narrative, which deals with the realm of experience where speakers seek to make sense of what happened; and (ii) research *on* narrative, which deals with the realm of narrative means, namely those narrative devices that are used to make sense of experience.

Data suitable for narrative analysis can come from a range of sources, including narrative interviews, life histories and autobiographies, among others. The key focus of such data is the telling of a story. So, narrative interviews, as distinct from other forms of interviews, are constructed so as to elicit stories from the interviewee.

Both Riessman (2008) and Bamberg (2012) distinguish three approaches to narrative analysis. These are:

1. The thematic approach: this approach focuses on the identification of plots and subplots in the stories and on integrating them into themes.
2. The structural approach: this approach focuses on the linguistic structure of the stories. It takes each clause and examines how it connects to the next and subsequent clauses, so as to build a sequence that provides a cohesive unit that reveals the meaning of the narrative.
3. The dialogical/performative approach: this approach focuses on the larger questions that situate the story or stories being told in their context. According to Bamberg (2012), this approach seeks to answer questions such as what is being accomplished by the story and why is it being told.

Bamberg (2012) provides an example applying these approaches to an extract of an interview with a 10-year-old boy about his interaction with a girl at preschool. Another example is provided by Richmond's (2002) analysis of an adult learner's story based on observations of the classes, focus group interviews and individual interviews with participants.

Classificatory methods of analysis

Methods of analysis involving classification of segments of qualitative data into codes have expanded significantly since the introduction of qualitative data analysis software. There are a range of such software packages, for instance Atlas Ti, NVivo and The Ethnograph, among others. These software packages enable codes to be stored, classified and enumerated, among other operations.

Codes and coding

Coding qualitative data is a method of classifying segments of the data into conceptual categories for the purpose of identifying themes that recur both within and across cases.

While there are many ways of defining codes, an early definition by Miles and Huberman (1994: 56) still captures the key ideas:

> Codes are tags or labels for assigning units of meaning to the descriptive or inferential information compiled during a study. Codes usually are attached to 'chunks' of varying size – words, phrases, sentences or whole paragraphs, connected or unconnected to a specific setting.

Coding is a way of summarizing qualitative data by reducing text to meaningful units that can be integrated into major themes to provide a comprehensive framework for interpreting findings.

Codes can either be predefined or a priori, or they can emerge from the data analysis (emergent codes). A priori codes can be derived from previous research or theory but they rely on a very clear view of what is expected from the data and may overlook aspects that are not expected. Emergent codes, on the other hand, are generated by the coding process itself and rely on the ingenuity and experience of the researcher to construct a set of codes that summarize the key aspects of the data.

Blair (2015) compared both types of coding in an analysis of focus group discussions and concluded that a combined approach yielded a more appropriate coding scheme.

Codes can also be classified according to their level of complexity. Miles and Huberman (1994) identified three main types of codes, varying in their level of complexity:

1. Descriptive codes: these are codes that assign descriptive labels to segments of text to provide convenient summaries of the content of the text. Descriptive codes entail minimal interpretation.
2. Interpretive codes: interpretive codes are those that go beyond description and entail some form of interpretation of the segment of text, such as inferring motives.
3. Pattern codes: these codes are designed to identify themes, relationships or explanations in the data.

These types of codes can be used in the one coding scheme. They are alternative ways of conceptualizing text and extracting meaning from the data.

Researchers will also need to adopt an approach to the coding process. A widely used approach, derived from grounded theory (Strauss and Corbin, 1998), involves the following three stages of coding:

1. Open coding: this is a form of emergent coding where codes are generated from the data.
2. Axial coding: this involves establishing relationships among codes formed during the open coding process. It identifies what open codes have in common and links them together by setting up higher level codes.
3. Selective coding: this is the final stage of coding where codes are integrated into a theoretical framework aimed at providing an explanatory framework for the coding scheme.

Grounded theory will be discussed in Chapter 16, but researchers can use these coding stages without necessarily subscribing to it. They provide a systematic way of refining and integrating codes to give a more complete picture of the data.

An example of a coding scheme is shown in Table 14.1. This scheme was constructed from data obtained from participants in a peer-mentoring programme for first-year arts and social science students at the University of New South Wales. These participants were interviewed following completion of the programme. As part of the interview, they were asked whether they experienced any problems with the programme and, if so, to describe the nature of the problems they experienced. The programme is described in Hall (2004, 2007). Coding was conducted using The Ethnograph, a computer software package for qualitative data analysis. This package enables the setting up of hierarchical coding schemes and this feature was used in the study. Software for the analysis of qualitative data will be discussed in the next section of this chapter.

Open coding was employed, followed by axial coding, to classify codes into categories, resulting in two levels of codes: the open codes arrived at through the initial coding process (level 1 codes) and the categorization of these codes through the axial coding process (level 2 codes).

Results of this analysis were used to revise the mentoring programme to address, as far as practicable, the problems identified.

Table 14.1 Coding of problems experienced in a peer-mentoring programme

Coding scheme for identification of problems experienced by mentees in a peer-mentoring programme

Level 2 codes	Level 1 codes	Description of level 1 code
Admin: Problems with the administration of the programme	Scheduling:	Problems with the timetabling of meetings, making attendance difficult
	Organization:	Problems with the organization of the programme
	Meetings:	Problems with the frequency of meetings
Mentor: Problems with the knowledge or style of the mentor	Unfriendly:	The mentor was too distant and lacked friendliness
	Knowledge:	The mentor was not sufficiently familiar with university requirements
Content: Problems with the content of the programme	Target:	The programme did not cover important issues relevant to the mentees
	Social:	There were not enough social events included in the programme

Coding can be conducted by one or more coders. Having more than one coder of the same data can contribute to overcoming the subjectivity inherent in the coding process.

Inter-coder reliability is a way of measuring agreement between coders. This is achieved by providing two coders with the code definitions and comparing their coding of the same selections from the data. Agreement is measured by calculating the proportion of times identical codes are assigned to the same segments of the data, as in the following formula:

$$\text{reliability of coding} = \frac{\text{number of agreements}}{\text{total number of segments coded}}$$

Inter-coder reliability of less than 70% suggests problems with the coding scheme.

The value of coding lies in its capacity to provide a comprehensive summary of the data. A disadvantage is that it runs the risk of losing meaning and context through fragmentation of the data by dividing it into segments for classification.

Content analysis

Content analysis is a method of classifying qualitative data similar to coding. It is used to classify text into categories, where the categories are usually predetermined. It has been applied to the analysis of media stereotypes, such as the portrayal of gender in magazines, newspapers, television and films.

Content analysis can involve word counts to establish the frequency with which particular words appear in a text. More commonly, though, it involves the ways in which concepts are used.

An example of a content analysis of anti-smoking videos on YouTube is provided in Box 14.2. This study examined the characteristics of the anti-smoking message and their impact on viewer response (Paek, Kim and Hove, 2010).

■ BOX 14.2 ■

A CONTENT ANALYSIS OF ANTI-SMOKING VIDEOS ON YOUTUBE

A study by Paek, Kim and Hove (2010) undertook a content analysis of 934 anti-smoking videos on YouTube. The videos were classified according to the following characteristics: message sensation appeal (MSV) and message appeal (threat, social and humour). The authors found that high levels of MSV attracted more viewers and generated higher levels of viewers' liking. Threat appeals, typically consisting of depicting the dangers of smoking in terms of health consequences, outnumbered social and humour appeals and attracted a greater viewer response.

The study used a priori categories to analyse the content of the videos, since these categories of MSV and message appeal were directly related to their research questions.

Qualitative comparative analysis (QCA)

Qualitative comparative analysis is an alternative approach to the analysis of qualitative data introduced by Charles Ragin in the 1980s (Ragin, 1987) and developed since then. It requires a relatively large number of cases (more than 10) where in each case an outcome can be specified along with conditions relevant to the explanation of the outcome. The aim of QCA is to establish a set of conditions that can provide a causal explanation of the outcome.

There are now three versions of QCA defined by the nature of the conditions and outcome. These are:

- crisp set QCA (csQCA), where the outcome and conditions are either present or absent – that is, defined as sets with values 0 (absent) or 1 (present)
- multi-value QCA (mvQCA), where the outcome and conditions can take on more than just two values
- fuzzy set QCA (fsQCA), where the outcome and conditions can take on a wide range of values.

The latter situation is more likely to be applicable in most social science situations. An example of a potential fuzzy set QCA problem is set out in Box 14.3.

━━━━━━━━━ **BOX 14.3** ━━━━━━━━━

AN EXAMPLE OF A RESEARCH PROBLEM FOR WHICH FUZZY SET QCA IS APPLICABLE

Problem: What conditions in cities lead to high levels of crime?
Cases: Cities in a particular country
Outcome: Crime rate in each city
Conditions: U: unemployment rate, P: population density, I: level of income inequality.

QCA as an approach to qualitative data analysis:

- is case based
- is comparative
- entails complex causality
- is based on set theory.

Each condition as well as the outcome for each case can be conceptualized as a set. Operations on sets are used to explore complex causality. A condition can be necessary, sufficient or INUS for the outcome, or, of course, none of these.

A condition is INUS if it is insufficient for producing the outcome by itself, but is a necessary part of a conjunction of conditions that is unnecessary but sufficient for producing the outcome.

Complex causality means that a combination of conditions is needed in order to explain the outcome. To establish these combinations, QCA software has been developed and will be outlined in the following section.

For further detail on conducting QCA analyses, the reader is referred to Schneider and Wagemann (2012).

COMPUTER SOFTWARE FOR QUALITATIVE DATA ANALYSIS

The development of computer software packages for the analysis of qualitative data has revolutionized such analysis by enabling large-scale projects to be analysed that were previously beyond the scope of manual methods of analysis.

These software packages for data analysis are referred to as computer-assisted qualitative data analysis software (CAQDAS). There is a wide range of such software packages, most of which enable coding, memoing, hierarchical coding, data linking and display, and many other features.

The major qualitative data analysis packages are summarized below:

Atlas Ti: Atlas Ti was developed by Thomas Muhr in 1993 and has gone through many revisions. It enables coding of text, graphic, audio and video data and contains a text editor for producing and editing memos. It also includes a theory builder. An example of the use of Atlas Ti in analysing interviews with primary school teachers in South Africa is provided by Smit (2002).

HyperResearch: HyperResearch was originally developed for Macintosh computers in 1990 (Hesse-Biber, Dupuis and Kinder, 1990). Version 4 was released in 2018 and is now cross-platform. It contains a code map and theory builder and enables analysis of textual, video, audio and graphical data.

NVivo: NVivo was developed by Lyn and Tom Richards in 1995 from LaTrobe University in Australia. It was originally called NUD*IST, an acronym for Non-numerical Unstructured Data Indexing, Searching and Theorising. It is now in its 12th edition. It enables coding, searching and retrieval of data from a variety of sources and includes hypothesis testing and theory-building facilities.

The Ethnograph: The Ethnograph is the oldest of the CAQDAS packages, having originally been developed in 1984. It enables coding, searching and retrieval of data and includes code families, memo writing and linked code searches.

MAXQDA: MAXQDA is another long-standing CAQDAS package, first released in 1989. It has been upgraded over the years and enables coding of a variety of data sources, including text, pdf files, audio or visual files, among others. It contains mapping facilities and analysis of mixed-methods data.

fs/QCA: this software has been in operation since 1992 and has undergone a number of revisions. It was developed specifically for conducting QCA. It can be downloaded from www.fsqca.com.

R Package QCA: this package can be downloaded from within R (at www.r-project.org) and performs QCA using crisp sets, fuzzy sets and multi-value QCA.

The above examples are just some of the software packages available for analysing qualitative data. No particular package stands out as a leader in the field so researchers need to explore options and choose the package with which they feel most comfortable.

CONCLUSION

The development of qualitative data analysis software has enabled significant changes to the way in which the analysis of qualitative data is conducted. This software enables code mapping, hierarchical coding and theory building.

Coding qualitative data runs the risk of losing meaning and context, so that researchers using this method need to continually review their coding schemes to ensure that this doesn't happen. If there is doubt about capturing meaning through a coding scheme, there is always the option of employing a holistic method, such as discourse analysis, conversation analysis or narrative analysis, to address this issue.

CHAPTER SUMMARY

In this chapter, approaches to the analysis of qualitative data have been outlined. Sources of qualitative data from both primary and secondary research have been outlined. Methods of analysing qualitative data are divided into those that employ holistic procedures and those that use classificatory methods. Holistic procedures include discourse analysis, conversation analysis and narrative analysis. Classificatory procedures include coding and content analysis.

Coding is a way of summarizing data into meaningful units that can provide a comprehensive framework for interpreting the data. Codes can either be predefined or derived from the data. Code types are descriptive, interpretive or pattern codes.

Coding strategies include open coding, axial coding and selective coding. Advocates of coding argue that it produces a comprehensive summary of the data, while critics argue that it fragments the data and loses meaning and context.

Coding has been facilitated by the advent of computer packages for the analysis of qualitative data.

FURTHER READING

Bazeley, P. and Jackson, K. (2013) *Qualitative Data Analysis with NVivo*. London: Sage Publications.
A detailed account of qualitative data analysis using a software data analysis package.

Flick, U. (ed.) (2014) *The Sage Handbook of Qualitative Data Analysis*. London: Sage Publications.
Contains chapters on most of the topics discussed in this chapter; an excellent resource.

Silver, C. and Lewins, A. (2014) *Using Software in Qualitative Research: A Step-by-Step Guide*, **2nd edition. London: Sage Publications.**
A guide to the use of computers in analysing qualitative data, with a summary of the major software packages.

COMPASSS (COMPArative Methods for Systematic cross-caSe analySis):
www.compasss.org
This website provides information on QCA, including courses, working papers and details of a wide range of software packages for conducting QCA.

15

MIXED-METHODS DATA ANALYSIS

INTRODUCTION

If all that was required in mixed-methods research was to report the qualitative and quantitative analyses, then there would be no need for this chapter. But the analysis of data from mixed-methods research is far more complex than this. Mixed-methods researchers seek to integrate the analysis of both quantitative and qualitative data to best reflect the value of each in answering the research questions.

In this chapter, methods of combining analyses of quantitative and qualitative data will be outlined and discussed.

FACTORS INFLUENCING ANALYSIS STRATEGIES

How data from mixed-methods research is analysed depends on a number of factors:

- The research questions to be addressed: types of research questions were outlined in Chapter 3. The purpose of all data analysis is to answer the research questions, and this is no different in mixed-methods research. As Onwuegbuzie and Leech (2006: 475) point out, 'research questions in mixed methods studies are *vitally* important because they, in large *part*, dictate the type of research design used, the sample size and sampling scheme employed, and the type of instruments administered as well as the data analysis techniques (i.e., statistical or qualitative) used.'
- Type of mixed-methods research design employed: mixed-methods research designs were outlined in Chapter 6. There, designs were classified into parallel and sequential designs, differing on whether the qualitative and quantitative data is collected concurrently or sequentially in time. Data analysis proceeds differently in each case.

- Priority of the component methods: the extent to which priority is given to either the qualitative or quantitative components in the research will impact on the way in which the data analysis is conducted.

OPTIONS FOR MIXED-METHODS DATA ANALYSIS

There are four broad options for mixed-methods data analysis available. Within these options, there is a range of possible variations, as will be discussed. The options are:

1. Parallel analysis of quantitative and qualitative data: in this option, data analysis is reported separately for quantitative and qualitative data and integration takes place at the discussion stage.
2. Sequential analysis of qualitative and quantitative data: this option involves analysing one form of data and using this analysis to frame the analysis of the other form.
3. Integration of quantitative and qualitative data analysis: this option involves generating themes from the research questions and analysing both quantitative and qualitative data within these themes, or linking qualitative and quantitative data in the one analysis.
4. Converting one form of data into the other: this option involves either converting quantitative data into qualitative data (qualitizing), or converting qualitative data into quantitative data (quantitizing). This is done in order to facilitate integration of the findings.

These methods will be discussed in more detail.

Parallel analysis

In the convergent parallel design outlined in Chapter 6, the quantitative and qualitative components are implemented independently and integration may not occur until the interpretation phase. This approach is most common in studies where the research questions are divided into separate and distinct qualitative and quantitative questions so that analysis proceeds by focusing on answering these questions by the appropriate data set. Any integration takes place at the interpretation stage. This process is depicted in Figure 15.1.

Parallel analysis is appropriate in cases where one form of data, for instance qualitative, may be used to enhance interpretation of the other, or where the methods are implemented separately with little interconnection.

An example of parallel mixed-methods data analysis is shown in Box 15.1, which describes a study by Bernardi, Keim and von der Lippe (2007) of social influences on fertility in cities in the former East and West Germany.

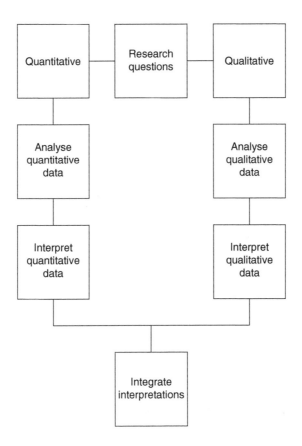

Figure 15.1 Parallel analysis of mixed-methods data

━━━━━━ BOX 15.1 ━━━━━━

AN EXAMPLE OF A PARALLEL ANALYSIS OF MIXED-METHODS DATA

Bernardi, Keim and von der Lippe (2007) reported a mixed-methods study of social influences on fertility in East (GDR) and West (FRG) Germany. They selected two German cities comparable in religious, historic and economic background – one from the former GDR and the other from the FRG. Within each city, they chose a quota sample of individuals together with one parent, the current partner and a close friend, where applicable. Each individual underwent an intensive interview focusing on expectations of childbearing, social relations, social networks

(Continued)

and demographic characteristics. Both qualitative data and quantitative data were derived from these interviews. The quantitative data was obtained in the social network grid and chart, and the qualitative data from the interviews. The qualitative data and the quantitative data were analysed separately and integrated in the discussion.

While useful for some research projects, this approach has been replaced, to some extent, by the integration methods discussed below.

Sequential analysis

Sequential analysis is appropriate to what has been called sequential designs in Chapter 6. These designs implement quantitative and qualitative methods in sequence where one set of data is analysed and the findings used to design a subsequent method. The analysis follows the design. Whichever method is implemented first is analysed first and feeds into the design and hence analysis of the subsequent method(s). This process is depicted in Figure 15.2.

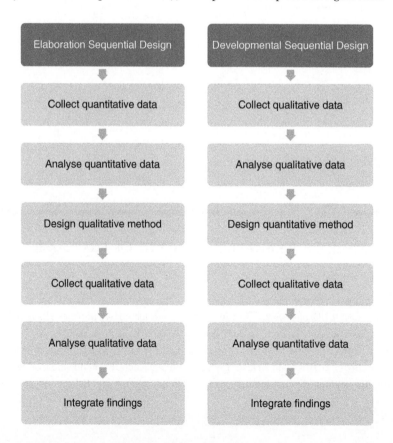

Figure 15.2   Sequential analysis of two mixed-methods designs

As outlined in Chapter 6, there are two types of sequential designs involving just two phases: an elaboration sequential design where the quantitative data is collected first and the qualitative method is usually designed to follow up on findings from the quantitative method; and a developmental sequential design where the qualitative data is collected first and the quantitative method is designed to generalize the qualitative findings by designing quantitative variables to measure the concepts developed in the qualitative stage. These two designs are shown separately in Figure 15.2.

There is also an iterative sequential design in which there are more than two phases of qualitative–quantitative methods following one another. This design is not shown in Figure 15.2 as it generates many possible combinations of design, data collection and data analysis phases.

An example of an elaboration sequential design is presented in Box 15.2. The study examined student persistence in a doctoral programme and was described in Chapter 6.

━━━━━ BOX 15.2 ━━━━━

AN EXAMPLE OF SEQUENTIAL ANALYSIS OF MIXED-METHODS DATA

Ivankova and Stick (2007) conducted an online survey to obtain quantitative data from 7-point Likert scales on ten variables deemed relevant to persistence in a doctoral programme on educational leadership in higher education. The quantitative data was analysed using discriminant function analysis to identify factors that predicted persistence. Five variables were identified as significant predictors, namely online learning environment, programme, student support services, faculty and self-motivation.

In the qualitative phase, a multiple case-study method was used involving interviews with four students, one from each group identified according to their status in the programme. The interview data was supplemented with additional information provided by the interviewees and gleaned from student files. Data was analysed using QSR N6 software, from which four themes emerged: quality of academic experiences, online learning environment, support and assistance, and student self-motivation. These themes were then integrated with the variables identified in the quantitative phase to provide a comprehensive account of programme persistence.

Integration methods

In this approach to data analysis, quantitative data and qualitative data are integrated either into themes generated by the research questions or linked in some way.

Integration of quantitative and qualitative data can be achieved by presenting data in joint displays. In such displays, themes or cases are identified and data from different sources placed side by side to facilitate comparison of the findings relating to these themes or cases. As Guetterman, Fetters and Creswell (2015: 555) point out, 'Meaningful integration allows researchers to realize the true benefits of mixed methods'.

The most frequently used type of joint display identified by Guetterman et al. (2015) was the 'themes by statistics' display, in which themes or quotes from the qualitative data are presented alongside categorized quantitative scores.

An example of a themes-by-statistics display is shown in Table 15.1 from a study of preschool inclusion (Li et al., 2000), in which findings from interviews and survey data are shown alongside themes generated from the research questions.

Table 15.1   An example of an integrated analysis of mixed-methods data

Theme	Interviews	Surveys
Programme's appropriateness for child	Factors affecting match between child's and family's needs: • acceptance by staff and children • likes activities for child • child likes programme • sees benefits or improvements	• 90% said very important for child to be in inclusive programme • 80% indicated child usually receives special services • 86% were satisfied with way in which child's educational goals were set
How and why child was placed in programme	Factors affecting choice: • visited and liked classroom teacher • convenience of location • flexibility in hours • good reputation of centre • concern if centre would accept child because of behaviour	Parents' most important reason for choosing programme: • offers special education services or therapies • provides opportunities for child to learn • provides opportunities for child to play with other children

Source: adapted from Li et al. (2000)

Conversion methods

In this approach, data is converted from one form into another, either by converting qualitative data into quantitative data (quantitizing) or by converting quantitative data into qualitative data (qualitizing). This is done to achieve integration of data in the analysis. These methods will be discussed separately.

Quantitizing

Quantitizing refers to the process of converting qualitative into quantitative data. This is done to facilitate comparisons of the quantitative and qualitative data by converting them into a common format. To do this, qualitative data is coded and the codes converted into numerical scales. These numerical scales are usually nominal scales representing the presence or absence of the code, but they may also be ordinal scales representing some measure of degree of presence.

As pointed out by Bazeley (2018, Ch. 8), quantifying qualitative data is designed to support the analysis of qualitative data, not to replace it. The purpose of collecting qualitative data in mixed-methods research is to provide in-depth accounts of events or experiences not available in quantitative data. To simply code such data into quantitative categories and neglect fuller analysis of this qualitative data is to overlook insights potentially embedded in this data.

It could be argued that rather than convert qualitative data into codes and numerical scales, the researcher could have constructed the numerical scales and included them in the quantitative method, thereby doing away with the need to collect the qualitative data. This argument, however, assumes that the researcher is already aware of all the potential codes that might arise from the qualitative data. It is more likely that the qualitative data generates codes which the researcher has not anticipated, thereby opening up new variables for analysis.

Coding was outlined in Chapter 14. For each segment of qualitative data coded, the simplest form of analysis is to record whether the code is present or absent. The number of times the code is present can then be counted and a table of codes by cases constructed.

Another quantitizing method is to rate qualitative data on a rating scale. This is appropriate for interview responses where respondents make evaluative comments such as expressing positive or negative views about an experience, event or proposal. These ratings can then be entered into a database alongside quantitative measures collected about the same phenomena.

As an example of quantitizing, Driscoll et al. (2007) reported two studies dealing with perceptions of vaccine safety issues among stakeholder groups. The second study reported by them is a sequential design involving a survey of staff of several federal agencies involved in vaccine safety followed by in-depth semi-structured interviews exploring perspectives on the purpose and utility of vaccine safety guidelines. The study is summarized in Box 15.3.

The authors concluded that without the follow-up interviews, the reasons for agency differences in ratings of usefulness of the vaccine guidelines would not have been revealed.

There are problems, however, in merging qualitative and quantitative data through quantitizing the qualitative data. These include the following:

1. Qualitative data is generally derived from different sampling schemes than quantitative data. While quantitative data is usually obtained from random samples of a population, qualitative data is more often obtained from purposely selected non-random samples of respondents exhibiting particular characteristics relevant to the research questions.
2. Quantitative data is usually obtained from large sample sizes to facilitate inferential statistical analysis, while qualitative data is obtained mainly from small samples because of the time consumed in collecting in-depth information.
3. Combining measures derived from quantitized qualitative data with measures obtained from quantitative data will likely breach the assumptions underlying inferential statistical methods, thereby limiting the range of data analysis methods available.

Despite these limitations, there is still a range of descriptive statistical methods available to compare the findings and reveal outcomes not available in the quantitative data alone. In the words of Sandelowski et al. (2009: 219), quantitizing, 'when used creatively, critically, and reflexively, can show the complexity of qualitative data'.

BOX 15.3

AN EXAMPLE OF QUANTITIZING QUALITATIVE RESPONSES IN A SEQUENTIAL DESIGN

Driscoll et al. (2007) report a sequential design involving a survey of staff of agencies with responsibilities for vaccine safety, in which a questionnaire was administered dealing with readability and utility of the vaccine safety guidelines. The analysis of this questionnaire revealed significant differences in satisfaction with the readability and utility of the guidelines by agency but did not explain the agency differences.

The follow-up interview responses were quantitized and related to the survey responses. The subsequent analysis of this combined analysis showed that agency officials satisfied with the guidelines viewed the scientific community as the major audience, while those officials who viewed the general public and policy makers as the main audiences, felt that the guidelines were too complicated to be understandable by such audiences.

Qualitizing

Qualitizing refers to the process of converting quantitative into qualitative data. This is done in order to identify categories from the quantitative data to facilitate analysis of the qualitative data within those categories.

Some methods of qualitizing quantitative data are as follows:

1. Dividing a single variable into categories based on a range of values of the variable. An example of this would be age group, where individuals are classified on the basis of their age, such as young (under 25), mature (25–39), middle aged (40–59) and elderly (60+).
2. Creating categories from a number of related variables or individuals through cluster analysis. This classificatory method groups variables or individuals together based on their similarities to form clusters which can be named based on the variables or individuals that group together to form each cluster.
3. Creating profiles based on similarities among individuals on their characteristics as measured by quantitative instruments. Tashakkori and Teddlie (1998) identified five types of profiles: average, comparative, modal, normative and holistic. These profiles can be formed through the use of cluster analysis applied to individuals.

Onwuegbuzie and Dickinson (2008) provide two examples of qualitizing, one using narrative profile formation and the other using cluster analysis.

CONCLUSION

The wide range of analysis options for mixed-methods research outlined in this chapter testify as to the complexity of this type of research. The task of combining quantitative and qualitative analyses to answer the research questions can be accomplished at the final interpretation phase, sequentially throughout the study, integrated at the analysis stage or by converting one type of data into the other and analysing them together. These methods are not mutually exclusive; they can be used in combinations, such as quantitizing along with integration, providing an even greater range of options for analysis.

CHAPTER SUMMARY

This chapter has dealt with the process of analysing data in mixed-methods research. Four options for mixed-methods data analysis were identified, namely parallel analysis, sequential analysis, integration and conversion methods. The latter involve converting qualitative to quantitative data (quantitizing) and converting quantitative to qualitative data (qualitizing).

Which approach is most suitable for a particular mixed-methods project will depend on the research questions to be answered, the design of the research and the extent to which priority is given to the component methods.

FURTHER READING

Bazeley, P. (2018) *Integrating Analyses in Mixed Methods Research*. London: Sage Publications.
A thorough account of the analysis of data in mixed-methods research.

Onwuegbuzie, A. J. and Teddlie, C. (2003) A framework for analyzing data in mixed methods research. In A. Tashakkori and C. Teddlie (eds), *Handbook of Mixed Methods in Social and Behavioral Research*. Thousand Oaks, CA: Sage Publications.
A comprehensive account of options for data analysis in mixed-methods research.

Sandelowski, M., Voils, C. I. and Knafl, G. (2009) On quantitizing. *Journal of Mixed Methods Research*, **3 (3), 208–222.**
A discussion of quantitizing that takes up important theoretical issues relating to the nature of mixed-methods data.

Teddlie, C. and Tashakkori, A. (2009) *Foundations of Mixed-Methods Research.* **Thousand Oaks, CA: Sage Publications.**
Chapter 11 outlines methods for quantitative, qualitative and mixed-methods data analysis.

REPORTING, PRESENTING AND IMPLEMENTING RESEARCH FINDINGS

Part 5 deals with the final stages in research, namely interpreting, reporting and implementing the research findings.

Chapter 16 examines the processes involved in interpreting findings, including the drawing of inferences from qualitative and quantitative data as well as from findings using mixed methods. The chapter concludes with a discussion of inference quality.

Chapter 17 deals with the communication of research findings through presentations and a written report. Approaches to writing reports for qualitative, quantitative and mixed-methods research are outlined, and problems encountered in writing reports discussed. Strategies for presenting research findings at conferences and to groups of stakeholders are also outlined.

Chapter 18 outlines issues involved in research utilization, including a discussion of evidence-based practice, underutilization of research and the role of the researcher in the implementation of findings.

16

INTERPRETING RESEARCH FINDINGS

INTRODUCTION

Once research data has been analysed, the findings need to be interpreted. This process can be regarded as the most creative part of the research project.

The main purpose of interpretation is to answer the research questions. Answering research questions requires drawing inferences from the data analysis. How this is done depends on the type of research questions asked. The major categories of research questions are quantitative and qualitative and within these categories there are further sub-categories, as outlined in Chapter 4. The inference process differs among these categories, as will be described in this chapter.

In mixed-methods research, inferences need to be drawn and integrated from both qualitative and quantitative data and this adds a degree of complexity to the process. Tashakkori and Teddlie (2008: 100) refer to this as a 'meta-inference' since it involves integrating inferences from the qualitative and quantitative findings from a mixed-methods study. Strategies for integrating data in mixed-methods research will be discussed.

Research questions may be formulated so as to test predictions from theories. In such cases, theory testing is the main purpose of the interpretation of findings. The role of theory in interpreting research findings will be discussed in this chapter.

The notion of inference is central to the interpretation of research findings, so an account of this will be developed first and then applied to quantitative, qualitative and mixed-methods findings. This will be followed by a discussion of inference quality.

THE ROLE OF INFERENCE IN INTERPRETING FINDINGS

As Miller (2003: 425) points out, an inference can be seen as both a process and a product. As a process, it refers to the procedures undertaken to interpret findings and as a product, it is the outcome of this interpretation. As a process, the drawing of inferences is the steps taken by a researcher to answer the research questions. How this is done will depend on how the research questions are formulated and on the nature of the findings being interpreted.

To understand the process of inference making, it is useful to consider the traditional distinctions that have been made about the types of inferences, so that the ways in which inferences are drawn in practice can be better understood.

Traditionally, two major types of inference drawing have been identified. These are **deductive** and **inductive inferences**. They are set out in Box 16.1. In research, deductive inferences are mainly applicable to deriving predictions from theory, whereas inductive inferences are used in generalizing from sample findings to populations in quantitative research, or from generalizing to a theory from regularities found in qualitative research.

A third type of inference was developed by Charles Pierce in the 19th century which he called *abduction*. This form of inference was developed in order to describe how scientists practically went about choosing hypotheses to explain their findings. Abduction then is a form of reasoning that infers a 'best explanation' for a set of observations. It is sometimes referred to as 'inference to the best explanation'.

Erzberger and Kelle (2003: 479–82) see **abductive inference** as being particularly useful in mixed-methods research when qualitative and quantitative findings are integrated. The process of integration can give rise to divergent findings that are not readily explained by existing theory or knowledge. They argue that, under such circumstances, abductive inference helps find new hypotheses to explain the apparently divergent findings.

This process of abductive inference will be discussed further in the section on inference in mixed-methods research later in this chapter.

═══════════ **BOX 16.1** ═══════════

DEDUCTIVE AND INDUCTIVE INFERENCE

Deductive inference

Deductive inference involves using logical principles to draw conclusions from a set of premises. If the premises are true, and the logical principles are followed, then the conclusion is necessarily true. This form of inference is used in deriving predictions from a theory rather than drawing inferences from research findings.

Inductive inference

Inductive inference involves generalizing from a set of specific cases to a general principle. If the specific cases all exhibit a particular characteristic, then it can be inductively inferred that all cases of this kind will exhibit this characteristic. Such an inference is not necessarily true since it is always possible to find cases that do not exhibit the characteristic.

Inference quality is critical to all research. **Tashakkori and Teddlie (2010)** argue that inference quality depends on two components which they call *design quality* and *interpretive rigour*.

Design quality refers to the quality of inputs to the research. These include the choice and design of the research methods used, the sampling procedure and the instruments used to collect data, all of which have been discussed in previous chapters. Interpretive rigour refers to the steps taken to interpret findings, the subject of this chapter.

The process of drawing inferences from findings differs for qualitative, quantitative and mixed-methods research. These will be outlined in the following sections.

INFERENCES IN QUALITATIVE RESEARCH

Qualitative data, as we have seen, takes a wide range of forms and is collected under a variety of research methods, such as case studies, observational studies, in-depth interviews and ethnographic research. It can consist of primary sources such as interview transcripts or field notes or secondary sources such as organizational documents, photos or videos.

Interpretation of such data is influenced by the paradigm adopted by the researcher (see Chapters 1 and 2). Interpretivists and constructivists are more likely to see qualitative data as reflecting multiple realities and to interpret the data as providing information about these realities through repeated examination of themes extracted from it. In such cases, inference may be to an existing theory or form components of theory construction, as in grounded theory (see Box 16.6).

Researchers adopting a realist paradigm are more likely to see qualitative data as providing evidence for causal mechanisms operating in the research situation. **Qualitative comparison analysis** (see Chapter 14) focuses on identifying causal mechanisms operating in case studies. It requires a moderate number of case studies, usually more than ten, in which an outcome is specified and the conditions that are expected to lead to that outcome identified. Application of the software mentioned in Chapter 14 enables specification of the best set of causal conditions leading to the outcome.

A similar approach to using qualitative methods to identify causal mechanisms has been developed by Beach and others (Beach and Pedersen, 2013, 2016). This method is referred to as process-tracing and involves tracing causal mechanisms within a case study.

Both approaches see causal mechanisms in social science as complex and see qualitative research as best suited to identifying these mechanisms. **Complex causation** is summarized in Box 16.2.

■■■■■■■ BOX 16.2 ■■■■■■■

CHARACTERISTICS OF COMPLEX CAUSATION

Complex causation is characterized by multiple causes determining an effect, as distinct from single cause–effect relationships. Such causes may operate as either–or causes or as conjunctural causes where the simultaneous occurrence of two or more causes produces the effect. A situation in which both either–or and conjunctural causation operates is referred to as a multiple conjunctural causation. In this case, two or more different combinations of conditions may produce the same effect. So, if A, B, C and D are conditions (causes) and Y is an outcome (effect), then a multiple conjunctural causation could be AB + CD → Y, where AB means the joint occurrence of conditions A and B, + indicates 'or' and → indicates 'produces' (see Berg-Schlosser et al., 2009 for further detail).

Since, in most qualitative research, cases or individuals are not chosen randomly from a population as in most quantitative research, findings cannot be generalized beyond the cases included in the study. This should not be seen as a drawback as case selection in qualitative research is made on grounds other than generalizability to a population, such as theoretical relevance, or, in some instances, the cases may exhaust the range of possible situations available for inclusion. Qualitative research is based on different rationales to quantitative research and inferences must be judged by criteria specific to those rationales.

INFERENCES IN QUANTITATIVE RESEARCH

Quantitative data can come from survey or experimental research where random samples are drawn from a population and the inference is to be made to that population, or it can be derived from existing statistical data such as census statistics or government statistical reports.

In the former case, inferences are what Miller (2003: 428) calls 'enumerative induction', or inductive generalization. The samples are drawn randomly with the intention of making generalizations to the population from which the samples are drawn. Such inferences are of three basic types:

1. Inferences about differences: inferences about differences are generalizations to a population that differences among two or more sample statistics are evidence of differences among the population versions of these statistics, referred to as population parameters. If, for example, the sample statistic calculated is a mean, say of a test score, and there are samples from two populations, say males and females, then the inference

from sample differences between the means is that differences exist between the mean test scores of males and females in the populations from which the samples were chosen. This inference is only made with a prescribed level of confidence expressed as a probability. (See Chapter 13.)

2. Inferences about relationships: relationships are measured by a correlation coefficient, as described in Chapter 13. Different measures of correlation are calculated from nominal, ordinal and interval scales but the inferential logic is the same. An observed relationship found in a sample is tested, using an appropriate statistical inference procedure, to decide whether this relationship is likely to be present in the population from which the sample is drawn.

3. Inferences about predictions: situations in which predictions are of interest are those in which a dependent variable, such as health status, can be predicted from a number of independent variables, such as body mass index, age, hours of sleep per night or hours of physical exercise undertaken per week. The prediction is formulated as a regression equation (see Chapter 13) and the sample regression equation tested for significance.

Once these statistical inferences are made, the results can be interpreted as providing an answer to the research question concerned.

These inferences are summarized in Table 16.1.

Table 16.1 Types of quantitative inferences

Inference type	Example
Differences	Do male and female school students in their final year differ in their attitudes towards successfully completing a university qualification?
Relationships	Is there a relationship between level of education and attitude towards gender discrimination?
Predictions	How well can school achievement be predicted from socio-economic status of the family, birth order of the student, size of family and place of residence?

In the case of existing statistics, statistical inference is not normally conducted as these statistics most likely will not have been calculated from random samples, or they will apply to the whole population as in census statistics. In such cases, the findings can be directly applied to answering the research question(s).

INFERENCES IN MIXED-METHODS RESEARCH

The inference process in mixed-methods research involves bringing together the inferences derived from the qualitative and quantitative strands. Tashakkori and Teddlie (2010) refer to this process as making *meta-inferences* – that is, making inferences from the inferences already drawn from the qualitative and quantitative findings.

Erzberger and Kelle (2003) use the methodological concept of *triangulation* to analyse the process of integration of research results from mixed-methods research. They point out that this concept is a metaphor derived from navigation, where an unknown position can be determined exactly from two known points, the distance between them and the angles that lines from these points make to the unknown point. In social research, triangulation provides no such certainty, so that use of the term is no more than a metaphor. In interpreting mixed-methods findings, triangulation is most commonly used to 'yield a fuller and more complete picture of the phenomenon concerned it brought together' (Erzberger and Kelle, 2003: 461). It has also been used to check the validity of an interpretation of findings from a single method by supplementing that method with another based on a different approach. As Erzberger and Kelle (2003: 461) point out, a convergence of findings may mean that both results could be biased in the same direction so that such convergence may not be evidence of validity. Hammersley (2008) lists a number of difficulties with this interpretation of triangulation besides that outlined above. These include the problem of how to respond to conflicting findings and the implicit assumption that there is a single reality that is revealed by the different methods of data collection.

When qualitative and quantitative methods are combined to answer a research question, there are three possible outcomes (Erzberger and Kelle, 2003):

1. Convergence: the results from the quantitative and qualitative findings lead to the same conclusion – that is, the findings converge on a single interpretation.
2. Complementarity: the results from the quantitative and qualitative findings may reveal different aspects of the subject of the research and these aspects may complement each other.
3. Divergence: the quantitative and qualitative findings may be divergent or contradictory.

Each of these outcomes will need to be handled differently.

Convergence

Convergence of findings from qualitative and quantitative research takes place when the quantitative and qualitative findings lead to the same conclusion. Erzberger and Kelle (2003) provide an example of this, as described in Box 16.3. In that example, findings from a survey and in-depth interviews were in substantial agreement. As mentioned above, this finding can either be interpreted as providing support for the validity of the findings, or as yielding a fuller picture of the phenomenon.

━━━━━ BOX 16.3 ━━━━━

AN EXAMPLE OF CONVERGENCE OF FINDINGS FROM QUALITATIVE AND QUANTITATIVE RESULTS

Erzberger and Kelle (2003: 469) report a mixed-methods study of post-Second World War employment patterns and attitudes to gender division of labour. The survey found that males saw themselves as the 'breadwinners' and their wives as having domestic responsibilities. This view was reinforced in extended in-depth interviews. They conclude that:

... no inconsistencies could be found between the actions of respondents related to their occupational life courses (empirically described by the records produced with standardized questionnaires), on the one hand and subjective interpretations of these actions (made visible through the qualitative data material), on the other.

Complementarity

Complementary findings of qualitative and quantitative research take place when each method provides only a partial account of the phenomenon under investigation. A more complete picture only emerges when the findings from the separate methods are integrated.

This is a common occurrence in many mixed-methods studies and is a convincing rationale for using mixed methods. Surveys and experiments can often gloss over detail that may be revealed in qualitative methods such as interviews or focus groups.

Divergence

Divergence of quantitative and qualitative findings is a challenge to interpreting mixed-methods research findings. There are two possible reasons for such divergence:

1. There are weaknesses in one or other of the methods used, resulting in the inadequate identification of concepts.
2. The methods have identified different aspects of the subject matter that reflect apparent contradictory outcomes.

The first of these reasons can be addressed by a careful examination of the methodologies used and by correcting any deficiencies found, by repeating the study with improved methods.

The second of these reasons presents us with a range of possibilities to resolve it. The contradictory outcomes could be due to an inadequate definition of the concepts and/or to poor theoretical development, leading to inappropriate predictions being deduced.

An example of the latter is provided in Box 16.4, which reports on a study of poverty in Guinea (Shaffer, 1998) in which surveys of households found that women were not more likely than men to be consumption poor, yet interviews conducted in one village found two dimensions of deprivation in which women were worse off than men, namely excessive workload and a lack of decision-making authority. The author concluded that measuring only consumption poverty misses other aspects of deprivation.

━━━━━━━ **BOX 16.4** ━━━━━━━

AN EXAMPLE OF DIVERGENCE IN FINDINGS BETWEEN QUANTITATIVE AND QUALITATIVE DATA

Shaffer (1998) reports on a study of gender and deprivation in a village in the Republic of Guinea. He first examined the existing evidence on poverty comparisons between males and females in Guinea and found that women were not more likely than men to be consumption poor, nor more likely to suffer greater levels of poverty on all the indices reported. The Participatory Poverty Assessment (PPA) conducted in the village found that women were worse off than men in the areas of decision-making authority and excessive workload. Shaffer concluded that the survey data focused too narrowly on consumption poverty and missed critical elements of women's deprivation.

───────────────

Cases in which inconsistent findings have been found can often be resolved by expanding the definition of the concept being investigated. In the example in Box 16.4, the inconsistency was due to different definitions of poverty being adopted in the qualitative and quantitative methods. The collection of both quantitative and qualitative data in these cases leads to the uncovering of a limited understanding of issues and the avoidance of incorrect conclusions being drawn from the use of just one data source.

THE ROLE OF SOCIAL THEORY IN INTERPRETING FINDINGS

Theory, whether stated explicitly or not, permeates all social research. As Hanson (1958) pointed out, all observations are theory laden. The view that observations can be objective, unbiased and value-free has long been discredited. This view was promoted by the positivists and outlined in Chapter 1. It has been replaced by a range of methodologies, all of which recognize the influence of values and theory on observations.

Theory can enter into the research process in several ways:

1. It can be implicit in the statement of the research question. In such cases, the research questions are stated without reference to theory, leaving the theoretical content implicit.
2. Research questions can be stated as the predictions from a social theory. In such cases, the answers to the research questions provide either confirmation or falsification of the theory. For this to be achieved, the theory needs to be developed to the point where unambiguous predictions can be derived from it in a form that can be tested by empirical evidence.
3. Research questions can involve the comparison of two or more theories. In such cases, the answers to the research questions decide which, if any, theories are supported by the findings. An example of this is provided in Box 16.5.

4. Theory can be constructed from the findings of the research – that is, each finding of the research project is interpreted as providing support for a theory that is being constructed. This process is followed in much qualitative research and is referred to as 'grounded theory' (see Box 16.6).

BOX 16.5

AN EXAMPLE OF RESEARCH DESIGNED TO DISCRIMINATE BETWEEN TWO THEORIES

Kraeger (2008) tested the predictions of social control theory and social learning theory in a study of male adolescent school students engaged in school sports programmes. He argued that social control theory predicts that engagement in school sports would reduce antisocial behaviour due to the values promoted by sports, such as teamwork, and the sanctions imposed on team members who exhibit deviant behaviour. Social learning theory, on the other hand, claims that antisocial behaviour is learned from interactions with peers and family. Violent behaviour is promoted in what is termed 'hyper-masculine' contact sports such as football, but not in other sports such as tennis. So Kraeger argued that social learning theory predicts the incidence of antisocial violent behaviour would be more prevalent in those engaged in the hyper-masculine contact sports. He compared male students involved in a range of high school sports and found that those involved in the hyper-masculine sports exhibited greater levels of violent behaviour than those involved in non-masculine sports, consistent with the predictions of social learning theory rather than social control theory.

As Popper (1959) and others have pointed out, finding evidence consistent with a theory doesn't mean that the theory is true, but finding disconfirming evidence falsifies the theory, unless the evidence has been misinterpreted or has been collected using faulty methods.

BOX 16.6

THE PRINCIPLES OF GROUNDED THEORY

Grounded theory was developed by Glaser and Strauss (1967) to provide a strategy for the development of theory from qualitative data. Rather than apply existing theories to understand data, theory was constructed from the analysis of the data through coding (see Chapter 14) and the development of categories from this coding. These categories are then interrelated to construct a theory.

(Continued)

Although Glaser and Strauss later disagreed over the detail of grounded theory development, the basic principles involve the use of coding qualitative data to allow for the emergence of a theory from this analysis (see Charmaz, 2006).

INFERENCE QUALITY

As mentioned above, Teddlie and Tashakkori (2009) use the term *interpretive rigour* to describe 'the degree to which credible interpretations have been made on the basis of obtained results' (p. 303). The criteria they suggest interpretations need to meet to achieve interpretive rigour are listed in Table 16.2.

Examining each interpretation by applying these criteria goes a long way towards ensuring confidence in the conclusions reached. This can't guarantee correctness of the conclusions, since it is not possible to anticipate all possible interpretations. It can only mean that, at the present state of knowledge in the field, the findings are credible.

Table 16.2   Criteria to achieve interpretive rigour in interpreting research findings

Criterion	Description
Interpretive consistency	The extent to which conclusions follow the findings and whether multiple conclusions based on the same results agree with each other
Explanation credibility	The extent to which conclusions are consistent with current theories and findings from other research
Interpretive agreement	How well are the conclusions accepted by other researchers?
Interpretive distinctiveness	The extent to which alternative interpretations of the findings can be ruled out
Integrative efficacy	The degree to which inferences from the results can be effectively integrated into a consistent conclusion
Integrative correspondence	In a mixed-methods study, integrative correspondence refers to the extent to which conclusions satisfy the initial purpose for using the mixed-methods design

Source: adapted from Teddlie and Tashakkori (2009, Ch. 12)

CONCLUSION

Interpreting findings is a critical part of the research process as it brings together all aspects of the research in arriving at conclusions about the relevance and meaning of the results.

Inferences follow a different pattern in quantitative and qualitative research, as described above, and these inferences need to be brought together in mixed-methods research so as to integrate the findings. This process requires a degree of ingenuity, particularly when findings from the qualitative and quantitative methods are inconsistent. Interpreting inconsistent findings are a challenge to the mixed-methods researcher, insofar as they point to limitations in either the design of one or more of the components, in the methods or in the theoretical formulations that have informed the interpretations that have led to the inconsistencies. Resolving these issues is what makes mixed-methods research worth doing as it exposes problems that single methods would not have uncovered and leads to more theoretically sophisticated conclusions.

CHAPTER SUMMARY

This chapter has dealt with the process of interpreting findings from quantitative, qualitative and mixed-methods research. Interpretation involves making inferences from research findings. The way in which inferences are drawn differ for qualitative, quantitative and mixed-methods research. They also depend on the way in which theory is incorporated into the research questions.

FURTHER READING

Corbin, J. and Strauss, A. (2015) *Basics of Qualitative Research: Techniques and Procedures for Developing Grounded Theory*, **4th edition. Thousand Oaks, CA: Sage Publications.**
A thorough account of the use of grounded theory in qualitative data analysis and interpretation.

Erzberger, C. and Kelle, U. (2003) Making inferences in mixed methods: the rules of integration. In A. Tashakkori and C. Teddlie (eds), *Handbook of Mixed Methods in Social and Behavioral Research*. **Thousand Oaks, CA: Sage Publications.**
A comprehensive discussion of inferences in mixed-methods research.

Teddlie, C. and Tashakkori, A. (2009) *Foundations of Mixed Methods Research: Integrating Quantitative and Qualitative Approaches in the Social and Behavioral Sciences*. **Thousand Oaks, CA: Sage Publications.**
Chapter 12 deals with the process of inference in research and examines the criteria for inference quality.

17

COMMUNICATING RESEARCH FINDINGS

INTRODUCTION

Once the data from a research project has been collected, analysed and interpreted, it needs to be communicated either to the research community as an article published in a scholarly journal, or to an organization that has commissioned the research or to a higher education institution as a thesis to be submitted for the award of a degree.

The way in which research is communicated will depend on how the research has been initiated:

- If it is a research project commissioned by an organization, it is likely that the organization will require a presentation to the stakeholders of the organization followed by a written report.
- If it is research that has been conducted within the auspices of a higher education institution or a research centre, then it will most likely be presented at a conference and then written as a research article for submission to an academic journal.
- If it is a thesis to be submitted for a higher degree, then it will be a written report set out in accordance with the guidelines of the institution. In such a case, the student may be required to defend the thesis before a committee.

In this chapter, these alternative formats for communicating research findings will be outlined and problems encountered in this process considered.

THE RESEARCH REPORT

Just about all research findings end up in a written report since this format provides a permanent record of the research and has been the accepted form of reporting research for centuries.

Despite developments in alternative forms of communication, this practice does not seem to be under any immediate challenge.

Written reports vary according to which of the above modes of initiation apply and whether the data is quantitative, qualitative or mixed. There is a greater variety in the writing of qualitative research than either quantitative or mixed-methods research, due no doubt to the greater range of viewpoints held by qualitative researchers.

Quantitative research shows the least variation in report format and is often used as the template for writing up all forms of research. For this reason, the quantitative research format will be outlined first.

Reporting quantitative research

The format generally accepted for writing quantitative research reports varies only slightly, depending on whether it is a thesis, a scholarly journal article or an applied research report. This format is set out in Table 17.1.

A thesis for a higher degree will likely contain more than one study so that each study could be reported in a separate chapter, with subsections corresponding to the introduction, method, results and discussion for the study. A concluding chapter would then be included to bring the findings of the separate studies together.

Table 17.1   Format for writing quantitative research reports

Section	Contents
Title page	Contains the title of the article or thesis and the author name(s) and affiliation(s)
Abstract or executive summary	A brief summary of the whole article or thesis. It is called an abstract in a scholarly journal article and an executive summary in an applied research report
Introduction	Sets out the background to the research and its aims and research questions. In a thesis, this is likely to be divided into two or more chapters, with one consisting of a literature review, followed by the aims and research questions
Method	Sets out the research method(s) employed in the study
Results	Includes information on how the data has been analysed and the results of this analysis
Discussion	Contains an interpretation of the findings by relating them to previous research and theory as appropriate

Section	Contents
Conclusion and/or recommendations	A concluding section setting out the major implications of the findings and suggestions for future research. Recommendations are often included here in a commissioned report
References or bibliography	A list of references referred to in the article or thesis in alphabetical order and set out in accordance with a format approved by the journal editors

Findings of quantitative research are usually presented in tables or graphs. These need to be structured to maximize effective communication of the key findings.

Graphs, if displayed effectively, are able to attract a reader's attention and can convey findings visually in a way that tables cannot. Henry (1998a) provides a set of principles for preparing graphs to maximize effectiveness. These principles are set out in Box 17.1.

Henry also points out that some graphs can hide information rather than reveal it. This is done by choice of units or by including too much information in one graph.

━━━━━ BOX 17.1 ━━━━━

GUIDELINES FOR PRESENTING INFORMATION IN GRAPHS

Henry (1998a) developed the following principles for presenting effective graphs:

1. Give primacy to the data: readers should be easily able to discern trends and patterns from the graph.
2. Design information-rich graphics: the complexity of the data should be readily seen from the graph.
3. Avoid distortion: ensure the choice of units in the graph does not distort differences.
4. Enhance clarity: avoid ambiguity.
5. Encourage important comparisons: ensure items that are to be compared are clearly placed in proximity.
6. Remember the audience: tailor the graph to the needs of the audience.

When presenting statistical tests of significance, ensure that these facilitate the flow of the argument and are not presented in obscure tables.

Reporting qualitative research

There is a wide variety of formats for presenting qualitative research findings. This is due to a number of factors, including the type of data collected, the paradigm adopted by the researcher, and the intended audience. Richardson (2003) sets out some principles to be considered in writing up qualitative research findings that open up a range of possible approaches.

Van Maanen (1988) identified three approaches to **ethnographic writing** (set out in Box 17.2), and the number of approaches has mushroomed since then.

============ BOX 17.2 ============

APPROACHES TO ETHNOGRAPHIC WRITING

Van Maanen (1988) identified three approaches to ethnographic writing, as follows:

- Realist tales: this approach is written in the third person and the researcher is absent from the content. It is close to the mode of writing in quantitative reports outlined in Table 17.1.
- Confessional tales: in this approach, the account incorporates the experiences of the researcher and is written from the viewpoint of the researcher. These tales are usually written in the first person.
- Impressionist tales: these are designed to achieve dramatic effect by being written as a story to convey the experience of the researcher.

Denzin (2003a, b) has championed *performance ethnography*, an approach which he says is 'situated in complex systems of discourse, where traditional, everyday, and avant-garde meanings of theater, film, video, ethnography, cinema, performance, text, and audience all circulate and inform one another' (Denzin, 2003a: 468). In this approach, the text takes the form of a performance, as in theatre, rallies, marches, and so on.

These few approaches only tap the surface of the range of options for reporting qualitative research. Richardson (2003) groups these emerging genres under the heading *creative analytic practices* (CAP) to set them apart from traditional reporting methods. Rather than being alternative approaches, Richardson sees them as the most valid representations of the social.

Reporting mixed-methods research

In mixed-methods research, reporting of the analyses of both quantitative and qualitative data needs to be integrated in some way. How this is done will depend on the mixed-methods design used and the way in which the data has been analysed. There are two options for presenting mixed methods:

1. Combine the findings from the qualitative and quantitative analyses and present them in an integrated form.

2. Present the findings from the qualitative and quantitative analyses separately and integrate them in the discussion.

Both these options were discussed in Chapter 15. Integration methods were outlined there and include presenting data in themes, with both qualitative and quantitative findings included under each theme (see Table 15.1), or by converting one form of data into the other (qualitizing or quantitizing) and analysing and presenting them together.

The report in such cases would not have separate sections for qualitative and quantitative data analyses but include each under single results and single discussion sections.

The second option of analysing and presenting qualitative and quantitative data separately is, as pointed out in Chapter 15, appropriate for sequential designs where the methods are conducted separately and in sequence.

An example of the separation of qualitative and quantitative analyses and discussion throughout the report is provided by an article by Way et al. (1994) (reprinted in Plano Clark and Creswell, 2008). In this study, the authors investigated the relationship between substance use and depression in students from two divergent high school cultures. The quantitative data was collected first through a survey of students from two high schools, one in a suburban location and the other in an urban location. They found that depression was significantly related to substance abuse (cigarette smoking, marijuana and hard drug use) in the suburban school but not in the urban school. To explore these findings, they interviewed students from both schools who had high depression scores. Analysis of the interviews found that depressed students in the two schools imputed different meanings to substance use. For example, suburban students were more likely to see substance use as an escape from problems, whereas urban students were more likely to see substance use as a cause of stress rather than an escape from it. Peer pressure to use substances was also experienced more among suburban than urban students.

Table 17.2 Structure of the mixed-method report

Sections and subsections			Contents
Introduction			Summary of research on the relationship between depression and substance use
Quantitative analysis	Method	Subjects	Describes the sampling method for selecting students
		Questionnaires	Describes the depression and substance use scales used
		Procedure	Describes the procedure for administering scales
	Results	Comparison across schools	Analysis of depression and substance use across schools
		Comparison within schools	Examines gender and grade differences within schools

(Continued)

Table 17.2 (Continued)

Sections and subsections			Contents
Qualitative analysis	Method	Subjects	Describes the choice of students to interview
		The interview	Describes the interview format
		Procedure	Describes how the interviews were conducted and analysed
	Results	Differences in substance use	Reports differences among the urban and suburban samples
		Differences in meaning	Identification of three common differences in meaning of substance use across the schools
Summary and Discussion			Discussion of the findings from both quantitative and qualitative analyses
Implications			Contains suggestions for further research
Notes			Footnotes used in the text
References			Contains the sources cited in the report

Source: Way et al. (1994)

The structure of the report of this study is set out in Table 17.2. The quantitative and qualitative components are described and analysed in separate sections of the report, and brought together in the summary and discussion.

The detailed structure of this report is included here to illustrate how a sequential mixed-method report is typically organized. Other examples can be found in Part II of *The Mixed Methods Reader* (Plano Clark and Creswell, 2008).

PROBLEMS ENCOUNTERED IN WRITING REPORTS

For many researchers, writing up a report or thesis can be the most difficult part of the whole process. There are a number of web-based resources providing advice on writing reports and most introductory research methods books also include advice (e.g. Bryman, 2015), so only a few suggestions will be included here:

1. List the proposed content in a series of bullet points. These are relatively easy to set up and they make the expansion of them into text easier to accomplish.
2. Take frequent breaks from writing. Sitting in front of a computer screen for a long time can be unproductive if ideas are not flowing. Engaging in a completely different activity during a break from writing enables time for ideas to form.
3. Don't be too meticulous about a first draft. It is more productive to get the main ideas in sequence completed without being too concerned about expression. This can be improved in a second draft.

Following submission, the writer may need to deal with feedback from editors in the case of an article, supervisors in the case of a thesis or a funding body in the case of a commissioned report. Comments, or even criticisms, from these sources can be helpful in revising the report. They can, however, be unhelpful if they seek to change the interpretation in a direction that you consider to be unsupported by the findings. This can happen in commissioned reports if the funding body perceives the report to imply criticism of their conduct or does not support their policy. In such cases, researchers need to consider the impact of any revisions they might make to accommodate such requests on their integrity and reputation. This can place a researcher in an extremely difficult situation, possibly necessitating legal advice.

PRESENTING RESEARCH FINDINGS

Research findings can also be presented at an academic conference or to a group of stakeholders. In each case, the presentation will most likely be limited in time and the composition of the audience will vary considerably in their backgrounds and knowledge of the area. For a presentation to be well received, these two factors will need to be considered. Some suggestions for doing this are as follows:

- Set up your presentation using presentation software. A set of slides covering the main points of your talk is essential to a successful presentation.
- Ensure your slides convey the information you wish to put across in a simple but systematic way.
- Do not include too much information on any one slide and ensure that you have sufficient time to comment on the content of each slide.
- Summarize the main findings without including too much technical detail.
- Leave time for questions at the end of your presentation but also invite participants to ask questions throughout.

A useful set of tips for presenting research at conferences, by Brian Campbell, can be found at the following Ex Ordo site: www.exordo.com/blog/presenting-at-a-conference

CONCLUSION

The final report of a research project conveys to its audience the findings and interpretations of them by the researcher. It is important for researchers to ensure the report is of a high standard and reflects the quality of the research undertaken, since this will have an impact on the reputation of the researcher.

CHAPTER SUMMARY

Communication of research findings can be via a presentation to an audience, a written report or both. Almost all research findings end up in a written report, the nature of which will depend on whether the research is:

- commissioned by an organization
- a scholarly project conducted within a higher education institution or research centre
- a thesis to be submitted for a higher degree.

The format of the report will also differ according to whether the research is quantitative, qualitative or mixed methods. Guidelines for each format have been included in this chapter.

Reporting mixed-methods findings has the added complexity of knowing how to integrate the qualitative and quantitative findings. This can be done separately with the interpretations integrated in the discussion, or the quantitative and qualitative findings can be integrated in the analysis either within themes derived from the research questions or by converting one form of data into the other and analysing them together.

Finally, some problems in writing up research and communicating them were identified and discussed.

FURTHER READING

Bryman, A. (2015) *Social Research Methods*, 5th edition. Oxford: Oxford University Press.
Chapter 28 provides some useful advice on writing research reports.

Henry, G. T. (1998) Graphing data. In L. Bickman and D. Rog (eds), *Handbook of Applied Social Research*. Thousand Oaks, CA: Sage Publications.
A good resource for displaying quantitative data.

Plano Clark, V. L. and Creswell, J. W. (eds) (2008) *The Mixed Methods Reader*. Thousand Oaks, CA: Sage Publications.
Part II contains a number of mixed-methods reports chosen to illustrate the variety of mixed-methods designs.

Richardson, L. (2003) Writing: A method of inquiry. In N. K. Denzin and Y. S. Lincoln (eds), *Collecting and Interpreting Qualitative Materials*, 2nd edition. Thousand Oaks, CA: Sage Publications.
A thought-provoking chapter on writing qualitative research.

18

TURNING RESEARCH RESULTS INTO PRACTICE

INTRODUCTION

Research findings can vary from purely basic research with little or no practical relevance to those that have quite specific implications for action. The latter is more likely to be characteristic of applied research, although basic research may have practical implications.

Where research does have implications for practice, the question remains as to how effectively these findings are implemented. The answer to this question appears to be not very well. There is a growing literature on underutilization of research and the reasons for it.

This final chapter will examine the utilization of social research and consider the role of the researcher in determining how, if at all, the findings of the research are implemented.

RESEARCH UTILIZATION

Research utilization refers to the implementation of research findings to improve policy or practice in human services. Research can be used in a variety of ways, as described in Table 18.1. Not all of these uses are legitimate since research findings can be misused as well as used constructively.

Table 18.1 Types of research utilization

Type of use	Description	Example
Instrumental use	Research findings are used to influence a policy or practice	A pill testing programme is introduced in concerts following evidence that pill testing reduces the harm caused by pills containing dangerous substances

(Continued)

Table 18.1 (Continued)

Type of use	Description	Example
Tactical use	Research findings are marshalled selectively by policy makers to justify a decision already made	A government minister cuts funding to a school programme and calls on the relevant department to find evidence that the programme isn't working
Conceptual use	Research influences how policy makers approach issues and problems	A government committee commissions research to find out how well a mental health programme is working
Process use	Being involved in research influences how practitioners understand how research is produced	Mental health workers consulted over research on programme delivery become more supportive of research

Tactical use is an example of a misuse of research findings in that it only includes research findings that support an action or policy, and ignores findings that don't support it.

The importance of such utilization of research stems from the focus, among decision makers in a wide range of fields, on **evidence-based practice** (EBP). This developed from the field of medicine in the 1980s when it was proposed that clinical decisions should be made on the basis of the best research evidence available (Rosenberg and Donald, 1995). The idea was extended to a wide range of fields beyond the health professions. The main characteristics of EBP are set out in Box 18.1.

━━━━━━━━ BOX 18.1 ━━━━━━━━

CHARACTERISTICS OF EVIDENCE-BASED PRACTICE (EBP)

Evidence-based practice (EBP) is a process in which decision making is based on the best available evidence derived from research findings. Although originating in clinical practice, it has been extended to fields beyond medicine, including allied health professions, education, psychology, social work and many others. The way in which EBP is implemented may differ in areas of application, but the following steps are common to most:

1. Locate the best available evidence relevant to the decision to be made. If the decision is to set up a rehabilitation programme, then evidence may come from the evaluation of similar programmes.
2. Appraise the evidence to ensure quality and relevance to the decision.
3. Implement the evidence in making the decision; for example, ensure that evaluation outcomes are incorporated into the rehabilitation programme.
4. Evaluate the outcome of the decision, such as in the case of a rehabilitation commission and evaluation of its implementation.

The extent to which such implementation of research actually takes place has been a matter for debate as both researchers and practitioners have identified what they call an 'implementation gap', namely the gap between the production of research relevant to policy or practice and the uptake of that research in improving them. Booth (1988) refers to this gap as underutilization of research.

Booth identified the following reasons for why research is underutilized:

1. The 'two communities' hypothesis: policy makers and social scientists live in different 'assumptive worlds' due to differences in reward systems, values, professional affiliations and other characteristics, making communication between them difficult.
2. Policy-maker-specific practices: policy makers need to negotiate with stakeholders when making decisions and are required to balance different demands and competing interests. This can conflict with the expectations of social scientists, who operate in a different environment.
3. Knowledge-specific research practice: social scientists are concerned with research quality, which may not coincide with the relevance demanded by policy makers.
4. Disenchantment: policy makers become disenchanted with the social scientific focus on academic standards to the neglect of relevance to practice.

An example of a combination of these problems, leading to underutilization of research, is described in Box 18.2.

The role of EBP is to overcome these limitations to research utilization in practice by bringing together researchers and practitioners to identify the best available compromises to produce and implement research in practice.

━━━━━━━━━ BOX 18.2 ━━━━━━━━━

AN EXAMPLE OF UNDERUTILIZATION OF RESEARCH

In 1994, the Australian Government was considering what restrictions, if any, should be imposed on the content of pay TV when it was made available to viewers. The Senate (the parliamentary upper house in Australia) established a Select Committee to report to parliament on this issue, particularly on whether R-rated material (Restricted) should be available on pay TV. The Senate Committee commissioned the Australian Broadcasting Authority (ABA) to conduct research to ascertain public opinion on whether R-rated material should be available. The questionnaire to be distributed to participants was reviewed by the Senate Committee, which requested changes to the question asking whether participants approved the availability of R-rated material on pay TV. The Committee wanted extreme examples of such material included in the question. The ABA refused to accommodate the concerns of the Committee, claiming that it jeopardized the academic integrity of the research. The findings of the research reported widespread support

(Continued)

for the availability of such material (Australian Broadcasting Authority, 1994), but the Senate Committee discounted the research and relied instead on submissions made by special interest groups opposed to the inclusion of R-rated material (Senate Select Committee on Community Standards Relevant to the Supply of Services Utilising Electronic Technology, 1995). The Senate Committee clearly wanted to bias the survey to maximize the achievement of a negative response to support its preconceived view about the issue. It was not about to let research findings get in the way of this view.

ROLE OF THE RESEARCHER IN IMPLEMENTING FINDINGS

Two extreme views are held on the involvement of the researcher. At one extreme, it is claimed that the researcher has no responsibility or involvement in how the research is used once it is published. According to this view, how research is used should be left up to the experts in implementing research findings. The expertise of the researcher is in conducting research, not in implementing it.

At the other extreme, action researchers maintain that research should be aimed at improving society and that it is the responsibility of the researcher not only to conduct research that is focused on social change, but also to follow up on seeing that the change implied by the research actually takes place. The characteristics of action research are described in Box 18.3.

■■■■ BOX 18.3 ■■■■

CHARACTERISTICS OF ACTION RESEARCH

Action research is research conducted with the aim of bringing about change to improve some aspect of social conditions. It is both participative and collaborative – participative in the sense that stakeholders are involved in all stages of the research, and collaborative in that participants are invited to contribute to the design and implementation of the study. Reflection on the outcomes is a key ingredient of action research in considering the impact of the research and working out ways to improve the outcome.

Action research is seen to be cyclic, with continuing improvement the aim. The cycle would look much like that shown in Figure 18.1.

A closely related version of action research is termed *participatory action research* (PAR). In this approach, there is a greater focus on participation by a range of stakeholders in the research. Kemmis and McTaggart (2003) identified seven key features of PAR, summarized as follows.

Participatory action research is:

1.   A social process insofar as it explores the relationship between the individual and the social.
2.   Participatory, in that it engages participants to examine and critically appraise their knowledge and how it constrains their action.

3. Practical and collaborative, in that it engages people in exploring how to improve their inter-actions by changing them.
4. Emancipatory, by helping people release themselves from the constraints imposed by social structures.
5. Critical of alienating discourses, modes of work and social relationships of power.
6. Recursive, by helping people change their practices through critical action and reflection.
7. Aimed at transforming both theory and practice through critical reasoning about their consequences.

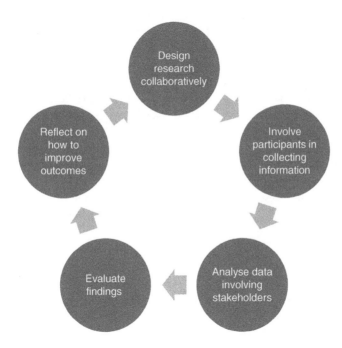

Figure 18.1   A portrayal of the action research cycle

There are, of course, positions between these two extremes. Researchers can, of course, nego-tiate with stakeholders and involve participants in research without being action researchers.

CONCLUSION

Researchers need to be clear about where they stand on the research utilization spectrum, since this will have an impact on their research project. If they take a position that their research should be aimed at improving some aspect of society, they will need to involve those stakeholders with influence to make the changes. This is the focus of participatory action research in which partici-pants are involved collaboratively with researchers throughout the research process.

Researchers are, of course, not obliged to concern themselves with how their research findings will be used. This position is typical of researchers who are concerned only with expanding knowledge in a field, or of many students undertaking a research project for a higher degree. Although for such researchers the contents of this chapter are not directly relevant, it is always possible that implementation issues may arise from any research findings so that some familiarity with research utilization issues can turn out to be important.

CHAPTER SUMMARY

Research utilization is the implementation of research findings to policy or practice. The emphasis among policy makers on evidence-based practice has intensified concern with the research use issue.

There is a variety of ways in which research can be used. These are described in Table 18.1 and include examples of effective use as well as misuse of research findings.

A focus on research use has been influenced by the evidence-based practice (EBP) development, where decision makers have insisted that policy and practice be based on the best available evidence derived from research.

Despite the emergence of EBP, there are still many examples of underutilization for reasons set out by Booth (1988), outlined above. Overcoming underutilization requires strong relationships to be formed between researchers and practitioners. One way of doing this is through the application of action research, which involves participants in all aspects of the research process and aims to improve outcomes for these participants as well as for society in general.

FURTHER READING

Kemmis, S. and McTaggart, R. (2003) Participatory action research. In N. K. Denzin and Y. S. Lincoln (eds), *Strategies of Qualitative Inquiry*. Thousand Oaks, CA: Sage Publications.
A thorough account of participatory action research; contains a very useful analysis of the notion of practice.

Nutley, S., Walter, I. and Davies, H. T. O. (2007) *Using Evidence: How Research Can Inform Public Service*. Bristol: Policy Press.
A comprehensive analysis of research utilization.

Reason, P. and Bradbury, H. (2008) *The SAGE Handbook of Action Research: Participative Inquiry and Practice*, 2nd edition. London: Sage Publications.
A handbook containing many useful chapters on action research.

Tseng, V. (2012) The uses of research in policy and practice. *Social Policy Report*, 26 (2), 1–16.
A good summary of research utilization issues.

GLOSSARY

Abductive inference   This is a form of inference in which an explanation of a set of observations is proposed on the grounds that it is the best explanation available. It is sometimes referred to as inference to the best explanation. Abductive inference was developed by the philosopher Charles Peirce in the late 19th century.

Action research   Action research is research conducted with the aim of bringing about change to improve some aspect of social conditions. It is both participative and collaborative: participative in the sense that stakeholders are involved in all stages of the research; and collaborative in that participants are invited to contribute to the design and implementation of the study. Reflection on the outcomes is a key ingredient of action research in considering the impact of the research and working out ways to improve the outcome.

Analysis of variance   This is an inferential statistical technique for testing for differences among means of any number of groups where the dependent variable is measured on an interval or a ratio scale. The method only tests whether all the group means in the population are equal. If the test leads to the rejection of this hypothesis, the researcher can conclude that there are differences but not state where those differences lie.

Applied research   This is research conducted to address specific issues or problems considered to be of practical significance. The focus of applied research is on problem solving rather than on expanding the knowledge base in a particular field.

Basic research   This is research conducted with the aim of extending knowledge in the field in which the research is conducted. It is curiosity driven, whereby researchers seek to fill gaps in knowledge as revealed in existing research.

Case study method   A case study is a research method that investigates a situation as it occurs in its real-life context. It can involve directly observing events as they occur, interviewing people or groups involved in the event, or obtaining secondary data describing the event.

Causality   A causal connection is one in which one event (the cause) brings about the occurrence of another event (the effect). For example, high blood alcohol level in drivers can be seen as a cause of motor vehicle accidents (although not the only cause). There are three requirements for establishing causality. For an event to be a cause of another, the following requirements must be met:

1. The two events must occur together (constant conjunction).
2. The cause must occur prior in time to the effect.
3. Other possible causes must be ruled out.

Chi-square test (of association) The chi-square test is a statistical inference procedure used to test for association between two variables when they are measured on ordinal or nominal scales.

Coding strategies Coding strategies are methods used to construct codes to analyse qualitative data. Three strategies have been identified:

1. Open coding: a strategy for constructing codes in the analysis of qualitative data where codes are generated from the data.
2. Axial coding: a strategy for constructing codes in the analysis of qualitative data which involves establishing relationships among codes formed during the open coding process. It identifies what open codes have in common and links them together by setting up higher level codes.
3. Selective coding: this is the final stage of coding where codes are integrated into a theoretical framework aimed at providing an explanatory framework for the coding scheme.

Complex causation Complex causation is characterized by multiple causes determining an effect as distinct from single cause–effect relationships. Such causes may operate as either–or causes or as conjunctural causes where the simultaneous occurrence of two or more causes produces the effect. A situation in which both either–or and conjunctural causation operates is referred to as multiple conjunctural causation. In this case, two or more different combinations of conditions may produce the same effect.

Conceptual framework The conceptual framework for a research project is the set of concepts used in the research project, including their definitions and type. It also includes the paradigm within which the researcher is operating, although this is not always made explicit.

Conflict theory Conflict theory sees social structures as products of conflict between social classes where the conflict arises from economic inequalities between these classes. It is seen to originate in the work of Karl Marx but has been developed by later theorists such as C. Wright Mills.

Constructivism Constructivism is a paradigm in which reality is seen to be socially constructed. It is adopted by some qualitative researchers who see social constructions as the subject matter of social science.

Content analysis Content analysis is a method of classifying qualitative data by classifying text into categories, where the categories are usually predetermined. It has been applied to the analysis of media stereotypes, such as the portrayal of gender in magazines, newspapers, television and films.

Conversation analysis Conversation analysis focuses on human interaction as it occurs naturally through talk. It involves a detailed analysis of conversations to provide an account of what happens in social interactions. It is based on the assumption that conversation is central to human interaction and is the primary means by which we relate to one another.

Correlation coefficient   A correlation coefficient is a measure of association between two variables. Where the variables are measured on interval/ratio scales, the measure of association used is normally the *Pearson product moment correlation*. For other measures, *Spearman's rho* can be used.

Critical realism   Critical realism is a paradigm that shares many features with post-positivism, in particular the existence of an external reality which can be accessed by the use of scientific method. It was formulated by the philosopher Roy Bhaskar in the 1970s and then termed transcendental realism. It differs from post-positivism in that it postulates unobservable events that can act as causes of observable ones.

Cross-sectional survey   This is a survey that is administered at a single point in time. A cross-sectional survey is usually designed to compare subsets of the population, such as males and females, on opinions or practices, such as alcohol consumption.

Deductive inference   Deductive inference involves using logical principles to draw conclusions from a set of premises. If the premises are true, and the logical principles are followed, the conclusion is necessarily true. This form of inference is used in deriving predictions from a theory rather than drawing inferences from research findings.

Dependent variable   A dependent variable is one which the researcher is seeking to explain or understand. It is seen as a consequence of the independent variables, such as performance on a simulated driving test where the independent variables might be number of hours of sleep deprivation (manipulated by the researcher) and age and gender of the participant (background variables).

Discourse analysis   Discourse analysis is an approach to the analysis of text that situates the text within the context in which it was produced. It seeks to interpret the text by examining the assumptions underlying its production. These assumptions are often hidden and require a critical analysis of the ways in which meaning is constructed by the linguistic formations that give rise to them. Social realities are seen as being constructed by language in the form of discourses.

Ethnographic writing   Three approaches to the writing of ethnographic reports are:

1. Realist tales: in this approach, the report is written in the third person and the researcher is absent from the content.
2. Confessional tales: here the account incorporates the experiences of the researcher and is written from the viewpoint of the researcher
3. Impressionist tales: these are designed to achieve dramatic effect by being written as a story to convey the experience of the researcher.

Ethnography   Ethnography is a research method involving the study of social groups or cultures through collecting information about the group or culture over time, both by direct observation and interviews with members.

Evidence-based practice (EBP) Evidence-based practice (EBP) is the process in which decision-making is based on the best available evidence derived from research findings. Although originating in clinical practice, it has been extended to fields beyond medicine, including allied health professions, education, psychology, social work and many others.

External validity External validity refers to the extent to which findings from a research study can be generalized to other populations or settings.

Feminist theory Feminist theory focuses on gender inequalities in societies where women have experienced discrimination in social, political and economic spheres. As a theoretical framework, feminist social theory was developed in the late 1960s by writers Shulamith Firestone, Betty Friedan and others.

Field study A field study is a data collection procedure involving observations of people or groups engaged in their normal everyday activities. Field studies often form part of the data collection in a case study.

Focus group interview A focus group interview is a form of group interview in which the interviewer, often referred to as the facilitator, directs questions to the group on a specific topic. Members of the group are usually chosen because of their involvement with the topic being discussed.

Historical-comparative research Historical-comparative research examines society and culture either within nations or across nations and either at a single point in time or across different time periods.

Independent variable An independent variable is one which is either manipulated by the researcher such as time spent awake in a sleep deprivation study, or a background variable, such as the age of participants, which is seen to be relevant to the research outcomes.

Index An index combines a number of distinct measures of a concept into a single score. Indexes are usually constructed from secondary data such as country statistical information. An example of an index is the Human Development Index (HDI), which combines life expectancy at birth, education level and income of a country to provide a measure of well-being in a country.

Individualistic explanation An individualistic explanation of a social phenomenon locates the explanation within the motives, values or intentions of individuals. Proponents of this approach argue that all social processes can be explained by recourse to individual actions and that there is no need to invoke higher-level structures in the explanation.

Inductive inference Inductive inference involves generalizing from a set of specific cases to a general principle. If the specific cases all exhibit a particular characteristic, then it can be inductively inferred that all cases of this kind will exhibit this characteristic. Such an inference is not necessarily true since it is always possible to find cases that do not exhibit the characteristic.

Inferential statistics   Inferential statistics are the procedures used to generalize from a sample to a population. For these procedures to be applicable, samples need to be randomly chosen from a population. The logic of inferential statistics is that it enables a generalization to be made to a population with a known level of confidence.

Internal validity   Internal validity refers to the extent to which a research study enables cause–effect relationships to be established from the findings of the study.

Interpretive rigour   Interpretive rigour refers to the extent to which interpretations made on the basis of research findings are credible.

Interpretive understanding   Interpretive understanding as a goal of theorizing is supported by those who claim that explanation is not appropriate for the social sciences. Instead, social research should be aimed at gaining an understanding of the meaning people attribute to their social experience. What is now called interpretive sociology was developed in the early 20th century by the German sociologists Max Weber and George Simmel. It was a reaction against positivism, which was seen by interpretive theorists as neglecting the real subject matter of social science, namely, the ways in which people make sense of their situations by attributing meaning to them.

Interpretivism   Interpretivism is a paradigm which focuses on the meaning and understanding of social reality as experienced by individuals. It is based on the premise that there is no single external reality but rather multiple realities that are constructed by individuals as they interact with their environment. The goal of social research is to uncover these realities.

Intervening variable   An intervening variable is one that mediates in some way the relationship between the independent and dependent variables. Intervening variables can be either **mediator** or **moderator** variables. A mediator variable is one that is affected by the independent variable and in turn affects the dependent variable. A moderator variable is one that affects the strength of the relationship between the independent and the dependent variables.

Kruskal-Wallis test   The Kruskal-Wallis test is a non-parametric method that tests whether two or more independent samples originate from the same distribution. It is used when requirements for the use of analysis of variance are not satisfied.

Likert scales   This technique for constructing a scale from multiple items was originally developed by Rensis Likert in 1932 and has survived to still be widely used in developing attitude scales. Items are chosen to represent levels of agreement and are rated on a scale from strongly agree to strongly disagree. Scores are assigned to each category and a total score is obtained by adding the score on each item in the scale. Items that discriminate between high and low scorers on the scale are retained in the final version and items that don't discriminate are deleted, leaving a scale consisting of items that are considered to measure the attitude well.

Longitudinal survey   This is a survey that is administered at more than one point in time. Longitudinal surveys are designed to track changes in attitude or behaviour over time.

Macro-level theory   Macro-level theory is at a high level of abstraction encompassing whole societies, social institutions or sectors of society, or historical periods. Researchers may generate their research topics from such theories but the concepts are too general to guide researchers in formulating specific research projects. Some macro-level theories are structural functionalism, conflict theory and social positions theory.

Measurement scales   Measurement scales used in the social sciences are as follows:

i.   Nominal scale: a nominal scale is one in which the concept is divided into categories that are mutually exclusive and exhaustive, such as gender, marital status or nationality. Nominal scales are the weakest form of measurement.
ii. Ordinal scale: an ordinal scale is one in which an order relationship exists among the values assigned to the concept. Level of education is an example of an ordinal scale.
iii. Interval scale: in an interval scale, distance between levels of the measurement are preserved. The classic example of an interval scale is temperature, as measured by the Fahrenheit or Celsius scales. In an interval scale, there is no absolute zero.
iv. Ratio scale: a ratio scale is one that preserves intervals, as in an interval scale, but in addition has an absolute zero. Height and weight are examples of ratio scales. The only arbitrary component in a ratio scale is the unit of measurement, such as centimetres or inches.

Micro-level theory   Micro-level theory focuses on the more specific aspects of social life and uses concepts that can more directly relate to the research project. An example of a micro-level theory is *self-efficacy theory*, derived from Bandura's social cognitive theory.

Mid-range theory   Mid-range theory deals with social processes at a societal level. The concepts involved are less general than those of macro theory but are still quite removed from the specific situations that researchers study.

Multiple-item scale   A multiple-item scale combines a number of separate questions into a single scale. Examples in common use include Likert scales and Rasch scales.

Narrative analysis   Narrative analysis is a method for interpreting stories contributed by individuals in either written or oral forms. It seeks to situate the stories in the wider culture within which they are created and to identify the ideologies embedded in them. Approaches to narrative analysis include:

i.   The thematic approach: this approach focuses on the identification of plots and subplots in the stories and integrating them into themes.
ii. The structural approach: this approach focuses on the linguistic structure of the stories. It takes each clause and examines how it connects to the next and subsequent clauses so as to build a sequence that provides a cohesive unit that reveals the meaning of the narrative.
iii. The dialogical/performative approach: this approach focuses on the larger questions that situate the story or stories being told in their context. The approach seeks to answer questions such as what is being accomplished by the story and why is it being told.

Non-parametric methods   These are inferential statistical methods used to test for differences among groups when analysis of variance is not applicable.

Non-probability sampling   Non-probability sampling refers to a variety of methods where sampled elements are chosen in a non-random manner, usually based on criteria set by the researcher. Such sampling procedures do not use random procedures for choosing sample elements, so that no generalization to a population is warranted. Methods of non-probability sampling include:

i.   Purposive sampling: purposive sampling involves choosing sample elements on the basis of their relevance to the research questions. These elements may be research sites in a multiple case study or particular individuals to be interviewed. The basis of choice is how well the sampled unit is likely to provide information that answers the research questions.

ii.   Theoretical sampling: theoretical sampling involves choosing sampling units that can be used to test a theory. In this form of sampling, the researcher derives predictions from a theory and then chooses a sample unit that satisfies the conditions for a test of the theory.

iii.   Convenience sampling: a convenience sample is one chosen by a researcher because of its ready accessibility. Convenience sampling involves including sample elements available to the researcher, either due to their being located in the proximity of the researcher or their being easily contacted, such as through Facebook.

iv.   Snowball sampling: a snowball sample is one where subsequent sampled elements depend on previously chosen elements, often through a referral process. The analogy is to a snowball gathering more snow and getting larger as it rolls downhill. Snowball sampling is used when participants are difficult to find because of the particular characteristics they possess that are either rare or hidden in a population.

Observational protocol   An observational protocol is a guide to observers, detailing what it is they should be observing and how to record their observations. It is used in field research where researchers observe events as they occur in 'real world' situations.

Paradigm   A paradigm is a broad concept about the nature of research and its philosophical underpinnings. In the social sciences, a paradigm has been defined variously as a world view, as an epistemological stance, as shared beliefs among a community of researchers and as a model example of quality research.

Parallel mixed-methods designs   These are mixed-methods designs in which the qualitative and quantitative methods are implemented concurrently. Variants of this design are:

i.   Convergent parallel design: in this design, the qualitative and quantitative methods are of equal status and are implemented independently, with integration occurring at the interpretation phase of the research.

ii.   Embedded parallel design: in this design, one method (e.g. the qualitative) is embedded in the other (e.g. the quantitative). Usually, the embedded component plays a minor role in the design.

Participant observation   This is a method of collecting information about the activities of groups or cultures where the researcher becomes a member of the group. The researcher may or may not reveal their research role. In the former case, the researcher is referred to as a *complete participant*, and referred to in the latter case as a *participant observer.*

Positivism   Positivism is a paradigm in which the aim of research is seen to involve objective, value-free observations of an external reality, in accordance with scientific method with a view to establishing cause–effect relationships.

Post-hoc comparison   This is an inferential statistical technique used when an analysis of variance leads to a rejection of the null hypothesis that all group means are not equal. A post-hoc test such as the Scheffe technique is used to locate the differences among the means.

Post-positivism   Post-positivism is a paradigm in which the aim of research is to attain both explanation and understanding of social reality through research employing a wide range of methods. It is a reformulation of positivism to modify the requirements of objectivity and value freedom to recognize the influence of values and subjectivity in observations.

Post-structuralism   Post-structuralism was a reaction against what was perceived to be a deterministic approach of structuralism. Social processes cannot be understood by locating them in a larger system but are better seen in relation to the discourses that construct knowledge about these processes. The development of post-structuralism is usually attributed to the work of Michel Foucault.

Primary and secondary sources   A *primary source* is a first-hand account of an event or situation as it occurred, whereas a *secondary source* is an analysis or reconstruction of that situation. Primary sources include diaries, autobiographies, legislation, government publications and original documents such as birth or death certificates. *Secondary sources* include newspaper reports of events, books reporting on events, and biographies. Both types of source are, however, secondary data in that they have been produced by others and not by the researcher.

Probability sampling   Probability sampling is a method where all members of a defined population have a known probability of selection in the sample. In most cases, the sampling is conducted using a random procedure. Probability sampling methods include the following:

i.   Simple random sampling: a simple random sample is one in which all members of the population from which the sample is chosen have a known, usually equal, probability of selection. This requires all elements of the population to be identified in some way so that they can be eligible for choice in a sample.
ii.   Cluster sampling: in cluster sampling, the population is divided into clusters. Such clusters are convenient ways of subdividing the population for easier access. Samples are chosen randomly from within the clusters.
iii.   Systematic sampling: a variation on simple random sampling is systematic sampling where one element of the population is chosen at random and then every kth member, where k is a whole number, is chosen thereafter until the sample size is reached. For this

to be achieved, the population needs to be ordered in some way. The number *k* is referred to as the sampling fraction.

Qualitative comparison analysis (QCA) Qualitative comparison analysis is an approach to the analysis of qualitative data in which data consists of events in which outcomes can be determined and the analysis consists of identifying conditions relevant to the explanation of the outcome. The aim of QCA is to establish a set of conditions that can provide a causal explanation of the outcome.

Qualitizing Qualitizing refers to the process of converting quantitative into qualitative data. This is done in order to identify categories from the quantitative data to facilitate analysis of the qualitative data within those categories.

Quantitizing Quantitizing refers to the process of converting qualitative into quantitative data. This is done to facilitate comparisons of the quantitative and qualitative data by converting them into a common format. To do this, qualitative data is coded and the codes converted into numerical scales.

Quasi-experiment This is an experimental method that shares all the conditions of the randomized control trial except that of random allocation. Quasi-experiments are conducted when randomization is not possible or is impractical. In a case control design, the groups are matched on some factor or factors, such as age, thought to be capable of influencing outcomes.

Randomized control trial This is an experimental method in which participants are assigned randomly to one or more treatment conditions or to a control condition. The treatment conditions are those in which participants receive some form of intervention such as a programme or other treatment, whereas the control group receives no, or the existing, treatment. The effects of the intervention are ascertained by comparing the experimental or treatment conditions with the control condition.

Rasch scales This technique was introduced by Rasch in 1960 in which he proposed a model for measuring both items and individuals on the one measurement scale. The technique is widely used in educational measurement.

Regression analysis Regression analysis is a statistical inference procedure used to predict a dependent variable from two or more independent variables, where all variables are normally measured on interval/ratio scales.

Reliability of measures Measurements need to meet the criteria of reliability and validity to be useful in research. There are several notions of both reliability and validity that apply to the measurement of social concepts:

i. Stability: stability refers to the extent to which the measure does not change over time. It is measured by the *test–retest method*. This involves taking the measure at two time periods and calculating the correlation between the two measures. A high correlation means that the test–retest reliability is high.

ii. Equivalence: equivalence refers to the extent to which the measure yields similar results to alternative measures of the same concept. It is also used to refer to the extent to which multiple items in a scale correlate with one another. For a multiple-item scale to measure a single concept such as an attitude, items need to correlate highly with one another and with the total score on the scale. The measure of equivalence used in such cases is Cronbach's alpha.

Research question   Research questions are those formulated by the researcher that the research project aims to answer. They are the main focus of the research. Research questions should be distinguished from aims and hypotheses. Aims are the broad statements of the purpose of the research and are more general than research questions, while hypotheses are more specific predictions about the outcomes of research.

Research utilization   Research utilization refers to the implementation of research findings to improve policy or practice in human services. It can take the following forms:

1. Instrumental use: research findings are used to influence a policy or practice.
2. Tactical use: research findings are marshalled selectively by policy makers to justify a decision already made.
3. Conceptual use: research influences how policy makers approach issues and problems.
4. Process use: being involved in research influences how practitioners understand how research is produced.

Sampling frame   A sampling frame is the list of all possible participants eligible to be included in a research project, referred to as the population. The sampling frame includes all elements of the population and identifies the means for accessing them.

Secondary data   Secondary data is data that exists prior to the research being undertaken. It can be data from previous studies, data collected by government agencies such as statistical information, or information held by organizations such as employment records, meeting records, and so on. It can either be publicly available, as is the case for most government agency data, or private, being owned by individuals or organizations. It can also be either quantitative, such as government statistical data, or qualitative, such as minutes of meetings or diary entries.

Semi-structured interview   Semi-structured interviews include predetermined questions, as in structured interviews, but permit the interviewer to ask follow-up questions on some topics for which additional information is considered necessary.

Sequential mixed-methods designs   These are designs in which the qualitative and quantitative methods are implemented sequentially in time. Variants of this design are as follows:

1. The elaboration sequential design: in this design, the quantitative method precedes the qualitative method. Usually, the qualitative method is designed to follow up on some of the findings in the quantitative method to provide further understanding or explanation.
2. The developmental sequential design: in this design, the qualitative method precedes the quantitative method. Usually, the quantitative method is designed to examine the generalizability of the findings of the qualitative method or to develop concepts identified in the qualitative stage.

3. The iterative sequential design: in this design, more than two methods are implemented sequentially with subsequent methods designed to explore findings in preceding methods.

Single-item scale   A single-item scale is one constructed from a rating scale or a single question providing a range of options from one extreme to the other. An example is a rating of job satisfaction.

Social desirability bias   Social desirability bias refers to a tendency for people to present a more socially desirable image of themselves to the researcher, rather than report their actual beliefs or behaviours.

Social positions theory   Blau (1977) sees social structure as a multidimensional space of social positions in which individuals are located and these positions are instrumental in determining social relations. Structural parameters such as age, race, education and socioeconomic status are the axes in the space that underlie the distinctions individuals make in their social relations.

Statistical conclusion validity   Statistical conclusion validity refers to the extent to which statistical inference procedures used in a study are adequate to detect relationships or differences among variables measured in the study.

Strategic research   Research conducted to expand knowledge in areas considered to be of national significance. It tends to be focused on policy areas considered to be important by governments such as health and education.

Structural explanation   A structural explanation is one in which an event is located within a larger system which imposes constraints on its occurrence. These constraints set limits on what actions are possible in a particular situation.

Structural functionalism   Functionalism sees society as being composed of a system of interrelated components which work together to bring about stability. These components satisfy the needs of the system as a whole and act to shape society. Functionalism as a theoretical methodology was developed by social theorists such as Emile Durkheim, Robert Merton and Talcott Parsons, among many others, in the early part of the 20th century.

Structuralism   Structuralism refers to the view that social processes can only be understood by their relation to overarching social systems or structures. This view was prominent in anthropology due to the work of Claude Lévi-Strauss, of Jacques Lacan in psychoanalytic theory and of Louis Althusser in social science.

Structured interview   A structured interview is one in which the questions to be asked of the interviewee are predetermined, with little scope for variation by the interviewer. Structured interviews are frequently used in case studies where the researcher usually has a clear idea of what questions need to be asked.

Survey method   A survey is a research method designed to collect information from a sample of individuals or groups, usually selected randomly from a defined population. The information collected is often attitudes, opinions, practices, knowledge or other matters, with a view to generalizing findings to the population from which the sample was drawn.

Symbolic interactionism   Symbolic interactionism is a framework that focuses on how individuals construct meaning through their communications with others. It is attributed to George Herbert Mead, but was developed by Herbert Blumer after Mead's death in 1931.

Theoretical framework   The theoretical framework is the connections that are proposed to exist among the concepts used in the study. It provides a framework for specific theories that share concepts and theoretical mechanisms. A theory is a specific version of a theoretical framework.

Triangulation   Triangulation is the use of multiple research methods to provide a more comprehensive understanding and/or explanation of the phenomenon being investigated than could be obtained by use of a single method. It is widely used as a justification for the use of mixed methods.

Unstructured interview   Unstructured interviews are those in which a general topic is specified but the questioning is left to the discretion of the interviewer. In such cases, the interview schedule would consist of an outline of the information needed from the interview and some suggested lines of questioning but would not include specific questions.

Validity of measures   Validity of measures refers to the extent to which measures actually measure what they are purported to measure. There are a number of alternative meanings of measurement validity:

Face validity: face validity refers to the judgement by users of the measure that it is a valid measure. That is, a measure has face validity if there is consensus among users that it is a valid measure of the concept. It is not a particularly useful notion of validity as there are many situations where wide agreement over a concept has turned out to be false.

Content validity: a measure has content validity if it includes all aspects of the concept being measured. For some concepts, areas in which the concept applies are not always obvious so that care needs to be taken in defining the concept to ensure such areas are included.

Construct validity: construct validity refers to the extent to which a measure of a concept does in fact measure the concept accurately. Construct validity is often inferred from a theory from which the concept is derived.

Criterion validity: a measure is said to have criterion validity if it correlates with a pre-existing criterion or predicts some future event regarded as a consequence of the concept being measured.

REFERENCES

Abend, G. (2008) The meaning of 'theory'. *Sociological Theory*, 26 (2), 176–199.

Ajzen, I. (1985) From intentions to actions: A theory of planned behavior. In J. Kuhl and J. Beckmann (eds), *Action Control: From Cognition to Behavior*. New York: Springer-Verlag.

Alireza, B. and Samuel, M. (2012) Headlines in newspaper editorials: A contrastive study. *International Research Journal of Social Sciences*, 1 (3), 1–7.

Allison, G. T. (1971) *Essence of Decision: Explaining the Cuban Missile Crisis*. Boston, MA: Little, Brown.

Anderton, D. L. and Cheney, E. (2004) Log-linear analysis. In M. Hardy and A. Bryman (eds), *Handbook of Data Analysis*. London: Sage Publications.

Angrosino, M. V. and de Perez, M. (2003) Rethinking observation. In N. K. Denzin and Y. S. Lincoln (eds), *Collecting and Interpreting Qualitative Materials*. Thousand Oaks, CA: Sage Publications.

Australian Broadcasting Authority (ABA) (1994) *R Classified Programs on Pay TV*. Canberra, ACT: Commonwealth of Australia.

Babbie, E. (2016) *The Practice of Social Research*, 14th edition. Boston, MA: Cengage Learning.

Bamberg, M. (2012) Narrative analysis. In H. Cooper, P. M. Camic, D. L. Long, A. T. Panter, D. Rindskopf and K. J. Sher (eds), *APA Handbook of Research Methods in Psychology, Vol. 2. Research designs: Quantitative, qualitative, neuropsychological, and biological*. Washington, DC: American Psychological Association.

Bales, R. (1950) *Interaction Process Analysis: A Method for the Analysis of Social Groups*. Cambridge, MA: Addison-Wesley.

Bandura, A. (2001) Social cognitive theory: An agentic perspective. *Annual Review of Psychology*, 52 (1), 1–26.

Bazeley, P. (2018) *Integrating Analyses in Mixed Methods Research*. London: Sage Publications.

Bazeley, P. and Jackson, K. (2013) *Qualitative Data Analysis with NVivo*. London: Sage Publications.

Beach, D. and Pedersen, R. B. (2013) *Process-tracing Methods: Foundations and Guidelines*. Ann Arbor, MI: University of Michigan Press.

Beach, D. and Pedersen, R. B. (2016) *Causal Case Studies: Comparing, Matching and Tracing*. Ann Arbor, MI: University of Michigan Press.

Berg-Schlosser, D., De Meur, G., Rihoux, B. and Ragin, C. (2009) Qualitative comparative analysis (QCA) as an approach. In B. Rihoux and C. Ragin (eds), *Configurational Comparative Methods: Qualitative Comparative Analysis (QCA) and Related Techniques*. Thousand Oaks, CA: Sage Publications.

Berkson, W. (1989) Testability in the social sciences. *Philosophy of Social Science*, 19, 157–171.

Bernardi, L., Keim, S. and von der Lippe, H. (2007) Social influence on fertility: A comparative mixed methods study in Eastern and Western Germany. *Journal of Mixed Methods Research*, 1 (1), 23–47.

Bhaskar, R. (1978) *A Realist Theory of Science*, 2nd edition. Brighton: Harvester Press.

Bickman, L. and Rog, D. (eds) (1998) *Handbook of Applied Social Research*. Thousand Oaks, CA: Sage Publications.

Biesta, G. (2010) Pragmatism and the philosophical foundations of mixed methods research. In A. Tashakkori and C. Teddlie (eds), *Handbook of Mixed Methods in Social and Behavioral Research*, 2nd edition. Thousand Oaks, CA: Sage Publications.

Blaikie, N. (2003) *Analyzing Quantitative Data*. London: Sage Publications.

Blair, E. (2015) A reflexive exploration of two qualitative data coding techniques. *Journal of Methods and Measurement in the Social Sciences*, 6 (1), 14–29.

Blau, P. (1977) A macrosociological theory of social structure. *The American Journal of Sociology*, 83 (1), 26–54.

Booth, T. (1988) *Developing Policy Research*. Avebury: Aldershot.

Braverman, M. (1996) Sources of survey error: Implications for evaluation studies. In M. T. Braverman and J. K. Slater (eds), *Advances in Survey Research: New Directions for Evaluation*, pp. 17–28.

Brazier, J., Roberts, J. and Deverill, M. (2002) The estimation of a preference-based measure of health from the SF-36. *Journal of Health Economics*, 21, 271–292.

Brinkerhoff, R. O. (2003) *The Success Case Method*. Oakland, CA: Berrett-Koehler Publishers.

Brownson, R. C., Brennan, L. K., Evenson, K. R. and Leviton, L. C. (2012) Lessons from a mixed-methods approach to evaluating active living by design. *American Journal of Preventive Medicine*, 43, 271–280.

Bryman, A. (2015) *Social Research Methods*, 5th edition. Oxford: Oxford University Press.

Bulmer, M. (ed.) (1978) *Social Policy Research*. London: Macmillan.

Bulmer, M. (1986) Types of research utilization: An overview. In M. Bulmer (ed.), *Social Science and Social Policy*. London: Allen & Unwin.

Bulmer, M. (ed.) (2003) *Questionnaires*. London: Sage Publications.

Bungum, T. J., Day, C. and Henry, L. J. (2005) The association of distraction and caution displayed by pedestrians at a lighted crosswalk. *Journal of Community Health*, 30, 269–279.

Burgess-Allen, J. and Owen-Smith, V. (2010) Using mind mapping in analysis of qualitative data. *Health Expectations*, 13, 406–415.

Campbell, D. T. and Stanley, J. C. (1963) Experimental and quasi-experimental designs for research on teaching. In N. L. Gage (ed.), *Handbook of Research on Teaching*. Chicago, IL: Rand McNally.

Campbell, D. T. and Stanley, J. C. (1966) *Experimental and Quasi-Experimental Design for Research*. Chicago, IL: Rand McNally.

Charmaz, C. (2006) *Constructing Grounded Theory: A Practical Guide through Qualitative Analysis*. London: Sage Publications.

Charon, J. M. (2010) *Symbolic Interactionism: An Introduction, an Interpretation, an Integration*, 10th edition. Boston, MA: Prentice-Hall.

Cohen, J. (1994) The earth is round (p < .05). *American Psychologist*, 49, 997–1003.

Converse, J. M. and Presser, S. (1986) *Survey Questions: Handcrafting the Standardized Questionnaire*. Thousand Oaks, CA: Sage Publications.

Cook, T. D. and Campbell, D. T. (1979) *Quasi-Experimentation: Design and Analysis Issues for Field Settings*. Boston, MA: Houghton Mifflin.

Cooper, H. (1998) *Synthesizing Research: A Guide for Literature Reviews*, 3rd edition. Thousand Oaks, CA: Sage Publications.

Corbin, J. and Strauss, A. (2015) *Basics of Qualitative Research: Techniques and Procedures for Developing Grounded Theory*, 4th edition. Thousand Oaks, CA: Sage Publications.

Creswell, J. W. and Plano Clark, V. L. (2011) *Designing and Conducting Mixed Methods Research*, 2nd edition. Thousand Oaks, CA: Sage Publications.

Creswell, J. W. and Plano Clark, V. L. (2007) *Designing and Conducting Mixed Methods Research*, 1st edition. Thousand Oaks, CA: Sage Publications.

Creswell, J. W., Fetters, M., Plano Clark, V. L. and Morales, A. (2009) Mixed methods intervention trials. In S. Andrew and E. Halcomb (eds), *Mixed Methods Research for Nursing and the Health Sciences*. Oxford: Blackwell.

Cummins, R. A. and Gullone, E. (2000) Why we should not use 5-point Likert scales: The case for subjective quality of life measurement. In *Proceedings of the Second International Conference on Quality of Life in Cities*. *Singapore*: National University of Singapore, pp. 74–93.

Cyr, J. (2017) The unique utility of focus groups for mixed methods research. *PS: Political Science and Politics*, 50 (4), 1038–1042.

Denzin, N. K. (2003a) The practices and politics of interpretation. In N. K. Denzin and Y. S. Lincoln (eds), *Collecting and Interpreting Qualitative Materials*, 2nd edition. Thousand Oaks, CA: Sage Publications.

Denzin, N. K. (2003b) *Performance Ethnography: Critical Pedagogy and the Politics of Culture*. Thousand Oaks, CA: Sage Publications.

Denzin, N. K. (2011) The politics of evidence. In N. K. Denzin and Y. S. Lincoln (eds), *The Sage Handbook of Qualitative Research*. London: Sage Publications.

deVaus, D. (2014) *Surveys in Social Research*, 6th edition. Sydney: Allen & Unwin.

Donaldson, S. (2001) Mediator and moderator analysis in program development. In S. Sussman (ed.), *Handbook of Program Development for Health Behavior Research and Practice*. Newbury Park, CA: Sage Publications.

Driscoll, D. L., Appiah-Yeboah, A., Salib, P. and Rupert, D. J. (2007) Merging qualitative and quantitative data in mixed methods research: How to and why not. *Ecological and Environmental Anthropology*, 3 (1), 19–28.

Erzberger, C. and Kelle, U. (2003) Making inferences in mixed methods: The rules of integration. In A. Tashakkori and C. Teddlie (eds), *Handbook of Mixed Methods in Social & Behavioral Research*. Thousand Oaks, CA: Sage Publications.

Esin, C., Fathi, M. and Squire, C. (2014) Narrative analysis: The constructionist approach. In U. Flick (ed.), *The Sage Handbook of Qualitative Data Analysis*. London: Sage Publications.

Fetters, M. D. (2016) 'Haven't we always been doing mixed methods research?': Lessons learned from the development of the horseless carriage. *Journal of Mixed Methods Research*, 10 (1), 3–11.

Fielding, N. G. (2003) *Interviewing*. London: Sage Publications.

Flick, U. (ed.) (2014) *The Sage Handbook of Qualitative Data Analysis*. London: Sage Publications.

Forrester, D., Copello, A., Waissbein, C. and Pokhrel, S. (2008) Evaluation of an intensive family preservation service for families affected by parental substance misuse. *Child Abuse Review*, 17, 410–426.

Foucault, M. (1970) *The Order of Things: An Archaeology of the Human Sciences*. London: Vintage Books.

Foucault, M. (1972) *The Archaeology of Knowledge*. London: Routledge.

Fowler, F. J. (1995) *Improving Survey Questions*. Thousand Oaks, CA: Sage Publications.

Gage, N. L. (1989) The paradigm wars and their aftermath: A 'historical' sketch of research on teaching since 1989. *Educational Researcher*, 4–10.

Galvan, J. L. (2017) *Writing Literature Reviews: A Guide for Students of the Social and Behavioral Sciences*, 7th edition. New York: Routledge.

Glaser, B. G. and Strauss, A. (1967) *Discovery of Grounded Theory: Strategies for Qualitative Research*. Mill Valley, CA: Sociology Press.

Golafshani, N. (2003) Understanding reliability and validity in qualitative research. *Qualitative Report*, 8(4), 597–606.

Gold, R. L. (1958) Roles in sociological fieldwork. *Social Forces*, 36, 217–223.

Greene, J. C. (2007) *Mixed Methods in Social Inquiry*. San Francisco, CA: Jossey-Bass.

Greene, J. C. and Hall, J. N. (2010) Dialectics and pragmatism. In A. Tashakkori and C. Teddlie (eds), *Handbook of Mixed Methods in Social and Behavioral Research*, 2nd edition. Thousand Oaks, CA: Sage Publications.

Greene, J. C., Caracelli, V. J. and Graham, W. F. (1989) Toward a conceptual framework for mixed-methods evaluation designs. *Educational Evaluation and Policy Analysis*, 11 (3), 255–274.

Guba, E. G. (1981) Criteria for assessing the trustworthiness of naturalistic inquiries. *Educational Communication and Technology Journal*, 29 (2), 75–91.

Guba, E. G. and Lincoln, Y. (1989) *Fourth Generation Evaluation*. Newbury Park, CA: Sage Publications.

Guetterman, T. C., Fetters, M. D. and Creswell, J. W. (2015) Integrating quantitative and qualitative results in health science mixed methods research through joint displays. *Annals of Family Medicine*, 13 (6), 554–561.

Hall, R. F. (1978) Student opinion of the General Studies programme at the University of New South Wales. *Vestes*, 21, 44–47.

Hall, R. (2004) Peer mentoring programs for first year undergraduate students. *Faculty Papers No. 2*. Faculty of Arts and Social Sciences, University of New South Wales.

Hall, R. (2007) Improving the peer mentoring experience through evaluation. *The Learning Assistance Review*, 12 (2), 7–18.

Hall, R. (2010) The work–study relationship: Experiences of full-time university students undertaking part-time work. *Journal of Education and Work*, 23 (5), 439–449.

Hall, R. (2013) Mixed-methods: In search of a paridigm. In T. Le and Q. Le (eds), *Conducting Research in a Changing and Challenging World*. New york: Nova Publishers.

Hammersley, M. (2008) Troubles with triangulation. In M. Bergman (ed.), *Advances in Mixed Methods Research: Theories and Applications*. Thousand Oaks, CA: Sage Publications.

Hammersley, M. (2011) *Methodology: Who Needs It?* London: Sage Publications.

Hammersley, M. and Atkinson, P. (2007) *Ethnography: Principles in Practice*, 3rd edition. London and New York: Routledge.

Hanson, N. R. (1958) *Patterns of Discovery: An Inquiry into the Conceptual Foundations of Science*. Cambridge: Cambridge University Press.

Hardy, M. and Bryman, A. (2004) *Handbook of Data Analysis*. London: Sage Publications.

Haslanger, S. (2016) What is a (social) structural explanation? *Philosophical Studies*, 173, 113–130.

Henry, G. T. (1998a) Graphing data. In L. Bickman and D. J. Rog (eds), *Handbook of Applied Social Research*. Thousand Oaks, CA: Sage Publications.

Henry, G. T. (1998b) Practical sampling. In L. Bickman and D. J. Rog (eds), *Handbook of Applied Social Research*. Thousand Oaks, CA: Sage Publications.

Hesse-Biber, S., Dupuis, P. and Kinder, S. (1990) HyperResearch: A computer program for the analysis of qualitative data using the Macintosh. *Qualitative Studies in Education*, 3 (2), 183–193.

Hickson, D. J., Butler, R. J., Cray, D., Mallory, G. R. and Wilson, D. C. (1986) *Top Decisions: Strategic Decision Making in Organisations*. New York: Basil Blackwell.

Howe, K. R. (1988) Against the quantitative–qualitative incompatibility thesis or dogmas die hard. *Educational Researcher*, 17 (8), 10–16.

Hughes, J. and Sharrock, W. (1997) *The Philosophy of Social Research*. Harlow: Longman.

Humphreys, L. (1970) *Tearoom Trade: Impersonal Sex in Public Places*. Chicago, IL: Aldine.

Imenda, S. (2014) Is there a conceptual difference between theoretical and conceptual frameworks? *Journal of Social Science*, 38 (2), 185–195.

Inglis, D., with Thorpe, C. (2012) *An Invitation to Social Theory*. Cambridge: Polity Press.

Ivankova, N. V. and Stick, S. L. (2007) Students' persistence in a distributed doctoral program in educational leadership in higher education: A mixed methods study. *Research in Higher Education*, 48 (1), 93–135.

Johnson, R. and Onwuegbuzie, A. (2004) Mixed methods research: A research paradigm whose time has come? *Educational Researcher*, 33, 14–26.

Kelle, U. (2015) Mixed methods and the problems of theory building and theory testing in the social sciences. In S. N. Hesse-Biber and R. Burke Johnson (eds), *The Oxford Handbook of Multimethod and Mixed Methods Research Inquiry*. Oxford: Oxford University Press.

Kemmis, S. and McTaggart, R. (2003) Participatory action research. In N. K. Denzin and Y. S. Lincoln (eds), *Strategies of Qualitative Inquiry*, 2nd edition. Thousand Oaks, CA: Sage Publications.

Kemper, E. A., Stringfield, S. and Teddlie, C. (2003) Mixed methods sampling strategies in social science research. In A. Tashakkori and C. Teddlie (eds), *Handbook of Mixed Methods in Social and Behavioral Research*. Thousand Oaks, CA: Sage Publications.

King, M. F. and Bruner, G. C. (2000) Social desirability bias: A neglected aspect of validity testing. *Psychology and Marketing*, 17 (2), 79–103.

Knorr-Cetina, K. D. (1981) Introduction: The micro-sociological challenges of macro-sociology – Towards a reconstruction of social theory and methodology. In K. Knorr-Cetina and A. V. Cicourel (eds), *Advances in Social Theory and Methodology: Toward an Integration of Micro- and Macro-Sociologies*. Boston, MA: Routledge & Kegan Paul.

Kraeger, D. A. (2008) Unnecessary roughness? School sports, peer networks and male adolescent violence. *American Sociological Review*, 72, 705–724.

Kuhn, T. (1970) *The Structure of Scientific Revolutions*, 2nd edition. Chicago: University of Chicago Press.

Lancaster, K., Ritter, A. and Matthew-Simmons, F. (2013) Young people's opinions on alcohol and other drug issues. ANCD research paper. Canberra, ACT: Australian National Council on Drugs.

Laney, D. (2001) *3D Data Management: Controlling data volume, velocity and variety*. Technical Report, META Group.

Laustsen, C. B., Larsen, L. T., Nielsn, M. W., Ravn, T. and Sorenson, M. P. (2017) *Social Theory: A Textbook*. Oxford: Routledge.

Lavrakas, P. (ed.) (2008) *Encyclopedia of Survey Research Methods*. London: Sage Publications.

Lee, J. P., Moore, R. S. and Martin, S. E. (2003) Unobtrusive observations of smoking in urban California bars. *Journal of Drug Issues*, 33, 983–999.

Leech, N. L. and Onwuegbuzie, A. J. (2009) A typology of mixed methods research designs. *Quality and Quantity*, 43, 265–275.

Li, S., Marquart, J. M. and Zercher, C. (2000) Conceptual issues and analytical strategies in mixed-method studies of preschool inclusion. *Journal of Early Intervention*, 23, 116–132.

Likert, R. (1932) A technique for the measurement of attitudes. *Archives of Psychology*, 22 (140), 55.

Lincoln, Y. S. and Guba, E. G. (1985) *Naturalistic Inquiry*. Beverly Hills, CA: Sage.

Lohr, S. (2013) The origins of 'Big Data': An etymological detective story. *The New York Times*, 1 February. Available at: https://bits.blogs.nytimes.com/2013/02/01/the-origins-of-big-data-an-etymological-detective-story (accessed 3 June 2019).

Low, S. M., Taplin, D. H and Lamb, M. (2005) Battery Park City: An ethnographic field study of the community impact of 9/11. *Urban Affairs Review*, 40 (5), 655–682.

Lynch, S. M. (2013) *Using Statistics in Social Research: A Concise Approach*. New York: Springer.

McDermott, M. (2006) *Working-class White*. Berkeley, CA: University of California Press.

McDonald, P. K., Thompson, P. M. and O'Connor, P. J. (2016) Profiling employees online: Shifting public–private boundaries in organisational life. *Human Resource Management Journal*, 26 (4), 541–556.

McEvoy, P. and Richards, D. (2006) A critical realist rationale for using a combination of quantitative and qualitative methods. *Journal of Research in Nursing*, 11 (1), 66–78.

McGill, M. (1997) Attraction and the Clients of Introduction Agencies. MA thesis, Macquarie University, North Ryde, NSW, Australia.

Madriz, E. (2003) Focus groups in feminist research. In N. K. Denzin and Y. S. Lincoln (eds), *Collecting and Interpreting Qualitative Materials*, 2nd edition. Thousand Oaks, CA: Sage Publications.

Malinowski, B. (1922) *Argonauts of the Western Pacific: An Account of Native Enterprise and Adventure in the Archipelagoes of Melanesian New Guinea*. London: Routledge & Kegan Paul.

Mark, M., Henry, G. and Julnes G. (2000) *Evaluation: An Integrated Framework for Understanding, Guiding and Improving Policies and Programs*. San Francisco, CA: Jossey-Bass.

Maxcy, S. J. (2003) Pragmatic threads in mixed methods research in the social sciences: The search for multiple modes of inquiry and the end of the philosophy of formalism. In A. Tashakkori and C. Teddlie (eds), *Handbook of Mixed Methods in Social and Behavioral Research*. Thousand Oaks, CA: Sage.

Maxwell, J. A. (2016) Expanding the history and range of mixed methods research. *Journal of Mixed Methods Research*, 10 (1), 12–27.

Maxwell, J. A. and Mittapalli, K. (2010) Realism as a stance for mixed methods research. In A. Tashakkori and C. Teddlie (eds), *Sage Handbook of Mixed Methods in Social and Behavioral Research*, 2nd edition. Thousand Oaks, CA: Sage Publications.

Mead, M. (1928) *Coming of Age in Samoa: A Psychological Study of Primitive Youth for Western Civilisation*. New York: William Morrow.

Mertens, D. M. (2003) Mixed methods and the politics of human research: The transformative–emancipatory perspective. In A. Tashakkori and C. Teddlie (eds), *Handbook of Mixed Methods in Social and Behavioral Research*. Thousand Oaks, CA: Sage Publications.

Mertens, D. M., Bledsoe, K. L., Sullivan, M. and Wilson, A. (2010) Utilization of mixed methods for transformational purposes. In A. Tashakkori and C. Teddlie (eds), *Sage Handbook of Mixed Methods in Social and Behavioral Research*, 2nd edition. Thousand Oaks, CA: Sage Publications.

Merton, R. K. (1949) *Social Theory and Social Structure*. Glencoe, IL: The Free Press.

Miles, I. and Irvine, J. (1979) The critique of official statistics. In J. Irvine, I. Miles and J. Evans (eds), *Demystifying Social Statistics*. London: Pluto Press.

Miles, M. B. and Huberman, A. M. (1994) *Qualitative Data Analysis*, 2nd edition. Thousand Oaks, CA: Sage Publications.

Miller, G. A. (1956) The magical number seven, plus or minus two: Some limits on our capacity for processing information. *The Psychological Review*, 63, 81–97.

Miller, S. (2003) Impact of mixed methods and design on inference quality. In A. Tashakkori and C. Teddlie (eds), *Handbook of Mixed Methods in Social and Behavioral Research*. Thousand Oaks, CA: Sage Publications.

Morgan, D. L. (2007) Paradigms lost and pragmatism regained: Methodological implications of combining qualitative and quantitative methods. *Journal of Mixed Methods Research*, 1, 48–76.

Morse, J. M. (2000) Editorial: Determining sample size. *Qualitative Health Research*, 10 (1), 3–5.

Morse, J. M. (2015) Critical analysis of strategies for determining rigor in qualitative inquiry. *Qualitative Health Research*, 25 (9), 1212–1222.

Mosteller, F. (1995) The Tennessee study of class size in the early school grades. *The Future of Children*, 5 (2), 113–127.

Nastasi, B. K., Hitchock, J. H. and Brown, L. M. (2010) An inclusive framework for conceptualizing mixed methods design typologies. In A. Tashakkori and C. Teddlie (eds), *Sage Handbook of Mixed Methods in Social and Behavioral Research*, 2nd edition. Thousand Oaks, CA: Sage Publications.

Neuman, W. L. (2011) *Social Research Methods: Qualitative and Quantitative Approaches*, 7th edition. Boston, MA: Pearson Education.

Newcomer, K. E., Hatry, H. P. and Wholey, J. S. (eds) (2015) *Handbook of Practical Program Evaluation*, 4th edition. Hoboken, NJ: John Wiley & Sons.

Nutley, S., Walter, I. and Davies, H. T. O. (2007) *Using Evidence: How Research Can Inform Public Service*. Bristol: Policy Press.

Onwuegbuzie, A. J. and Dickinson, W. B. (2008) Mixed methods analysis and information visualization: Graphical display for effective communication of research results. *The Qualitative Report*, 13 (2), 204–225.

Onwuegbuzie, A. J. and Leech, N. L. (2006) Linking research questions to mixed methods data analysis procedures I. *The Qualitative Report*, 11 (3), 474–498.

Onwuegbuzie, A. J. and Teddlie, C. (2003) A framework for analyzing data in mixed methods research. In A. Tashakkori and C. Teddlie (eds), *Handbook of Mixed Methods in Social and Behavioral Research*. Thousand Oaks, CA: Sage Publications.

Paek, H.-J., Kim, K. and Hove, T. (2010) Content analysis of anti-smoking videos on YouTube: Message sensation value, message appeals, and their relationships with viewer responses. *Health Education Research*, 25 (6), 1085–1099.

Parke, J. and Griffiths, M. (2008) Participant and non-participant observation in gambling. *Enquire*, 1 (1), 61–74.

Phillippi, J. and Lauderdale, J. (2018) A guide to field notes for qualitative research: Context and conversation. *Qualitative Health Research*, 28 (3), 381–388.

Plano Clark, V. L. and Creswell, J. W. (eds) (2008) *The Mixed Methods Reader*. Thousand Oaks, CA: Sage Publications.

Polkinghorne, D. E. (1988) *Narrative Knowing and the Human Sciences*. Albany, NY: State University of New York Press.

Popper, K. (1959) *The Logic of Scientific Discovery*. New York: Basic Books.

Porcellato, L., Dughill, L. and Springett, J. (2002) Using focus groups to explore children's perceptions of smoking: Reflections on practice. *Health Education*, 102 (6), 310–320.

Przeworski, A. and Teune, H. (1973) Equivalence in cross-national research. In D. P. Warwick and S. Osherson (eds), *Comparative Research Methods*. Englewood Cliffs, NJ: Prentice-Hall.

Ragin, C. C. (1987) *The Comparative Method: Moving beyond Qualitative and Quantitative Strategies*. Los Angeles, CA: University of California Press.

Ragin, C. C. and Amoroso, L. M. (2011) *Constructing Social Research: The Unity and Diversity of Method*, 2nd edition. Thousand Oaks, CA: Sage Publications.

Rasch, G. (1980) *Probabilistic Models for Some Intelligence and Attainment Tests*. Copenhagen, Danish Institute for Educational Research, expanded edition. Chicago: University of Chicago Press.

Reason, P. and Bradbury, H. (2008) *The SAGE Handbook of Action Research: Participative Inquiry and Practice*, 2nd edition. London: Sage Publications.

Reed, A. E., Mikels, J. A. and Lockenhoff, C. E. (2012) Choosing with confidence: Self-efficacy and preferences for choice. *Judgment and Decision Making*, 7 (2), 173–180.

Reichhardt, C. S. and Rallis, S. F. (eds) (1994) The qualitative–quantitative debate: New perspectives. *New Directions for Program Evaluation*, No. 61. San Francisco, CA: Jossey-Bass.

Richardson, L. (2003) Writing: A method of inquiry. In N. K. Denzin and Y. S. Lincoln (eds), *Collecting and Interpreting Qualitative Materials*, 2nd edition. Thousand Oaks, CA: Sage Publications.

Richmond, H. J. (2002) Learner's lives: A narrative analysis. *The Qualitative Report*, 7 (3), 1–14.

Riessman, C. K. (2008) *Narrative Methods for the Human Sciences*. London: Sage Publications.

Risjord, M. (2019) Middle-range theories as models: New criteria for analysis and evaluation. *Nursing Philosophy*, 20 (1), e12225.

Roh, S. and Choo, T. M. (2008) Looking inside zone V: Testing social disorganization theory in suburban areas. *Western Criminological Review*, 9 (1), 1–16.

Rosenberg, W. and Donald, A. (1995) Evidence-based medicine: An approach to clinical problem-solving. *British Medical Journal*, 310, 1122–1126.

Rossi, P. H, Lipsey, M. W. and Freeman, H. E. (2004) *Evaluation: A Systematic Approach*, 7th edition. Thousand Oaks, CA: Sage Publications.

Russell, B. (1945) *A History of Western Philosophy*. Forage Village, MA: Simon & Schuster.

Ryan, G. W. and Bernard, R. (2003) Data management and analysis methods. In N. K. Denzin and Y. S. Lincoln (eds), *Collecting and Interpreting Qualitative Materials*, 2nd edition. Thousand Oaks, CA: Sage Publications.

Sacks, H., Schegloff, E. A. and Jefferson, G. (1974) A simplest systematics of turn-taking for conversation. *Language*, 50, 696–735.

Sale, J. E. M., Lohfeld, L. H. and Brazil, K. (2002) Revisiting the quantitative–qualitative debate: Implications for mixed-methods research. *Quality & Quantity*, 36, 43–53.

Sandelowski, M., Voils, C. I. and Knafl, G. (2009) On quantitizing. *Journal of Mixed Methods Research*, 3 (3), 208–222.

Schneider, C. Q. and Wagemann, C. (2012) *Set-theoretic Methods for the Social Sciences: A Guide to Qualitative Comparative Analysis*. Cambridge: Cambridge University Press.

Schoemaker, P. J., Tankard, J. W. Jr. and Lasora, D. L. (2004) *How to Build Social Science Theories*. Thousand Oaks, CA: Sage Publications.

Schuman, H. and Presser, S. (1981) *Questions and Answers in Attitude Surveys: Experiments on Question Form, Wording and Context*. San Diego, CA: Academic Press.

Schwandt, T. A. (2003) Three epistemological stances for qualitative inquiry: Interpretivism, hermeneutics and social constructionism. In N. K. Denzin and Y. S. Lincoln (eds), *The Landscape of Qualitative Research: Theories and Issues*, 2nd edition. Thousand Oaks, CA: Sage Publications.

Senate Select Committee on Community Standards Relevant to the Supply of Services Utilising Electronic Technologies (1995) *Report on R-Rated Material on Pay TV*. Canberra, ACT: Commonwealth of Australia.

Shaffer, P. (1998) Gender, poverty and deprivation: Evidence from the Republic of Guinea. *World Development*, 26 (12), 2119–2135.

Sidnell, J. and Stivers, T. (eds) (2012) *The Handbook of Conversation Analysis*. Oxford: Wiley-Blackwell.

Silver, C. and Lewins, A. (2014) *Using Software in Qualitative Research: A Step-by-Step Guide*, 2nd edition. London: Sage Publications.

Siniscalco, M. T. and Auriat, N. (2005) *Questionnaire Design*. Paris: International Institute for Educational Planning/UNESCO. Available at: http://unesdoc.unesco.org/images/0021/002145/214555E.pdf

Smit, B. (2002) Atlas.Ti for qualitative data analysis. *Perspectives on Education*, 20 (3), 65–75.

Stevens, S. S. (1946) On the theory of scales of measurement. *Science*, 103, 677–680.

Stewart, C. J. (2014) *Interviewing: Principles and Practices*, 14th edition. New York: McGraw-Hill.

Strauss, A. and Corbin, J. (1998) *Basics of Qualitative Research*, 2nd edition. Oxford: Blackwell.

Tashakkori, A. and Teddlie, C. (1998) *Mixed Methodology: Combining Qualitative and Quantitative Approaches*. Thousand Oaks, CA: Sage Publications.

Tashakkori, A. and Teddlie, C. (eds) (2003) *Handbook of Mixed Methods in Social and Behavioral Research*. Thousand Oaks, CA: Sage Publications.

Tashakkori, A. and Teddlie, C. (2008) Quality of inferences in mixed methods research: Calling for an integrative framework. In M. Bergman (ed.), *Advances in Mixed Methods Research: Theories and Applications*. Thousand Oaks, CA: Sage Publications.

Tashakkori, A. and Teddlie, C. (eds) (2010) *Sage Handbook of Mixed Methods in Social and Behavioral Research*, 2nd edition. Thousand Oaks, CA: Sage Publications.

Teddlie, C. and Tashakkori, A. (2009) *Foundations of Mixed Methods Research*. Thousand Oaks, CA: Sage Publications.

Teddlie, C. and Tashakkori, A. (2010) The past and future of mixed methods research: From data triangulation to mixed model designs. In A. Tashakkori and C. Teddlie (eds), *Sage Handbook of Mixed Methods in Social and Behavioral Research*, 2nd edition. Thousand Oaks, CA: Sage Publications.

Tedlock, B. (2003) Ethnography and ethnographic representation. In N. K. Denzin and Y. S. Lincoln (eds), *Strategies of Qualitative Inquiry*, 2nd edition. Thousand Oaks, CA: Sage Publications.

Thorgersen-Ntoumani, C. and Fox, K. R. (2005) Physical activity and mental well-being typologies in corporate employees: A mixed methods approach. *Work & Stress*, 19 (1), 50–67.

Tischler, V., Rademeyer, A. and Vostanis, P. (2007) Mothers experiencing homelessness: Mental health, support and social care needs. *Health and Social Care in the Community*, 15 (3), 246–253.

Toerien, M. (2014) Conversations and conversation analysis. In U. Flick (ed.), *The Sage Handbook of Qualitative Data Analysis*. London: Sage Publications.

Tseng, V. (2012) The uses of research in policy and practice. *Social Policy Report*, 26 (2), 1–16.

Van Maanen, J. (1988) *Tales of the Field: On Writing Ethnography*. Chicago, IL: University of Chicago Press.

Victor, C. R., Ross, F. and Axford, J. (2004) Capturing lay perspectives in a randomized control trial of a health promotion intervention for people with osteoarthritis of the knee. *Journal of Evaluation in Clinical Practice*, 10 (1), 63–70.

Viterna, J. and Fallon, K. M. (2008) Democratization, women's movements, and gender-equitable states: A framework for comparison. *American Sociological Review*, 73 (4), 668–689.

Way, N., Stauber, H. Y., Nakkula, M. J. and London, P. (1994) Depression and substance use in two divergent high school cultures: A quantitative and qualitative analysis. *Journal of Youth and Adolescence*, 23 (3), 331–357.

Wheeldon, J. and Faubert, J. (2009) Framing experience: Concept maps, mind maps, and data collection in qualitative research. *International Journal of Qualitative Methods*, 8 (3), 68–83.

White, P. (2009) *Developing Research Questions: A Guide for Social Scientists*. Houndmills, Basingstoke: Palgrave Macmillan.

Willig, C. (2008) A phenomenological investigation of the experience of taking part in extreme sport. *Journal of Health Psychology*, 13 (5), 690–702.

Willig, C. (2014) Discourses and discourse analysis. In U. Flick (ed.), *The Sage Handbook of Qualitative Data Analysis*. London: Sage Publications.

Wilson, R. E., Gosling, S. D. and Graham, L. T. (2012) A review of Facebook research in the social sciences. *Perspectives on Psychological Sciences*, 7 (3), 203–220.

Wodak, R. and Meyer, M. (eds) (2016) *Methods of Critical Discourse Studies*. London: Sage Publications.

Wolfinger, N. H. (2002) On writing fieldnotes: Collection strategies and background expectancies. *Qualitative Research*, 2 (1), 85–95.

Yin, R. K. (1984) *Case Study Research*. Thousand Oaks, CA: Sage Publications.

Yin, R. K. (2003) *Applications of Case Study Research*, 2nd edition. Thousand Oaks, CA: Sage Publications.

Yin, R. K. (2009) *Case Study Research: Design and Methods*, 4th edition. Thousand Oaks, CA: Sage Publications.

Yin, R. K. (2014) *Case Study Research: Design and Methods*, 5th edition. Thousand Oaks, CA: Sage Publications.

Zerbe, W. J. and Paulhus, D. L. (1987) Social desirable responding in organisational behavior: A reconception. *Academy of Management Review*, 12, 250–264.

INDEX